Contentious Performances

How can we get inside popular collective struggles and explain how they work? *Contentious Performances* presents a distinctive approach to analyzing such struggles, drawing especially on incomparably rich evidence from Great Britain between 1758 and 1834.

The book accomplishes three main objectives. First, it presents a logic and method for describing contentious events, occasions on which people publicly make consequential claims on each other. Second, it shows how that logic yields superior explanations of the dynamics in such events, both individually and in the aggregate. Third, it illustrates its methods and arguments by means of detailed analyses of contentious events in Great Britain from 1758 to 1834.

Charles Tilly (1929–2008), who was Joseph L. Buttenwieser Professor of Social Science, Columbia University, authored, co-authored, edited, or co-edited more than fifty published books and monographs. He also published between six hundred and seven hundred scholarly articles, reviews, review essays, comments, chapters in edited collections, and prefaces, not counting reprints, translations, and working papers. His most recently published books are *Trust and Rule* (2005); *Why?* (2006); *Oxford Handbook of Contextual Political Analysis* (co-authored and co-edited with Robert Goodin, 2006); *Contentious Politics* (co-authored with Sidney Tarrow, 2006); *Democracy* (2007); *Explaining Social Processes* (2008); and *Credit and Blame* (2008). He was a member of the National Academy of Sciences, the American Academy of Arts and Sciences, the American Philosophical Society, and the Ordre des Palmes Académiques. He received numerous international prizes and honorary degrees.

Cambridge Studies in Contentious Politics

Editors

Mark Beissinger   *Princeton University*

Jack A. Goldstone   *George Mason University*

Doug McAdam   *Stanford University and Center for Advanced Study in the Behavioral Sciences*

Suzanne Staggenborg   *McGill University*

Sidney Tarrow   *Cornell University*

Charles Tilly   *Columbia University*

Elisabeth J. Wood   *Yale University*

Deborah Yashar   *Princeton University*

Ronald R. Aminzade et al., *Silence and Voice in the Study of Contentious Politics*

Javier Auyero, *Routine Politics and Violence in Argentina: The Gray Zone of State Power*

Clifford Bob, *The Marketing of Rebellion: Insurgents, Media, and International Activism*

Charles D. Brockett, *Political Movements and Violence in Central America*

Gerald F. Davis, Doug McAdam, W. Richard Scott, and Mayer N. Zald, editors, *Social Movements and Organization Theory*

Jack A. Goldstone, editor, *States, Parties, and Social Movements*

Doug McAdam, Sidney Tarrow, and Charles Tilly, *Dynamics of Contention*

Sharon Nepstad, *War Resistance and the Plowshares Movement*

Kevin J. O'Brien and Lianjiang Li, *Rightful Resistance in Rural China*

Silvia Pedraza, *Political Disaffection in Cuba's Revolution and Exodus*

Sidney Tarrow, *The New Transnational Activism*

Ralph Thaxton, *Catastrophe and Contention in Rural China: Mao's Great Leap Forward Famine and the Origins of Righteous Resistance in Da Fo Village*

Charles Tilly, *The Politics of Collective Violence*

Charles Tilly, *Contention and Democracy in Europe, 1650–2000*

Stuart A. Wright, *Patriots, Politics, and the Oklahoma City Bombing*

Deborah Yashar, *Contesting Citizenship in Latin America: The Rise of Indigenous Movements and the Postliberal Challenge*

Contentious Performances

CHARLES TILLY

CAMBRIDGE
UNIVERSITY PRESS

CAMBRIDGE UNIVERSITY PRESS
Cambridge, New York, Melbourne, Madrid, Cape Town, Singapore, São Paulo, Delhi

Cambridge University Press
32 Avenue of the Americas, New York, NY 10013-2473, USA

www.cambridge.org
Information on this title: www.cambridge.org/9780521731522

First published 2008

Printed in the United States of America

A catalog record for this publication is available from the British Library.

Library of Congress Cataloging in Publication Data
Tilly, Charles.
  Contentious performances / Charles Tilly.
    p.   cm. – (Cambridge studies in contentious politics)
  Includes bibliographical references and index.
  ISBN 978-0-521-51584-9 (hardback) – ISBN 978-0-521-73152-2 (pbk.)
  1. Collective behavior.   2. Political psychology.   3. Political sociology.
  4. Demonstrations.   5. Protest movements.   6. Political violence.
  7. Great Britain – History – 1714–1837.   I. Title.
  HM866.T55 2008
  306.20941'09033–dc22   2008005765

ISBN 978-0-521-51584-9 hardback
ISBN 978-0-521-73152-2 paperback

Contents

Boxes, Figures, and Tables

Boxes

Figures

Tables

Preface

For me, the ideas in this book began to crystallize three decades ago. Looking at the history of popular contention in France from the 17th to the 20th centuries, I couldn't help noticing two related anomalies. First, although ordinary people found vigorously vital ways of making their voices heard in the midst of repressive regimes, they clung to the same few forms of collective expression and modified those forms only slowly. Seizure of high-priced food, assaults on tax collectors, and resistance to unjustified rent increases followed the same routines year after year during the 17th century, just as street demonstrations and mass meetings repeated themselves almost stereotypically during the 20th century. Given the richness and particularism of French popular culture, one might have expected an almost infinite variety of contentious performances.

Second, ordinary people never engaged in a wide variety of technically feasible ways of making collective claims that ordinary people elsewhere and in other times had readily employed. Those 17th-century French villagers did not strike, picket, or strip themselves naked in public protest. Nor did their 20th-century successors engage in suicide bombing, coups d'état, or ecstatic religious rituals. It occurred to me that in general participants in uprisings and local struggles followed available scripts, adapted those scripts, but only changed them bit by bit. A metaphor came readily to mind: like troupes of street musicians, those French people drew their claim-making performances from standardized, limited repertoires. I first published the idea in 1977.[1]

---

[1] Charles Tilly, "Getting It Together in Burgundy, 1675–1975," *Theory and Society* 4 (1977): 479–504.

To my surprise and delight, the metaphor caught on. Analysts of contention began using the notion of repertoire widely. Then I began to recognize the drawbacks of success. I had developed the repertoire notion in the course of retrieving and cataloging thousands of "contentious gatherings" that occurred in one or another of five French regions between 1600 and 1975. I could easily document the repetitions, the transformations, and the absences from my catalogs of episodes. Although I was reasonably confident that it described my evidence well, I meant the term "repertoire" to present a provocative hypothesis for other analysts of contention to test on their own systematic catalogs. After all, in a public debate we held around that time, influential collective action theorist Mancur Olson responded to my presentation of repertoires by calling them a "dangerous idea." But by and large analysts of popular struggles who did not share Olson's collective action persuasion simply adopted the term to signal the repetitive character of claim making without thinking through what evidence would confirm or deny that repertoires actually facilitated and channeled claim making in the manner of theatrical scripts and standard jazz tunes.

Despite my repeated calls for empirical verification, modification, or falsification of the repertoire idea,[2] no one responded with evidence in hand. I reluctantly decided I would have to undertake the testing myself. The result is this book, an extended effort to explicate, verify, and refine the twinned concepts of performance and repertoire. As their originator, I am not the ideal judge of the ideas' validity. But my effort will, I hope, spur more skeptical analysts of contentious politics to bring their own evidence and procedures to bear on performances and repertoires. The study of contentious politics can only benefit from the crossfire.

Students of popular struggle will immediately recognize this book as a product of an explanatory program that Doug McAdam, Sidney Tarrow, and I started advocating during the 1990s.[3] Our collaboration on the

---

[2] E.g., Charles Tilly, "Contentious Repertoires in Great Britain, 1758–1834," *Social Science History* 17 (1993): 253–280.

[3] E.g., Doug McAdam, Sidney Tarrow, and Charles Tilly, "To Map Contentious Politics," *Mobilization* 1 (1996): 17–34; McAdam, Tarrow, and Tilly, *Dynamics of Contention.* Cambridge: Cambridge University Press, 2001. For a sample of works in the Dynamics of Contention tradition, broadly defined, see the later volumes of the Cambridge (University Press) Studies in Contentious Politics series: Ronald R. Aminzade et al., *Silence and Voice in the Study of Contentious Politics* (2001); Jack A. Goldstone, ed., *States, Parties, and Social Movements* (2003); Charles Tilly, *The Politics of Collective Violence* (2003); Charles Tilly, *Contention and Democracy in Europe, 1650–2000* (2004); Sidney Tarrow, *The New Transnational*

subject began in conversations at a 1995 Amsterdam meeting designed to ease me into retirement. The meeting failed in that regard, but succeeded famously in initiating new connections among students of contentious politics.[4]

The Dynamics of Contention (DOC) Program had several distinctive features: identification of "contentious politics," rather than collective action, protest, or conflict, as the object of study; insistence on a dynamic, relational understanding of contention; preference for the systematic and comparative study of multiple contentious episodes; and employment of mechanisms and processes – environmental, dispositional, and relational – as fundamental explanations. The program stirred up a good deal of controversy, but eventually took its place as a major alternative to the covering law and dispositional accounts of contention that had hitherto prevailed. For fear that too much complexity would discourage my readers, I have suppressed the specification of mechanisms and processes that underlies every analysis in the book and have radically limited references to parallel work in the DOC tradition. In compensation, the book clearly identifies contentious politics as its object of explanation, offers a deeply dynamic and relational account of contention, and rejoices in the systematic and comparative study of multiple contentious episodes.

With some regret, I decided not to engage the vast, chaotic, sparsely connected literature on performance as an organizing aspect of social life.[5] The close study of contentious performances has important lessons to teach that literature and can benefit from sorting out the competing

Activism (2005); Charles D. Brockett, *Political Movements and Violence in Central America* (2005); Deborah J. Yashar, *Contesting Citizenship in Latin America* (2005); Gerald F. Davis, Doug McAdam, W. Richard Scott, and Mayer N. Zald, eds., *Social Movements and Organization Theory* (2005); Clifford Bob, *The Marketing of Rebellion* (2005); Kevin J. O'Brien and Lianjiang Li, *Rightful Resistance in Rural China* (2006); Javier Auyero, *Routine Politics and Violence in Argentina* (2007); Stuart A. Wright, *Patriots, Politics, and the Oklahoma City Bombing* (2007); and Silvia Pedraza, *Political Disaffection in Cuba's Revolution and Exodus* (2007).

[4] Papers from the meeting appeared in Michael P. Hanagan, Leslie Page Moch, and Wayne te Brake, eds., *Challenging Authority: The Historical Study of Contentious Politics*. Minneapolis: University of Minnesota Press, 1998.

[5] See, e.g., Jeffrey C. Alexander, Bernhard Giesen, and Jason L. Mast, eds., *Social Performance: Symbolic Action, Cultural Pragmatics, and Ritual*. Cambridge: Cambridge University Press, 2006; Peter Burke, "Performing History: The Importance of Occasions," *Rethinking History* 9 (2005): 35–52; Michel Callon, ed., *The Laws of the Markets*. Oxford: Blackwell, 1998; and R. Keith Sawyer, *Group Creativity: Music, Theater, Collaboration*. Mahwah, NJ: Lawrence Erlbaum Associates, 2003.

theoretical perspectives that have arisen within the literature. But again I concluded that sustained discussions of performance as a general feature of social life would greatly complicate the book without advancing its main arguments significantly.

When I have already written on precisely one point or another, I have not hesitated to lift material from my earlier publications. Perhaps 10 percent of this book's text adapts paragraphs previously published in my *Popular Contention in Great Britain, 1758–1834* (Cambridge, MA: Harvard University Press, 1995; revised paperback edition Boulder, CO: Paradigm Publishers, 2005), my *Social Movements 1768–2004* (Boulder, CO: Paradigm Publishers, 2004), my *Regimes and Repertoires* (Chicago: University of Chicago Press, 2006), or in Charles Tilly and Sidney Tarrow, *Contentious Politics* (Boulder, CO: Paradigm Publishers, 2006).

For advice, information, criticism, and encouragement, I am grateful to Mark Beissinger, Ernesto Castañeda, Sam Clark, Roberto Franzosi, Roy Licklider, Clark McPhail, Nicholas Toloudis, Takeshi Wada, Elisabeth Wood, Lesley Wood, Viviana Zelizer, an anonymous reader for Cambridge University Press, and the many students at the University of Michigan and the New School for Social Research who worked on the Great Britain Study. Once again, Sidney Tarrow made demands for revision that I could not fulfill. One of my fondest hopes is that some day I'll write a book of which Sid approves.

* * *

Charles Tilly died on April 29, 2008, after a lengthy battle with cancer and shortly after he finished writing *Contentious Performances*. Cambridge University Press is most grateful to both Chris Tilly of the University of Massachusetts and Sidney Tarrow of Cornell University, who read the page proofs, and to Sidney Tarrow who also reviewed the copyedited manuscript.

Lewis Bateman, Senior Editor
Political Science and History

Contentious Performances

1

Claims as Performances

In London, magazines, newspapers, and pamphlets proliferated during the middle decades of the 18th century. For an increasingly literate urban population, they mixed together vital visions of world affairs, national politics, news of high society, and everyday events. The *Gentleman's Magazine*, edited by "Sylvanus Urban, Gent.," began publication in 1731. Among other features, each monthly issue of the magazine contained a miscellaneous chronicle of events likely to interest its cosmopolitan readers. The events often concerned contacts of ordinary people – workers and others who had no particular connections to power at a national scale – with genuine wielders of power.

For Monday the 9th of May, 1768, the chronicle reported these items from the London streets:

A numerous body of watermen assembled before the mansion house, and laid their complaint before the lord-mayor, who advised them, to appoint proper persons to draw up a petition to parliament, which his lordship promised them he would present; upon which they gave him three huzzas and went quietly home.

The same night a large mob of another kind assembled before the mansion-house, carrying a gallows with a boot hanging to it, and a red cap; but on some of the ringleaders being secured by the peace-officers, the rest dispersed.

This day the hatters *struck*, and refused to work till their wages are raised.

What should 21st-century readers make of these 18th-century reports? Today's readers need some essential background. In London, a great port, the watermen – dock workers and boatmen who serviced ships on the Thames – worked within easy walking distance of the City of London's center. The Lord Mayor of London maintained his headquarters in Mansion House, not far from the Thames' docks.

The year 1768 brought political turmoil to London: sailors, watermen, and other workers made repeated demands on their employers and on public authorities, as many people opposed the British crown's repressive policies in the American colonies vocally. Meanwhile, the rakish aristocratic demagogue John Wilkes returned from exile, went to prison, won multiple parliamentary elections while incarcerated, received repeated rebuffs from Parliament itself, and gained wide popular support as a speaker for popular liberties.

What about the three events of May 9th? In the first, a large delegation of watermen asked the Lord Mayor to support their demands for higher wages. He agreed to communicate a properly drafted humble petition to Parliament. The assembled workers closed with the three cheers that today have become a mere cliché but then signified viva voce approval of a person or an action. (Three loud groans in chorus then signified collective disapproval.)

The second event takes more glossing. The crowd was acting out its opposition to the king's Scottish advisor Lord Bute, who was leading the crown's repressive policies in England and America; it mimed the execution of Bute, using a Scotch bonnet and a punning boot as a stand-in for the advisor. John Wilkes's supporters, who included silk weavers from nearby Spitalfields, often vented their disapproval of royal authorities in just such street theater.

In the third, the *Gentleman's Magazine*'s description of the hatters' action italicized the word "struck." The term was a generalization taken from sailors' striking of sails on ships they refused to man until the masters met their demands for better wages and working conditions. Only later did the word "strike" come to cover any collective withdrawal of labor from an enterprise or a craft. In their time, all three events broadcast familiar, comprehensible themes. In all three, ordinary people made claims on holders of power. They staged contentious performances. But they did so in three very different ways.

Jump forward two-thirds of a century. On the 28th of January 1834, London's metropolitan newspaper the *Morning Chronicle* carried the following advertisement in the name of the Central Anti–Corn Law Society:

ABOLITION OF THE CORN LAWS. – A PUBLIC MEETING will be held at the Crown and Anchor Tavern, Strand, on Friday next, January 31, at Twelve at Noon, for the purpose of deciding on the most efficient Means of obtaining a Removal of the Bread Tax Grievance. Colonel Perronet Thompson will take the Chair at One o'clock precisely.

Since 1797, the Corn Laws had imposed a tariff on imported grain up to a high level of British prices, thereby protecting the sellers and imposing higher prices on the buyers of grain or bread. An 1828 revision had set a sliding scale, but retained the tariff. Opponents called it the Bread Tax. According to the *Morning Chronicle* of February 1st, participants in the meeting expressed disappointment that no lords or members of Parliament had shown up.

After speeches, the meeting approved a petition to Parliament including this passage:

That your Petitioners believe and are firmly convinced, by the exercise of such experience and judgment as in their several occupations and modes of life they have acquired, that the limitation of industry and employment produced by the Corn Laws is the great cause of the National Distress, and of the sufferings and dangers incurred by the different classes of the community.

That your Petitioners have seen no instance in history of the numerous classes in any nation submitting to sufferings approaching in manner and degree to those endured by the people of this country, after the cause and nature of their evils had become familiarly known to them; and that it is consequently highly desirable to the lovers of peace and order of society, among whom your Petitioners are, that measures should be taken for effecting the inevitable change, with the least disturbance to the general quiet of the community.

The obsequious second paragraph conveyed a veiled threat: inattention to the people's needs might foster a revolution like those that had recently overturned the governments of France and Belgium. The petition did go to Parliament, but missed its mark by far. Not until a dozen years later, in 1846, did the Anti–Corn Law League reach its goal of free trade in grain. But throughout all that time, opponents of the Bread Tax continued to meet, debate, petition, lobby, and make statements to the press.

As compared with the events of 1768, notice three features of the 1834 Crown and Anchor gathering. First, it took the form of an indoor public meeting, with prior announcement, elected chair, parliamentary procedure, and cheers for statements the audience approved. Second, unlike the Lord Mayor's mediation for watermen in 1768, its leaders communicated directly with Parliament. Third, it ended (as everyone expected) with voted approval of a petition subsequently signed by many of the participants.

Four handpicked events from London can't establish the general pattern of change in such public events for the whole country between the 1760s and the 1830s. As we will see in detail later, over the two-thirds of a century between them, decorous public meetings in the Anti–Corn Law style became much more prevalent in Great Britain. During the 18th century patrons and other intermediaries regularly stood between ordinary people and national authorities, as in the Lord Mayor's offer to pass on the watermen's petition. During the 19th century, however, popular communication with Britain's rulers, especially Parliament and its members, became much more common. Direct action against moral and political offenders, whether violent or nonviolent, gave way to meetings, demonstrations, and other nonviolent expressions of collective disapproval. On the way from the 18th to the 19th century, Britons were creating many forms of collective voice that we 21st-century political observers still notice in relatively democratic countries.

Nevertheless, some things remained the same. Both in 1768 and in 1834, Londoners were engaging in collective performances that contemporaries then found familiar. Newspapers and magazines took the existence of such events more or less for granted. They didn't ask, "What in the world are these ordinary people doing?" They asked chiefly who took part, over what issues, and how. The two gatherings at Mansion House, the hatters' strike, and the Anti–Corn Law meeting all voiced collective claims on people or institutions outside the number of those who gathered to make the claims. The fact that the claims bore on someone else's interests (rather than simply blowing off steam) made them contentious. Whether addressing government officials directly or drawing in governments as third parties, they also involved political power. The events of 1768 and 1834 belong to contentious politics.

Our four vignettes from London raise profound, unresolved questions about contentious politics in Britain and at large. Within Britain, why did the claim makers use these particular ways of voicing collective claims rather than others that would have been technically possible, such as suicide bombing or armed insurrection? Over the period from 1768 to 1834, how and why did the standard ways of making collective claims change so decisively? More generally, what accounts for variation and change in the forms of collective claim making wherever it occurs?

As a general answer, this book treats collective contention as a product of learned and historically grounded performances. In a given time and place, people learn a limited number of claim-making performances, then mostly stick with those performances when the time to make claims arrives. Contentious performances change incrementally as a result of accumulating experience and external constraints. But in the short run they strongly limit the choices available to would-be makers of claims. In some settings, suicide bombing or armed insurrection look like two of the major options. Not so in 18th- and 19th-century Great Britain. This book asks why and how that is the case.

The book also has a methodological lesson to teach. Many historians and social scientists think they must make sharp choices between quantitative and qualitative methods, between formal analysis and literary storytelling, between narrowly conceived pursuit of explanations and broadly conceived interpretations. On one side, epidemiology; on the other side, narrative. The materials and methods of this book identify a middle ground where logical rigor meets the nuances of human interaction. It shows how the stories in which most reports of contention come packaged – including the stories from London in 1768 and 1834 – lend themselves to systematic description and analysis. Before plunging too deeply into method, however, we should clarify the subject matter: contentious politics.

Contentious Politics

Although we can obviously identify differences, the four British events converged in many ways. What did they have in common? They all made claims on other people, used public performances to do so, drew on inherited forms of collective action and invented new ones, forged alliances with influential members of their respective political regimes, took advantage of existing political regime opportunities, and helped create new opportunities to advance their claims. They engaged in contentious politics.

Contentious politics involves interactions in which actors make claims bearing on someone else's interests, in which governments appear either as targets, initiators of claims, or third parties. Contentious politics thus brings together three familiar features of social life: contention, collective action, and politics.

Contention involves making claims that bear on someone else's interests. Claims run from negative to positive. People make claims with such words as condemn, oppose, resist, demand, beseech, support, and reward. They also make claims with actions such as attacking, expelling, defacing, cursing, cheering, throwing flowers, singing songs, and carrying heroes on their shoulders. In everyday life, contention ranges from small matters like which football team we should support to bigger questions such as whether grandpa rightly divided his inheritance among us, his heirs. But it also takes place in chess matches, competition among retail stores, and struggles of defense lawyers with presiding judges.

In the simplest version of contention, one party makes claims on another. The parties are often persons, but one or the other can also be a group or even an institution; you can make a claim on your boss, or file a claim on the government for worker's compensation. In the elementary version, we can think of one party as a subject (the maker of a claim) and the other as an object (the receiver of a claim). Claims always involve at least one subject reaching visibly toward at least one object. You (subject) ask your sister (object) to pay back the money she borrowed from you yesterday. But claims range from timid requests to strident demands to direct attacks, just so long as they would, if realized, somehow affect the object's well-being, the object's interests. Often three or more parties are involved, as when you demand that your sister pay you back the money she was about to hand over to a friend. Contention always brings together subjects, objects, and claims.

Collective action means coordinating efforts on behalf of shared interests or programs. Baseball teams engage in collective action, but so do choirs, neighborhood associations, and neighbors who track down a child molester. When you go to church or take a job selling hamburgers in a fast-food emporium, you enter an organization that is carrying on collective action. But most of the collective action involved occurs with no significant contention and no government involvement. The bulk of collective action takes place outside of contentious politics.

Most contention also occurs outside of politics. We enter the realm of politics when we interact with agents of governments, either dealing with them directly or engaging in activities bearing on governmental rights, regulations, and interests. Politics likewise ranges from fairly routine matters such as applying for a driver's license to momentous questions such as whether the country should go to war. But most of politics involves little or no contention. Most of the time, people register for benefits, answer census takers, cash government checks, or show their passports to immigration officers without making significant claims on other people.

The presence or absence of governments in collective contention makes a difference for three big reasons. First, people who control governments gain advantages over people who don't. Even where the government is weak, controlling it gives you the means of collecting taxes, distributing resources, and regulating other people's behavior. As a result, political contention puts at risk, however slightly, the advantages of those who currently enjoy governmental power.

Second, governments always make rules governing collective contention: who can make what collective claims, by what means, with what outcomes. Even weak governments have some influence over the prevailing forms of claim making, and they resist anyone else who attempts to build up competitive centers of power within their territories.

Third, governments control substantial coercive means: armies, police forces, courts, prisons, and the like. The availability of governmental coercion gives an edge to political contention that rarely exists outside of the political arena. In political contention, large-scale violence always remains a possibility, however faint. Contention connected to governments does resemble contention in families, sports, churches, and businesses in some regards. This book sometimes calls attention to those parallels. But it singles out government-connected contention because of these distinctive political properties.

Let me rule out a possible misunderstanding at once. Restriction of contentious politics to claim making that somehow involves governments by no means implies that governments must figure as the makers or receivers of contentious claims. On the contrary, as the book proceeds we will encounter a wide range of contention in which non-governmental actors confront each other and make claims on religious, economic, ethnic, or other non-governmental holders of power. In 1768, the watermen first directed their claims against dockside employers, and only then asked government officials to intervene in their dispute. The minimum government involvement consists of monitoring and regulating public contention, and preparing to step in if the claim making gets unruly.

Here is another possible misunderstanding. Many people use the term "social movement" broadly to cover all sorts of struggle, from intellectual currents to rural rebellions. But, as we will soon see, as it grew up in western countries the social movement actually brought together a very limited range of claim-making performances: creation of special-purpose associations, public meetings, petition drives, street demonstrations, and a few more. It specifically excluded most varieties of armed attack as well as a wide variety of nonviolent actions, such as shaming ceremonies and magical rituals. The distinction matters. One of this book's main aims is to show how different sorts of performance, including social movement performances, vary and change.

Episodes, Performances, and Repertoires

Astute social movement analyst Francesca Polletta points out that movement participants often describe major episodes as products of spontaneous inspiration: "It was like a fever." That description contradicts the testimony of both veteran organizers and close students of particular movements. Both of them stress the social connections and organizing efforts that go into any effective collective action. The background includes life experiences of individual participants, but it also includes their social locations. Polletta adds that the cultural milieu provides languages and symbols through which participants and observers make sense of the collective action. Speaking of the American civil rights movement, Polletta remarks:

> To account for the emergence of a mobilizing identity on black college campuses and the development of such identities more broadly, we need to examine not only the instrumental framing efforts of established groups and movement organizations but also the larger cultural context in which an idiom of student activism made sense. Then we need to capture the diffuse, non-institutionalized discursive processes through which a rationale for protest, or a set of rationales, gained currency. (Polletta 2006: 37)

The civil rights movement, then, did not consist simply of spontaneous actions by heroic individuals. It involved life experiences, deliberate organizing, and concerted episodes of claim making.

Any close observer of contentious politics witnesses a continuous stream of interaction. Whether gathering with like-minded people or not, participants in claim making not only make publicly visible collective claims on other people but also recruit like-minded folks to their cause, plan their strategies in private, and dig up information that will help them. In many cases, they engage in other activities that likewise advance their cause: contribute money and time to help fellow members, wear badges or colors advertising their affiliation, sell polemical books or pamphlets, argue with opponents they meet at work, and more.

In some broad sense, all these activities belong to contentious politics. Yet we won't get far in explaining the variation and change of contentious politics without making preliminary distinctions among three classes of activity: 1) routine social life, 2) contention-connected social interaction and 3) public participation in collective making of claims. Students of social movements and of other forms of contentious politics therefore face a serious question: where should we draw the line between what we are explaining and what explains it?

For some purposes, we will treat 2) and 3) as what we are trying to explain, and change and variation in 1) as part of the explanation. If, for example, we are examining the contentious politics of American feminism over the last half-century, we are quite likely to pinpoint consciousness-raising women's groups – a clear case of contention-connected social interaction, but not usually of public activity – as something to explain along with public collective claim making such as street marches and petition drives (Beckwith 2001, Katzenstein 1998, Whittier 1995). We will then treat change and variation in routine social life such as employment, education, child-raising, and household economic activity as partial causes of change and variation in organized feminism. In this sort of analysis, the stream of contentious politics we are trying to explain includes both contention-connected social interaction and public participation in claim making. Call this a thick object of explanation.

Suppose, on the other hand, that we are trying to explain how the march on Washington became such a powerful way to promote an American cause (Barber 2002, Hall 2007). We thus single out a thin object of explanation. Then we will do better to treat changes in the first and second elements – routine social life and contention-connected social interaction – as causes of change in the third: public participation in the making of claims. On Saturday, 27 January 2007, for example, participants in a Washington Mall demonstration against the Iraq War included not only "tens of thousands of protesters" from across the United States but also political leaders and such celebrities as Jane Fonda, Susan Sarandon, and Tim Robbins (Urbina 2007).

A full explanation of participation in the January 2007 Washington march would locate the demonstrators in everyday American life (the first element above), but it would also concern the second element: who recruited participants and how. In such cases, the stream of contention we are trying to explain includes all marches on Washington. We may also want to compare that stream with other streams, including marches on state capitals, street marches in general, and delegations to Washington that do not engage in street marches. Or we might undertake international comparisons. In Great Britain, for example, the march on London has a history running back hundreds of years (Reiss 2007a). The stream of contentious politics we are then explaining still consists of public participation in collective making of claims, and the explanations still concern routine social life and contention-connected social interaction.

Similarly, analysts of strikes typically make strong distinctions between strike episodes as such and what happens in work settings that generate – or, for that matter, fail to generate – strikes. Where they draw lines between episodes and contexts significantly affects the inferences they can draw about causal mechanisms and processes. In the broad view, change and variation in contention-connected interaction become part of what analysts are explaining. In the narrower view, both routine social life and contention-connected interaction become part of the explanation for public, collective making of claims. This book generally takes the narrower view. It singles out thin objects of explanation. It identifies a thin object of explanation, but strives to get it right.

In either case, we will usually get a better grip on the cause-effect dynamics involved by cutting the big streams into episodes: bounded sequences of continuous interaction, usually produced by an investigator chopping up longer streams of contention into segments for purposes of systematic observation, comparison, and explanation. Let us say we already know what stream of contention we want to explain, and whether it contains a thick or a thin object of explanation. How to identify episodes still remains a knotty conceptual and theoretical problem. Analysts face hard choices among three very different approaches to delineating episodes:

1. Trying to reconstruct what participants in contention experience as a single episode, for example, by taking self-reports of staged events or campaigns as units of observation
2. Adopting conventions that already appear in reporting media, for example, what newspapers count as riots or police count as encounters with rioters
3. Letting observed interactions and their interruptions delimit episodes, for example, by regrouping available accounts into one-day segments of interaction

Each has its advocates, its advantages, and its obvious limitations. But the choice among them does not depend on common sense or convenience so much as on conflicting conceptions of what analysts are actually studying. Each implies a somewhat different line of explanation for contentious politics.

In the first alternative, the actors' consciousness becomes central; analysts often think of their topic as something like "protest" or "resistance." In that case, analysts might find interesting how participants in contention organize their perceptions and memories. But the real explanatory news concerns shifts in consciousness.

In the second, culture and convention become more prominent; analysts are trying to locate contentious interaction within the available categories of its time-place setting. Now (as Polletta's treatment of American social movements suggests) explanation will have to feature change and variation in existing idioms, categories, and practices, including the idioms, categories, and practices of reporting media.

In the third, observed interactions prevail. Analysts are seeking to identify common properties of contention across different forms of consciousness and various time-place settings. They are less willing to let actors' consciousness or local culture determine what will count as a unit of observation, and more willing to assign limits to episodes on the basis of observed interactions. For example, many analysts of contentious politics try to determine under what conditions and how governmental repression reduces levels of collective action, while others are hoping to identify regularities in every sort of human gathering (Davenport 2007, Davenport, Johnston, and Mueller 2005, McPhail 2006). While giving ample attention to consciousness and culture, this book stresses the advantages of concentrating on observed interactions.

Questions about contentious public political performances have brought this book into being. We are asking how and why gatherings outside of officials' headquarters, collective seizures of food, armed attacks, street marches, and a wide variety of other claim-making performances rise, fall, and change. We witness a changing interplay between continuity and improvisation. On one side, people who make contentious claims in a given time and place draw on a very limited repertoire of performances. Most of the performances are sufficiently familiar that participants know more or less how to behave and what to expect. London's skilled workers of the 1760s knew about assembling outside Mansion House and calling on the Lord Mayor, just as middle-class Londoners of the 1830s knew how to conduct a public meeting and how to send Parliament a petition. Those performances only change slowly and incrementally. But they do change continuously; even the public meetings of 1834 look somewhat different from the public meetings of 1768.

On the other side, no two contentious performances mirror each other perfectly. Indeed, they would lose some of their effect if they operated like precision military drill. Participants improvise constantly in two different ways: figuring out how to shape the available routines to communicate the claims they are currently pursuing, and responding to other people's reactions as they make the claims. They interact with other participants, onlookers, objects of claims, competitors, and authorities. In the process, they introduce minor innovations into established forms. Most of those innovations disappear as the event ends. But some stick. As a result, some performances disappear, others come into being, and most others modify incrementally.

To be sure, radical innovations sometimes occur suddenly and spread rapidly. The marches and popular assemblies of the early French Revolution adapted features of previous French claim making, but broke substantially with the resistance and rebellion of the earlier 18th century (Markoff 1996a, Tilly 1986). In the American civil rights movement, bus boycotts and sit-ins certainly had precedents, but they multiplied, mutated, and then standardized with impressive speed (McAdam 1999). Rapid changes in political contexts offer more stimuli to radical, rapid innovation in performances. But most of the time political contexts change incrementally. As a result, so do performances.

This book represents political contexts in three main ways: as regimes; within regimes, as political opportunity structures; and within political opportunity structures, as sketches of the strategic situations faced by claim-making actors. Regime means relations between a government and the major political actors within its jurisdiction plus relations among those actors; we have already encountered the British government and such actors as the Lord Mayor, Parliament, organized workers, and opponents of the Corn Laws. Political opportunity structure (as Chapter 4 says in much greater detail) consists of opportunities and threats posed for claim making on the part of one or many actors by changes in regime openness, coherence of the national elite, stability of political alignments, availability of allies for potential claimants, and regime repression or facilitation with respect to possible forms of claim making. Finally, sketches of strategic situations close in on the positions and relations of crucial actors as they approach the making of collective claims.

Despite paying repeated attention to political contexts, the book as a whole takes a resolutely bottom-up perspective. That is true with respect to evidence as well as analysis. The evidence presented overwhelmingly concerns the characteristics and actions of claim-making actors rather than the objects or regulators of their claims; public authorities, merchants, members of Parliament, and political brokers occupy less space in the evidence than do the characteristics and actions of ordinary participants in contentious politics. Accordingly, the analysis itself provides much less insight into elite strategizing and elite response to contentious claims than to how relatively ordinary people get involved. We focus on continuity and improvisation in the means that people employ in making collective claims on each other and on authorities.

How can we explain the combination of continuity and improvisation? This book combines two different strategies. The first is to analyze contentious performances as a class of communications that evolve in something like the same way that language evolves: through incremental transformation in use. The second is to look closely at evidence on how contentious claim making actually works. This chapter began with cases from Great Britain between the 1750s and the 1840s because the largest single body of evidence the book analyzes comes from a systematic examination of British contention during that period. But discussions in the rest of the book also bring in the best systematic work other investigators have done. In particular, the book takes advantage of a forty-year-old practice in the study of contentious politics: creation of uniform catalogs to describe one sort of claim making or another.

Catalogs of events have predominated in recent quantitative work on contentious politics (Franzosi 1995, 1998, McAdam 1999, Olzak 1992, Rucht, Koopmans, and Neidhardt 1999, Rucht and Ohlemacher 1992, Tarrow 1989, Tilly 1995, 2004a, Tilly and Tarrow 2006: appendices, Wada 2003, 2004). Catalogs formalize the observation of contentious interaction, and thus facilitate both careful theorizing and systematic comparison (Tilly 2002a). Such catalogs implicitly favor abstract, uniform units of observation. Our four London events of 1768–1834 actually came from a theoretically motivated event catalog: an enumeration of 8,088 "contentious gatherings" (CGs) that occurred somewhere in Great Britain during twenty scattered years spread from 1758 to 1834 (Tilly 1995).

Much more about the catalog later. For now, it matters that the catalog identified individual episodes from continuous reading of multiple British periodicals over the twenty years. From the more continuous stream of British contention it selected public gatherings during which people made visible collective claims on other people outside their own number. With abundant evidence drawn from other sources, my collaborators and I located the CGs in their time-place settings as we sought to explain their change and variation. We attempted to pinpoint how and why British popular claim making varied from setting to setting, how and why it underwent deep change between the 1750s and the 1830s.

Seen in context, our CGs told a dramatic story of changes in Britain's forms of popular struggle between the 1750s and 1830s. "Drama" is the right word. We can capture some of the recurrent, historically embedded character of contentious politics by means of two related theatrical metaphors: performances and repertoires.[1] Once we look closely at collective making of claims, we see that particular instances improvise on shared scripts. Presentation of a petition, taking of a hostage, or mounting of a demonstration constitutes a performance linking at least two actors, a claimant and an object of claims. Innovation occurs incessantly on the small scale, but effective claims depend on a recognizable relation to their setting, to relations between the parties, and to previous uses of the claim-making form.

Performances clump into repertoires of claim-making routines that apply to the same claimant-object pairs: bosses and workers, peasants and landlords, rival nationalist factions, and many more. Existence of a repertoire means that a given claimant has more than one way to make collective claims on the object. The same people who march through the streets also sometimes petition, the same people who conduct armed raids on each other also sometimes meet to negotiate. The theatrical metaphor calls attention to the clustered, learned, yet improvisational character of people's interactions as they make and receive each other's claims. Claim making usually resembles jazz and commedia dell'arte rather than ritual reading of scripture. Like a jazz trio or an improvising theater group, people who participate in contentious politics normally have several pieces they can play, but not an infinity (Sawyer 2001). Within that limited array, the players choose which pieces they will perform here and now, in what order.

Repertoires vary from place to place, time to time, and pair to pair. But on the whole, when people make collective claims, they innovate within

---

[1] For a historically informed explication and critique of performance as a metaphor, see Burke 2005. For descriptions and surveys of contentious performances and repertoires (by no means all of them using these terms), see Archer 1990, Barber 2002, Beckwith 2000, Beissinger 1998, Borland 2004, Bourguinat 2002, Casquete 2006, Chabot 2000, Chabot and Duyvendak 2002, Duyvendak, van der Heijden, Koopmans, and Wijmans 1992, Ekiert and Kubik 1999, Ellingson 1995, Ennis 1987, Esherick and Wasserstrom 1990, Eyerman 2006, Farrell 2000, Fillieule 1997, Garrett 2006, Granjon 2002, Greiff 1997, Hanagan 1999, Heerma van Voss 2001, Hertel 2006, Jarman 1997, Lafargue 1996, Lee 2007, Lofland and Fink 1982, McPhee 1988, Mueller 1999, Munro 2005, Oberschall 1994, Péchu 2006, Pigenet and Tartakowsky 2003, Plotz 2000, Plows, Wall, and Doherty 2004, Reiss 2007b, Robert 1996, Rolfe 2005, Salvatore 2001, Scalmer 2002a, 2002b, Schwedler 2005, Sowell 1998, Steinberg 1999a and b, Stinchcombe 1999, Szabó 1996, Tarrow 1989, 1998, 2005, Tartakowsky 1997, 2004, Thornton 2002, Traugott 1995, Vasi 2006, Wada 2004, and Wood 2004.

limits set by the repertoire already established for their place, time, and pair. Social movement activists in today's European cities adopt some mixture of public meetings, press statements, demonstrations, and petitions, but stay away from suicide bombing, hostage taking, and self-immolation. Their repertoire draws on a long history of previous struggles (Tilly 2004b).

Weak and Strong Repertoires

In principle, the words "performance" and "repertoire" could merely serve as metaphors. They could simply signal that participants in contentious politics commonly dramatize their claims rather than treating them as routine transactions like ordering products on the Internet. In principle, we could imagine repertoires varying from non-existent to rigid, depending on the extent to which one experience with the making of collective claims affects the next experience:

- No repertoire: One performance doesn't affect or predict the next, either because collective actors do whatever will be most efficient for them in the circumstances or (at the opposite extreme) because their actions simply express the emotions of the moment; individual reflexes and instant judgments behave in this way, responding largely to wired-in routines.
- Weak repertoire: Some repetition occurs from one episode to another, because habit and limited imagination make repetition easier than innovation; casual conversation and walking through crowded streets often conform to this model.
- Strong repertoire: In something like the style of theatrical performers, participants in contention are enacting available scripts within which they innovate, mostly in small ways; parliamentary debates and classroom oral reports frequently proceed in this manner.
- Rigid repertoire: Participants repeat the same few routines over and over as exactly as they can; military drill and language-learning exercises commonly display this rigidity.

We arrive at this book's broadest generalization: although in principle any of these descriptions could – and sometimes does – apply to claim making, overwhelmingly public collective contention involves strong repertoires. It involves collective learning and incessant adaptation.

The theatrical metaphor fails us in one important regard. Unlike the imagined situation of actors on a stage before a darkened house, all participants in contention learn continuously as they interact. That includes claimants, objects of claims, third parties, and observers. What's more, they arrive at settlements that last beyond the current episode. They do not merely drop the curtain and walk away. As a consequence of interaction and bargains struck, the prior path of collective claim making constrains its subsequent forms. It influences the issues, settings, and outcomes of popular struggle. The particular path of contention affects what happens next because each shared effort to press claims lays down a settlement among parties to the transaction, a memory of the interaction, new information about the likely outcomes of different sorts of interactions, and a changed network of relations within and among participants.

The hypothesis of strong repertoires has powerful implications for the analysis of contentious politics. First, it implies that performances and repertoires are causally and symbolically coherent phenomena. A causally coherent phenomenon results from the same basic mechanisms and produces similar effects across a wide range of circumstances. Political brokerage, for example, operates in essentially the same manner regardless of scale and circumstances: brokers connect two or more previously less connected sites and thus facilitate their political coordination (Tilly 2003, Tilly and Tarrow 2006).

A symbolically coherent phenomenon results from human action that classifies events as similar whether or not they are causally coherent. In other publications I have argued that all processes people call revolutions do not conform to the same causal laws, yet once people label a certain process as revolutionary the process – for example, the series of struggles that in retrospect people call the French Revolution – becomes available as a shared symbol and model for action (Tilly 1993). The hypothesis of strong repertoires translates into a claim of both causal and symbolic coherence for performances and repertoires.

Second, the hypothesis implies constraint. Performances and repertoires do not simply serve as convenient labels for regularities in contention. The previous existence of a performance such as petitioning Parliament or striking a ship's sails channels subsequent actions of watermen or sailors toward innovative enactments of similar performances and away from other performances of which they would be technically capable. The establishment of a repertoire of citizen-ruler interactions including petitioning, delegating, mounting satirical skits, and staging public celebrations disposes subsequent citizens and rulers to choose among these performances (rather than reaching out for entirely different performances) when they make claims on each other. Here, rephrased, are this book's organizing arguments: performances and repertoires are causally coherent. They are symbolically coherent. And their existence constrains collective claim making.

Later chapters document these generalizations for a wide range of contention. In order to examine them closely, we need further distinctions among four possible levels of uniformity: actions, interactions, performances, and repertoires. Conceivably the main regularities could occur at the level of specific actions, with participants in collective claims learning to cheer, march, smash, shoot, and run away without necessarily putting them into coherent connections with each other (McPhail 1991, Sugimoto 1981). Possibly they learn interactions, so smashing a person differs significantly from smashing a shop window, just as cheering your own group's leader occurs differently from cheering a national hero. Again, participants could learn whole interactive performances such as street marches and infantry skirmishes. Finally, we could imagine learning at the level of an entire repertoire, as when social movement participants learn more or less simultaneously to meet, march, picket, pamphlet, and petition, as well as learning which combination of these interactions will produce what effects.

The levels matter. If learning occurs chiefly at the level of specific actions, we can rely heavily on individual psychology, including neuroscience and perhaps even evolutionary psychology, for our explanations. If interactions take center stage, explanations will have to reach further into interpersonal processes, although they can still remain small in scale. If people learn performances collectively, our explanations will have to include a good deal more coordination and shared understanding, some of it large enough in scale to include most or all of the participants in a given episode. If repertoires turn out to be the chief sites of learning, we analysts will have to allow for extensive coordination, large-scale indoctrination, and collective adoption of strategic logics.

The rest of this book argues that learning occurs at all four levels, but pride of place goes to the level of performances. Participants in contentious politics certainly learn how to perform individual actions such as marching and smashing. They also learn to differentiate interactions clearly from each other; they always learn, for example, to separate "us" from "them," even though who qualifies as "us" and "them" shifts frequently in the flux of contentious politics. They usually learn repertoire-level strategic logics that govern the choice to initiate, mix, and match different performances in a certain kind of claim making. They become more knowledgeable in those strategic logics, furthermore, to the extent that they become specialists and/or leaders in contentious politics.

Most of all, participants in contentious politics learn how to match performances with local circumstances, to play their own parts within those performances, and to modify performances in the light of their effects. As a result, performances vary and change in partial independence of repertoires. Street demonstrations, for an obvious case in point, belong to the repertoires of social movement activists who are communicating their programs to authorities and the general public. But they likewise belong to the repertoires of some groups of workers who also engage in strikes, slow-downs, and grievance meetings to confront their employers. Street demonstrations therefore vary somewhat in form and content depending on whether social movement activists or workers are staging them.

If that is true, it sets a challenging explanatory agenda. For it means we must explain variation and change in

Origins, feasibility, and efficacy of individual actions that occur within contentious performances

Origins, feasibility, and efficacy of individual interactions that occur within contentious performances

Articulation of actions and interactions with each other in the course of contentious performances

Origins, feasibility, and efficacy of whole performances

Articulation of performances within repertoires

In strong repertoires, all of these elements interact with one another. Communications innovations such as cellular telephones and Internet connections, for example, make rapid communication easier in the heat of action. They affect the origins, feasibility, and efficacy of individual actions. The viability of individual actions in turn shapes the origins, feasibility, and efficacy of whole performances such as simultaneous street demonstrations in multiple locations. But effects also flow in the opposite direction: the emergence of antislavery mobilizations across the Atlantic during the late 18th century and of anti-globalization mobilizations across the world during the early 21st century both promoted invention of claim-making actions that would travel well from one site to another and would lend themselves to simultaneous performance in separate locations.

As we will see in detail later on, the organization of national political regimes strongly affects the content of contentious repertoires. In particular, two factors make a large difference: the capacity of the government to intervene in everyday affairs and the regime's degree of democracy. On the whole, agents of high-capacity regimes like that of 19th-century Britain play much larger parts in day-to-day contention than do agents of low-capacity regimes, hence higher proportions of all contentious events orient toward those agents. In general, democratic regimes tolerate a wider range of claim-making actions than undemocratic regimes. They do so at the price of placing a clear boundary between acceptable and unacceptable forms of action and intervening aggressively against the forbidden forms. Later we will watch closely the interplay between Great Britain's partial democratization and deep transformations of its contentious politics between 1750 and 1840.

Formal Descriptions of Performances and Repertoires

European and American governments began collecting official reports on work stoppages during the later 19th century. From that point on, statistically minded analysts began conducting quantitative analyses of industrial conflict based on government data (Franzosi 1989, 1995, Haimson and Tilly 1989, Korpi and Shalev 1979, 1980, Shorter and Tilly 1974). During the 1920s and 1930s, pioneers such as my great teacher Pitirim Sorokin constructed chronologies for wars and revolutions (Sorokin 1962 [1937]). Not until after World War II, however, did analysts dealing with other forms of struggle start constructing parallel data sets for revolutions, coups d'état, international wars, civil wars, and domestic collective violence (Cioffi-Revilla 1990, Rucht, Koopmans, and Neidhardt 1999, Rule and Tilly 1965, Sarkees, Wayman, and Singer 2003, Tillema 1991, Tilly 1969). For many years, investigators sought to do one of two things with those collections: either to explain place-to-place variation in the intensity of conflict or to analyze fluctuations over time. For those purposes, simple counts of whole events served reasonably well. They served well, that is, so long as investigators could agree on what counted as an individual event (Olzak 1989, Tilly 2002a).

By and large, analysts who did simple counts worried little about performances and repertoires. To be sure, students of strikes distinguished strikes from lockouts, wildcats from formally registered walkouts, and successful from unsuccessful stoppages. Similarly, studies of collective violence typically employed classifications of intensity (how many killed and wounded, how much property damage) and form (street fights, violent demonstrations, uprisings, and more). They analyzed classified event counts. For them, cross-tabulations and correlations provided information on the nature and characteristic settings of different sorts of claims. Yet on the whole they included too little evidence for serious examination of the questions we are pursuing here: the origins, feasibility, and efficacy of individual actions; the articulation of performances within repertoires; and so on.

Austrian social historian Gerhard Botz, for example, prepared a chronology of strikes and "violent political events" for Austria from 1918 to 1938. The violent events came mainly from his reading of three Viennese newspapers – the *Reichspost*, *Arbeiter-Zeitung*, and *Neue Freie Presse* – over the entire period. Botz then added strike data from 1946 to 1976 (Botz 1983, 1987). He combined two methods: 1) analytic narratives placing the selected events in Austria's political history and 2) regression analyses relating fluctuations in violent events (1918–1938) and strikes (1918–1938, 1946–1976) to economic growth, unemployment, and trade union membership. Like many other studies in this vein, the quantitative analyses show mainly a broad tendency for strike activity to rise and fall with employment, union membership, and prosperity.

About the same time that Botz was working in Austria, Swiss sociologist-historian Hanspeter Kriesi and his colleagues were cataloging what they called "political activation events" in Switzerland from 1945 to 1978. They combed newspapers, political yearbooks, historical works, archives, strike statistics, and leftist literature collections for occasions on which ordinary citizens initiated collective, public claims over specific political issues (Kriesi, Levy, Ganguillet, and Zwicky 1981: 16–33). They also examined the public responses to those 3,553 events. Their extensive quantitative analyses of the data showed that the Swiss system encouraged plenty of citizen participation (see Frey and Stutzer 2002, Trechsel 2000), but also gave a very cold shoulder to marginal groups and stridently anti-government activists (Kriesi, Levy, Ganguillet, and Zwicky 1981: 596–598).

With these results as a background, Kriesi recruited another group of collaborators for a large-scale international comparison of "protest events" in France, Germany, the Netherlands, and Switzerland. They read the Monday issues of four national newspapers from 1975 through 1989, spotting "politically motivated unconventional actions" (Kriesi, Koopmans, Duyvendak, and Giugni 1995: 263; see also Kriesi 1993). They found 7,116 of them, about 120 per country per year. They meant to determine whether the form of the political opportunity structure – for example, very fragmented in Switzerland, highly centralized in France – affected the character and intensity of social movements. Their answer, backed by extensive data: yes, it does. Switzerland provided many more niches for small, differentiated protests, while France gave the advantage to nationally coordinated political activity. The Kriesi and collaborators study represents a sophisticated use of the classified event count, which in recent decades has become the standard method for making descriptions of contentious episodes available for quantitative analysis.[2]

No doubt the largest single classified event count for contentious politics in existence is Prodat (for Protest Data), in which Dieter Rucht and collaborators have assembled records for almost 15 thousand "protest actions" in Germany from 1950 through 1997.[3] Table 1-1 presents the overall counts. In the set, petition drives, marches, and static demonstrations account for more than half the events and more than 90 percent of all participants. But the range runs from brawls to hunger strikes and beyond. Still, Rucht himself points out the data's limitations:

Such findings can be expanded and differentiated further on the basis of information from protest event analysis, but in essence, they are limited to external features. They tell us little or nothing about the organizational effort of preparing and staging protest marches, the tactical considerations of the organizers, the socio-structural composition of the group of participants and their attitudes, and the direct and indirect impact of the marches. These require other sociological methods, such as participant observation, the questioning of organizers and participants, detailed case studies looking at themes and conflict, media analyses, and, finally, analyses of political decision-making processes. (Rucht 2007: 57; see also Rucht 1991, Rucht and Neidhardt 1998)

For all their other virtues, then, none of these massive investigations offered much opportunity to look inside contentious performances and discern their dynamics. Some investigators, however, have come closer. Driven by a general interest in how collective behavior works, Clark

---

[2] E.g., Beissinger 2002, Brockett 2005, Duyvendak 1994, Ekiert and Kubik 1999, Fillieule 1997, Giugni 1995, Imig and Tarrow 2001, Koopmans 1995, Lindenberger 1995, López-Maya, Smilde, and Stephany 2002, Robert 1996, Rucht and Koopmans 1999, Rucht, Koopmans, and Neidhardt 1999, Rucht and Ohlemacher 1992, Soule 1997, 1999, Tartakowsky 1997, and Tilly, Tilly, and Tilly 1975.

[3] More specialized catalogs, however, sometimes amass large numbers; for example, Danielle Tartatkowsky catalogs about 15,000 French street demonstrations from 1918 to 1968, whereas Edward Shorter and I analyzed data on about 100,000 French strikes from 1830 to 1968 (Tartakowsky 1997, Shorter and Tilly 1974).

Table 1-1. *Forms of Contention and Their Participants in Germany, 1950–1997*

Form	Actions (%)	Participants (%)
Petition, open letter, etc.	19.5	35.7
March	18.0	21.4
Static demonstration	15.6	34.0
Strike	12.0	5.1
Serious damage to property	5.5	0.0
Disturbance, obstruction	4.5	0.7
Legal proceedings	3.7	0.1
Assembly, teach-in	3.4	1.9
Occupation	3.2	0.1
Non-verbal protest	2.6	0.1
Blockade, sit-in	2.6	0.2
Flyer	2.3	0.1
Brawl, mêlée	1.6	0.1
Damage to property	1.5	0.0
Hunger strike	1.2	0.0
Press conference	1.0	0.0
Assault	1.0	0.0
Appeal	0.2	0.3
Defamation	0.1	0.0
Larceny, break-in	0.1	0.0
Manslaughter, murder	0.1	0.0
Other	0.3	0.0
Total %	100.0	100.0
Total number	14,686	68,156,452

Source: Rucht 2007: 52.

McPhail took the first steps toward a general account not just of contentious events but of all occasions on which people assemble, act together, and disperse. In 1983, McPhail personally observed forty-six political demonstrations in Washington, DC. He broke them down into specific types of gathering, more than one of which sometimes occurred in the same demonstration. The distribution of the seventy-five gatherings he saw looked like this: rally (34), march (19), vigil (10), picket (6), rally-picket–civil disobedience (3), rally–civil disobedience (1), picket–civil disobedience (1), and civil disobedience (1) (McPhail 1991: 183). McPhail's observed repertoire thus consisted of five distinct performances: rally, march, vigil, picket, and civil disobedience. Mostly the performances occurred separately, but sometimes they combined.

McPhail proposed to group individual gatherings of these sorts into larger sets: events like demonstrations, campaigns involving multiple events, waves including both individual events and campaigns, and trends. He nevertheless attached particular importance to the fine structure of gatherings:

If comparatively few sociologists have given attention to what people do collectively within gatherings, an increasing number have given attention to larger units of analysis, at more macro levels of analysis, e.g. gatherings, events, campaigns, waves, and trends. The relationships between what people do collectively at micro and macro levels of analysis are too important to ignore. These must be considered in relation to rather than at odds with one another (McPhail 1991: 186; see also McPhail 2006, McPhail and Miller 1973, and McPhail and Wohlstein 1983).

Later, McPhail became more ambitious and fine-grained. He decomposed actions and interactions into four broad categories: facing, voicing, manipulating, and locomotion. Joint actions (e.g., simultaneous facing in the same direction) and interactions (e.g., joining hands) counted as collective action (McPhail, Schweingruber, and Ceobanu 2006). Next McPhail and his collaborators broke each one down with finer and finer distinctions. Voicing, for example, first divided into verbalizing and vocalizing, with vocalizing further subdivided into cheering, booing, oohing-ohhing-ahhing, and whistling. A code sheet then permitted observers to record how many people in some assembly were performing each action or interaction at a given point in time and space (Schweingruber and McPhail 1999: 466).

Multiple observers and their code sheets thus aggregated into overall characterizations of action and interaction distributions for different episodes. They showed, for example, how much more frequently people cheered in a rally than in a march (Schweingruber and McPhail 1999: 480). The procedure centers attention on actions and especially interactions as the elementary particles of collective performances. McPhail's promising line of research has not so far yielded either a coherent theory of performances and repertoires or a feasible method for aggregating and disaggregating descriptions of contentious performances into the sorts of characteristics studied by Botz, Kriesi, and other users of classified event counts. But it heads in the right direction.

International relations specialists have come at the problem from a somewhat different angle: transcribing international actions such as diplomatic exchanges and military attacks uniformly and voluminously from standard news sources. Political scientist Philip Schrodt and his collaborators have devised methods for making simple transcriptions of newswire reports. Schrodt called the system KEDS, the Kansas Event Data System. As Schrodt describes it,

> KEDS relies on shallow parsing of sentences – primarily identifying proper nouns (which may be compound), verbs and direct objects within a verb phrase – rather than using full syntactical analysis. As a consequence it makes errors on complex sentences or sentences using unusual grammatical constructions, but has proven to be quite robust in correctly coding the types of English sentences typically found in the lead sentences of newswire reports. On early-1990s hardware, the system coded about 70 events per second, which seemed at the time to be a huge improvement over human coding projects, which typically have a sustained output of five to ten events per coder per hour. (Schrodt 2006: 5)

A technical cousin of KEDS called the VRA (Virtual Research Associates) System likewise processes the leads or first sentences of online news reports, recording subject, verb, and object (Bond 2006). In principle, these related approaches could eventually produce a fast, sophisticated way to assemble detailed accounts of contentious performances and repertoires. For the moment, however, they have not come close to solving the problems of aggregation and disaggregation inherent in any such effort.

So far, Sidney Tarrow, Roberto Franzosi, and Takeshi Wada have come closest. Tarrow examined Italy's cycle of protest from 1965 to 1975, for which the national newspaper *Corriere della Sera* yielded 4,980 "protest events." "Since I was interested in actions that exceeded routine expectations and in which the participants revealed a collective goal," Tarrow tells us, "I collected information on 'protest events,' a category which included strikes, demonstrations, petitions, delegations, and violence, but which excluded contentious behaviour which revealed no collective claims on other actors. I defined the protest event as a disruptive direct action on behalf of collective interests, in which claims were made against some other group, elites, or authorities" (Tarrow 1989: 359).

Like most of his predecessors, Tarrow produced a single machine-readable record for each event. But he enriched the enterprise in three important ways. First, he incorporated textual descriptions at a number of critical points – summaries of events, grievances, policy responses, and more. That made it possible to refine his classified counts without returning to the original newspaper sources. Second, within the record he placed checklists in which two or more features could coexist. As a result, he was able to analyze not only the overall distribution of events but also the frequency of such features as different forms of violence – clashes with police, violent conflict, property damage, violent attacks, rampages, and random violence (Tarrow 1989: 78). Third, Tarrow also created an index of "intensity" by combining and weighting the frequencies of different sorts of action, for example, petitions versus physical violence. Thus cross-classifications of broad event types with specific forms of action brought Tarrow closer to a systematic description of performances, if not of repertoires.

Tarrow consulted me before starting his collection of evidence on Italian contentious events. So did Roberto Franzosi. Franzosi once spent a year working closely with members of my research group. Although he eventually developed his own sophisticated system for recording events, he started his analysis of Italian conflicts since 1919 with a logic my own work has followed closely (Franzosi 2004a: 39). The logic uses observed combinations of subject, verb, and object – which Franzosi calls "semantic triplets" – to identify interactions, then attaches further information to the triplets.

On 30 August 1920, workers at Milan's Romeo metalworking plant responded to a management lockout by occupying the factory (Franzosi 2004a: 66). The occupation started a great wave of sitdown strikes – *occupazioni delle fabbriche* – that eventually became a model for sitdowns in France, the United States, and elsewhere.

Franzosi shows that he can meaningfully reduce the complex story in the Genoese newspaper *Il Lavoro* to these phases:

firm announces lockout
workers do not accept decision
labor leaders decide factory occupation
workers do not leave plant (Franzosi 2004a: 78)

This plus further information tagged to these spare elements makes it possible for Franzosi to produce rich analyses first of the single episode and then of many episodes: network representations of relations among the actors, classifications of participants' actions and their sequences, time-series of different sorts of events, and much more. Packed into the general-purpose data storage and retrieval system Franzosi has developed (Franzosi 2004b), the information becomes available for a great variety of pairings.

Properly handled, as Franzosi says, even simple counts tell complex stories. For example, Franzosi's frequency distribution of the most common actors from 1919 to 1922 identifies an astonishing shift: from heavy involvement of workers and trade unions during the revolutionary years of 1919 and 1920 to their rapid decline; from near-absence of political activists (including Fascists) to their utter prevalence; and no more than a weak presence of government officials as Mussolini's Fascists began their ascent to power (Franzosi 2004a: 82–84). Those counts then send canny analyst Franzosi back to look more closely at how different actors within these categories interacted and what claims they made.

Takeshi Wada's work on Mexican politics between 1964 and 2000 displays many affinities with both Tarrow's and Franzosi's analyses of Italian contention (Wada 2003, 2004; Wada wrote his doctoral dissertation under my direction). Wada drew accounts of protest events from the daily newspapers *Excélsior*, *Unomásuno*, and *La Jornada* for twenty-nine-day periods spanning national elections over the thirty-seven years, a total of thirteen electoral periods. From the newspapers he identified 2,832 events, some linked together in campaigns, for a total of 1,797 campaigns. Wada's subject-verb-object-claim transcriptions made it possible for him to employ sophisticated network models of who made claims on whom. Overall, they reveal a sharp politicization of Mexico's collective claim making as the country's partial democratization proceeded. From claims on business, landowners, and universities, protesters moved to making increasingly strong claims on the government itself.

According to Wada's analysis, the weakening of network ties among the elite (especially as concentrated within the longtime ruling party PRI) provided an opportunity for claimants to divide their rulers. It thus advanced the partial democratization of the 1990s. Technically, Wada broke free of many restrictions imposed by classified event counts. That technical freedom opened the way to a sophisticated treatment of interaction in Mexican politics.

The innovations of McPhail, Tarrow, Franzosi, and Wada offer three lessons for analysts of contentious politics. First, it is practically feasible to record and analyze the internal dynamics of contentious episodes instead of settling for classified event counts. Second, the recording of particular verbs rather than general characterization of the action is crucial for that practical purpose. Third, verbs with objects make it possible to move from individualistic analyses to treatments of connections among contentious actors.

Detecting Performances and Repertoires

Note the implications. Transcribing episodes action-by-action does not simply provide more detailed descriptions of events. It frees the analyst from simple aggregate counts of events coded as strikes, meetings, demonstrations, and the like. The freedom runs in two directions: toward the possibility of reclassifying episodes on the basis of more detailed knowledge, and away from the aggregation of whole episodes toward the comparison and linking of actors, actions, interactions, locations, and issues, plus all the other elements of performances and repertoires.

This book pivots on the use of refined event descriptions to explain how actions, interactions, performances, and repertoires vary and change. How can we face that mighty challenge? Before anything else, we should look for signs that repertoires actually exist. Among signs that repertoires actually exist, the most telling would be these:

- In particular times and places, performances cluster into a limited number of recurrent, well-defined types.
- For a given set of actors and issues, those performances change relatively little from one round of action to the next.
- Participants in contention give evidence that they are aware of those performances by giving names to them, referring to previous actions of the same kind, giving each other instructions, adopting divisions of labor that require prior consultation or experience, anticipating each other's actions, and/or terminating actions more or less simultaneously.
- Within the range defined by all contentious actions that a given set of actors carry on, substantial blanks appear; combinations of actions clearly lying within the technical reach of participants never occur.
- Within a set of connected actors, each significant pair of actors has its own repertoire. In the pair, claim-making actors make choices within the existing repertoire.
- The more connected the histories of actors outside of contention, the more similar their repertoires.

In many cases like Wada's analysis of Mexican democratization we might also expect to pinpoint significant shifts in performances and repertoires as political opportunity structures change. We might then ask more detailed questions about the transition:

- How much of the change occurred by means of the evolution of existing performances, how much through changes in the relative salience of already-existing performances, how much through the rapid introduction of new performances?
- How uneven was the shift across regions, issues, and groups, and why?
- To what extent did the shift result from changes in the distribution of contention across regions, issues, and groups?
- To what extent did changes result from coordinate transformations or substitutions of whole performances rather than specific elements of performances?
- How large a difference did governmental repression and facilitation make?
- Did repertoire changes make it easier for some actors to act or to get results, and harder for others?

Some of these questions are easy, some of them difficult, but all are answerable in principle.

Yet certain problems remain troubling. Many of them cluster around questions of outcomes and effectiveness. Do innovations associated with successful pressing of contentious claims, for instance, tend to reappear in the next round of claim making? Without evidence on outcomes we can rarely judge effectiveness, but reports of contentious episodes often stop as the participants disperse. It usually takes more work to determine how authorities, competitors, spectators, and objects of claims responded, and an even greater effort to discern the impact of an episode on the general public.

Thin documentation of outcomes, in its turn, renders judgments of effectiveness risky. It has never been easy to trace the effectiveness of contention, especially when the presumed effects lie outside the action itself, concern multiple actors, and occur incrementally.[4] We must do

---

[4] See Amenta 2006, Andrews 2004, Banaszak 1999, Button 1978, DeNardo 1985, Gamson 1990, Giugni, McAdam, and Tilly 1999, Gran and Hein 2005, Ibarra 2003, Jenkins 1985, Linders 2004, Luders 2006, Mansbridge 1986, Markoff 1997, McAdam and Su 2002, McCammon, Campbell, Granberg, and Mowery 2001, McVeigh, Welch, and Bjarnason 2003, Schumaker 1978, Skocpol 1992, Snyder 1976, 1978, Soule and Olzak 2004, Stearns and Almeida 2004, Tamayo 1999, Tilly and Wood 2003, and Wisler and Giugni 1999.

three difficult things: 1) catalog the political gains and losses of certain actors separately from the descriptions of contention itself, 2) spread those gains and losses across multiple events, and 3) work out alternative testable models of the relationship between action and external outcome.

Again, large arguments concerning the effects of changing interests, organization, culture, and political position of potential political actors require long-term observations going far beyond the perimeters of contentious gatherings, indeed of contention in general. Although in a sense most political and social history concerns just such issues, the challenge of documenting such changes and their links to contentious action for even a small proportion of all potential actors looms enormous. It's even worse than that: in the long run, crucial arguments also concern potential actors that do not act, regions that harbor little or no contention, and situations in which interests are at stake, but contention remains minimal.

Finally, the explanatory approach this chapter has sketched invokes collective awareness, learning, and adaptation. Take the street demonstration. If it developed from such earlier forms of collective action as religious processions, military parades, and excursions by fraternal orders, part of the process must have included deliberate borrowing and adaptation, followed by consolidation of the new form. It also must have involved negotiation with authorities over participants' rights to borrow and adapt those established routines. How can we capture such a complex process over thousands of externally described episodes?

This book makes the attempt by emphasizing history. Well documented historical accounts have two great advantages for our purposes. First, they allow us to draw on historians' expertise in reconstructing the political, economic, and social contexts of contentious politics as we search for explanations of change and variation. Second, they involve streams of struggle that have run their course and wrought their consequences. In historical retrospect, we have a chance to detect recurrent patterns. That is why the book emphasizes the history of Great Britain during the 18th and 19th centuries, as well as undertaking recurrent comparisons with Ireland, France, Britain's 18th-century North American colonies, and other historical instances. They place contentious performances in historical-comparative perspective.

Chapters to come address these issues: a first main section treats variation and change in repertoires. Chapter 2 looks more closely at the systematic description of performances and repertoires, Chapter 3 at how performances and repertoires change, and Chapter 4 at campaigns – organized pursuit of programs through multiple performances. The book's second half then shifts to more specialized but no less interesting topics: the invention of the social movement and its repertoire (Chapter 5), how change and variation in national regimes and economies affects contentious repertoires (Chapter 6), and larger historical-comparative perspectives on repertoire change (Chapter 7). A concluding chapter (Chapter 8) braids these diverse strands together. By the end, we should have a much clearer picture of how and why so much variation and change in how people make contentious claims occurred in the past, and continue to occur today.

2

How to Detect and Describe Performances
and Repertoires

The classified counts approach to contentious performances assembles
catalogs of events, categorizes them, and computes frequencies of those
events by time and place. One of the most impressive recent analyses in
this tradition pinned down how nationalist mobilization helped shatter
the Soviet Union. Concentrating on the crucial years from 1987 to 1992,
Soviet specialist Mark Beissinger and his research team assembled massive
evidence on Soviet and post-Soviet contention. His event catalogs
included both relatively peaceful demonstrations and viciously violent
confrontations.

Beissinger used his collection of episodes to untangle the disintegration
of the Soviet state. As he put it:

The fundamental unit of analysis in this study is the contentious event. Although
by no means the only method for dissecting contention, event analysis is widely
recognized as a tool for studying waves of mobilization. It is essentially a way of
tracking over time the rise and fall of particular types of events and the features
associated with them. (Beissinger 2002: 42)

An experienced analyst of Soviet politics, Beissinger wanted to explain the
enormous rise of separatist nationalism in the Soviet Union after 1986.
Successful bids for independence on the part of former Soviet republics
blew the union apart by 1991.

Beissinger could have written an interpretive history of the whole
process. He chose instead to center his analysis on two large catalogs of
episodes from the beginning of 1987 to August 1991: one of 5,067 protest
demonstrations with at least one hundred participants, the other of 2,173
incidents in which at least fifteen people attacked persons or property.
He further classified the violent events as 1) ethnic riots, 2) communal

violence, 3) pogroms, and 4) ethnic warfare. Beissinger also prepared catalogs of strikes and of demonstrations before 1987, but concentrated his analysis on the two large files.

In preparing those two catalogs, Beissinger and his collaborators consulted 150 different sources, including Russian-language newspapers, wire services, compilations by Soviet dissidents, émigré publications, and reports of foreign monitoring services. They were able to show that by the later 1980s the street demonstration – which sometimes turned into a violent clash – had become a standard performance in the shaken Soviet Union.

Setting the catalogs against his own knowledge of Soviet politics, Beissinger was able to show how initial demands for internal reforms of the Soviet Union gave way to bids for regional autonomy and independence, by no means all of them successful. Early successes of demands for independence in such places as Estonia and Latvia encouraged further demands across a wide range of republics and increasing violence as unsuccessful claimants faced competition and repression.

Between 1987 and 1991, across the USSR many regionally organized nationalities began to make collective claims for autonomy or independence. By 1992, fifteen of them had managed to secede from the union and gain international certification as sovereign states. When Beissinger was analyzing his event catalogs, one of the many things he did was to chart the frequency with which members of different Soviet nationalities staged protest demonstrations month-by-month from 1987 through 1991 (Beissinger 2002: 84). For the most active, these were the peak months:

Armenians	May 1988
Estonians	November 1988
Moldavians	February 1989
Russians	January 1990
Crimean Tatars	April 1990
Ukrainians	November 1990
Latvians	December 1990
Lithuanians	December 1990
Azerbaijanis	December 1990
Georgians	September 1991

The Soviet Union had built these categories and their boundaries into its governing structure, for example, by treating Ukraine and Lithuania as distinct units of rule with some degree of autonomy on such questions as language and cultural expression. As a result, all existed as established interests. They easily created activist groups claiming to speak for all Ukrainians, all Lithuanians, and so on down the list. Brokerage brought together different clusters within a given nationality into a temporarily unified actor.

Other political actors were also at work in the disintegrating Soviet Union: Soviet leader Mikhail Gorbachev, Russian leader (and later Russian president) Boris Yeltsin, emerging industrial tycoons, the government's security service, and more. Yet by itself this simple chronology tells an important tale about the sequence of flight from the USSR. On the union's edge and supported by powerful neighbors, Armenians and Estonians acted early and successfully, securing quick outside support for their claims to become independent states. Then the rush began. It peaked at the end of 1990. Of these major actors, all but the Tatars of the Crimea (who ended up inside Ukraine) eventually won independence.

Beissinger points out that demonstrations and attacks did occur occasionally in the Soviet Union before Gorbachev began his reform programs. In April 1965, for example, 100 thousand people gathered in Yerevan, Armenia, to commemorate victims of the Ottoman expulsion and massacre of Armenians fifty years earlier (Beissinger 2002: 71). Under that repressive regime, however, both demonstrations and collective attacks by anyone other than state authorities remained very rare. The script ran differently after 1985. Once such Soviet Republics as Estonia and Armenia started edging toward independence with foreign support, leaders of titular nationalities across the Soviet Union began making demands for autonomy or independence. Figure 2-1 describes monthly changes from 1987 through 1992.

An initially peaceful process soon radicalized and escalated. In principle, a straightforward cycle could have occurred: a decentralized USSR could have granted partial autonomy to a certain number of titular nationalities, incorporated them into its governing structure, repressed the more unruly and threatening claimants, and returned to a revised version of Soviet business as usual. At one point, Gorbachev actually tried to do just this, but failed. Instead, fifteen nationalities gained total independence, others acquired rights they had never enjoyed under Soviet

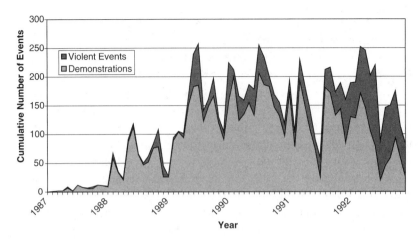

Figure 2-1 Demonstrations and Violent Events in the Soviet Union and Successor States, 1987–1992 (Source: Mark Beissinger)

rule, and what Beissinger calls a "tide of nationalism" emerged. In the process, the regime known as the Soviet Union disappeared. Beissinger says of the violent events in Figure 2-1:

In all, I have been able to identify thirty-two major waves of nationalist violence in the former USSR during the 1987–92 period, part of sixteen larger ethnonationalist conflicts involving violence during these years. Only in four of these conflicts (the Azerbaijani-Armenian conflict, the Georgian-Ossetian conflict, the Georgian-Abkhaz conflict, and the Moldovan-Transdniestr conflict) did violence become a self-sustaining strategy of contesting state boundaries, with relatively short waves of violence growing increasingly protracted over time. In all other cases, violent mobilization remained short-lived. What distinguished conflicts in which mass violence grew sustained from those in which violence ceased to proliferate was the relationship of state institutions to the production of violence. (Beissinger 2002: 309)

Notice, for instance, the quick acceleration of nationalist claims in 1989, after Armenians, Estonians, and Moldavians had already made strong bids for autonomy. Beissinger explains the sequence as a consequence of a modified political cycle: early risers, on the average, either gained some advantages or demobilized peacefully. But those who persisted despite previous failures or arrived on the scene late encountered rising resistance and engaged increasingly in claim making that incited or entailed violence. If the latecomers' program centered on political autonomy or independence, violence from both sides occurred more often. Figure 2-1 clearly displays the rising ratio of violent events to peaceful demonstrations as the cycle proceeded.

Coupled with deep knowledge of the context, then, relatively simple classified event counts can provide crucial evidence on major political processes. Beissinger's event catalogs do not, however, make it possible to do two crucial things: 1) look inside individual episodes to analyze the interplay of actors, actions, interactions, and contentious claims and 2) examine exactly how one episode affects the next. For those purposes, we need more refined evidence on performances and repertoires. This chapter describes ways of achieving that refinement. It does so by returning to a study that the work of Franzosi and Wada has surpassed in technical finesse. I present an older model because I know it well, and I can draw readily on the evidence it produced.

The Great Britain Study

Pinning down performances and repertoires by means of event catalogs requires a vigorous but vital technical effort. Over about ten years, research groups at the University of Michigan and the New School for Social Research worked with me to create a systematic body of evidence on actions, interactions, performances, repertoires, and their settings in Great Britain between 1758 and 1834. We invented a series of interactive routines that allowed our researchers to converse with a mainframe computer, store extensive summaries of hand-edited files in a relational data base, and retrieve information from and about contentious gatherings (CGs) in an almost infinite variety of ways (Schweitzer and Simmons 1981). We called our enterprise the Great Britain Study (GBS).

The central data set we produced includes machine-readable descriptions for 8,088 CGs that occurred in southeastern England (Kent, Middlesex, Surrey, or Sussex) during thirteen selected years from 1758 to 1820, or anywhere in Great Britain (England, Scotland, and Wales, but not Ireland) from 1828 to 1834. In this study, a CG is an occasion on which ten or more people gathered in a publicly accessible place and visibly made claims that, if realized, would affect the interests of at least one person outside their number. In principle, CGs include almost all events that authorities, observers, or historians of the time would have called "riots" or "disturbances" as well as even more that would fall under such headings as "public meeting," "procession," and "demonstration."

Our standardized descriptions of CGs come from periodicals: the *Annual Register*, *Gentleman's Magazine*, *London Chronicle*, *Morning Chronicle*, *Times of London*, *Hansard's Parliamentary Debates*, *Mirror of Parliament*, and *Votes and Proceedings of Parliament*; we read these periodicals exhaustively for the years in question plus January to June 1835. Although we frequently consulted both published historical work and archival sources such as the papers of the Home Office in interpreting our evidence, the machine-readable descriptions transcribed material from the periodicals alone. We did not try to find every event about which information was available or even a representative sample of such events. Instead, we assembled a complete enumeration of those described in standard periodicals whose principles of selection we could examine, and sometimes even test.

Our group created a kind of assembly line: one researcher scanned periodicals for reports of likely qualifying events, another assembled those reports into dossiers of qualifying and non-qualifying CGs, a third hand-transcribed the reports onto preliminary code sheets, an editor reviewed the summary, the next person entered the material in a computer conversation, and so on to a finished entry in the database. Obviously, we could not simply automate the assembly line, as the newswire analysts described in Chapter 1 almost have. On average, we had 2.6 accounts from our periodicals for each CG. That meant we often had to piece together incomplete stories and sometimes had to adjudicate disagreements over such aspects as how many people participated. We also spent plenty of time looking up obscure place names in gazetteers and personal names in histories or biographical dictionaries. Now and then, transcribers made mistakes. Editors had to catch them. In short, it took plenty of conscious, intelligent effort to produce faithful but reduced transcriptions of our sources.

The computer-stored records for CGs break into separate sections:

- A general description of each event (8,088 machine-readable records)
- A description of each formation – each person or set of persons who acted distinguishably during the event (27,184 records)
- Supplementary information on the geographical or numerical size of any formation, when available (18,413 records)
- A summary of each distinguishable action by any formation, including the actor(s), the crucial verb, the object(s) of the action (where applicable), and an excerpt of the text(s) from which we drew actor, verb, and object (50,875 records)

- Excerpts from detailed texts from which we drew summary descriptions of actions (76,189 records)
- Identification of each source of the account (21,030 records)
- Identification of each location in which the action occurred, including county, town, parish, place, and position within a one-hundred-meter grid square map of Great Britain (11,054 records)
- A set of verbal comments on the event, or on difficulties in its transcription (5,450 records)
- Special files listing all alternative names for formations and all individuals mentioned in any account (28,995 formation names, 26,318 individual names)

Except for straightforward items such as date, day of the week, and county names, the records do not contain codes in the usual sense of the term. On the whole, we transcribed words from the texts or (when that was not feasible) paraphrases of those words. Think of formation names: instead of coding names given to formations in broad categories, we transcribed the actual words used in our sources. For example, the transcription of each action includes the actor's name, a verb characterizing the action, and (in the roughly 52 percent of cases in which there was an object) the object's name.

Here is a simple case. In its issue of 24–26 January 1758, the *London Chronicle* reported that

some Persons assembled in a riotous Manner on Tower-Hill, and broke several Windows, Candles not being soon enough lighted in Honour of the King of Prussia's Birth Day. The same night the Mob committed great Violences in Surry-Street in the Strand, particularly at the Coach-Office, not a Window was left with a whole Pane of Glass.

During the European conflicts historians eventually called the Seven Years' War, Britain had recently allied with Prussia, which temporarily made the King of Prussia a popular hero in London. Lighting candles in windows then signaled the occupants' support for a public celebration. People often marked their disapproval of a building's occupants by breaking windows. We interpreted the "some persons" as insufficient evidence that ten or more people had gathered in the same place before the attack on the Coach Office, but took "mob" as indicating at least ten persons got together at the office. The machine-readable transcription of the actions in question therefore ran like this:

Transcription	Subject	Verb	Object
the same night the mob (gathered)	mob	#gather	none
the mob committed great violences in Surry-Street, in the Strand, particularly at the Coach-Office, not a window was left with a whole pane of glass	mob	#break	owner of Coach-Office
	mob	#end	none

In this case, the #gather, #break, and #end indicate that we inferred the verb from the narrative rather than finding it directly in the text. Most of the time, however, the texts themselves supplied verbs.

We did take a few editorial liberties. We defined the event itself as starting when interaction began between the first pair of participating formations (including absent objects of claims, such as Parliament), and ending when interaction ended. That led to two further adaptations: 1) dividing actions reported in our sources into three segments – before, during, and after the event – but recording all of them and 2) supplying the verb "END" at the event's termination when our sources failed to report how the participants ceased interacting and/or dispersed. That second maneuver placed 5,936 ENDs in the machine-readable action record – almost 12 percent of all verbs, and almost 75 percent of all events.

Lovers of conventional historical narratives may find this approach to transcription of narratives mechanistic or reductionist. It certainly makes the evidence available for systematic analysis in ways that storytelling alone does not. In my view, however, the GBS transcription actually permits a richer, more subtle attachment of episodes to their contexts than sequential narratives allow. It does so by facilitating the connection of particular elements – the formations, actions, locations, and so on – both to their counterparts in other episodes and to the larger contexts within which they occur. In that sense, the method is anti-reductionist and expansive.

We also produced a number of other machine-readable files, including a transcription of Kent's directory of London trades for various years between 1758 and 1828, county census data, descriptions of London-area parishes, assemblies of ten or more people between 1758 and 1820 that did not qualify as CGs, a transcription of 1830s Swing events from *Captain Swing* by E. J. Hobsbawm and George Rudé, and a catalog of CGs drawn from a large number of published historical works. In addition, we accumulated massive files of microfilm, photocopy, and notes from British archives, notably including a complete set of county files from the Home Office for 1828–1834. All of these have played their parts in the analysis of changing claim making.

Figure 2-2 presents simple annual counts of CGs for the four counties of the London region. The enormous increase in numbers after 1811 combines a reporting effect with a major transformation of contention. So far as I can tell from detailed comparisons with local sources and local historians, our reliance on national periodicals meant that a smaller proportion of local events – especially labor disputes – entered our catalogs of 18th-century years. But the sheer volume of public claim making did shoot up after the Napoleonic Wars, as the state's wartime repression relaxed. At the same time, locally distinctive forms of conflict such as struggles over village commons and rivalries between trade groups gave way to nationally oriented claims. As a result, London-based periodicals paid increasing attention to contention wherever it occurred.

Unlike investigations singling out events in advance for their importance (whatever the criterion of importance), this sort of inquiry leads almost inevitably to a sense of déjà vu, to a realization that the events in any particular time and place fall into a limited number of categories, repeating themselves with only minor variations. The ideas of performance and repertoire almost force themselves on a reader of our event catalog.

Yet different settings and periods produce different arrays of events: collective seizures of grain, invasions of enclosed fields, and attacks on gamekeepers in one place and time; sacking of houses, satirical processions, and sending of delegations in another; demonstrations, strikes, and mass meetings in yet another. The prevailing forms of action likewise vary by the social class of the actors (burghers dealing with nobles act differently from peasants dealing with burghers), the contentious issues at hand (disciplining a fellow worker differs from seeking royal favors), and the immediate occasion for gathering (festival, election, meeting of legislative assembly, etc.). The arrays of actions obviously bear a coherent relationship to the social organization and routine politics of their settings.

The study builds in some risky epistemological and ontological wagers (Tilly and Goodin 2006). Epistemologically, this line of investigation bets that periodicals (at least in Great Britain during the 18th and 19th centuries) report enough of political contention sufficiently well for systematic

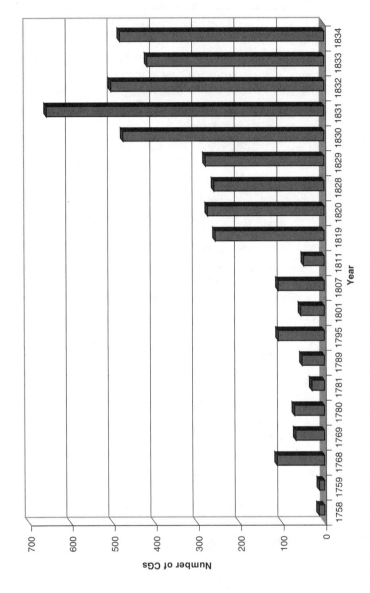

Figure 2-2 Contentious Gatherings in the London Region, 1758–1834

analysis of large-scale change and variation in contentious performances and repertoires. It goes further, assuming that canny investigators can infer causes and effects of political contention from relationships between public performances and their settings and from relationships among performances as well. Such an approach rejects a common belief: that only by probing the consciousness of individual and collective actors can we develop reliable causal accounts of their actions.

Ontologically, this sort of event-based study wagers on the likelihood that public political performances constitute causally coherent and distinguishable phenomena – that, for example, we can arrive at valid histories of the strike, the forcible seizure of food, or the public meeting in Great Britain. On the other hand, it denies that public political performances defined in these terms form universal categories for which we might be able to formulate covering laws of the type "All strikes everywhere are X and result from Y." Indeed, I initiated the study of Great Britain after long immersion in French history precisely because it seemed to me that the two regimes had fostered different patterns of variation and change in contention (Tilly 1986). Eventually this and other comparisons led me to the conclusion that analysts of political phenomena should not be searching for broad transnational empirical generalizations but for the causal mechanisms and processes that in different combinations, sequences, and initial conditions produce political variation and change (Tilly 2001).

To say the least, many other analysts of political contention reject one or another of these wagers (see, e.g., Goodwin and Jasper 2004, *Mobilization* 2003, Wells 2000). At least the bets have two great virtues. First, they make clearer than usual the assumptions about knowledge and reality readers must accept (however tentatively) in order to credit the findings of the British study and others like it. Second, if correct, they set challenging but feasible terms for explanatory comparison of contention in different times and places. That includes examining how contentious repertoires changed in Great Britain during the country's momentous transformations of the 18th and 19th centuries.

Changing Repertoires

In the case of Great Britain between the 1750s and 1830s, we can distinguish sharply between the repertoires prevailing at the beginning and the end. Performances that occurred frequently in the Southeast during the 18th century's middle decades included:

Smashing windows of householders who failed to illuminate

Breaking up of theaters at unsatisfactory performances

Collective seizures of food, often coupled with sacking the premises of the merchant

Fights between hunters and gamekeepers

Battles between smugglers and royal officers

Verbal and physical attacks on malefactors seen in the street or displayed in the pillory

Pulling down and/or sacking of dangerous or offensive houses

Donkeying, or otherwise humiliating, workers who violated collective agreements

Ridicule and/or destruction of symbols, effigies, and/or property of public figures or moral offenders

Liberation of prisoners

Mutinies of pressed military men

Taking sides at public executions

Workers' marches to public authorities in trade disputes

Outside of the Southeast, the comparable list includes not only all of these but also destruction of tollgates, invasions of enclosed land, and disruptions of public ceremonies and festivals (Bohstedt 1983, Brewer 1976, Brewer and Styles 1980, Charlesworth 1983, Harrison 1988, Hayter 1978, Stevenson 1979).

To simplify greatly, we might think of a characteristic British "18th-century" repertoire involving:

- People's frequent employment of the authorities' normal means of action, either as caricature or as a deliberate, if temporary, assumption of the authorities' prerogatives in the name of the local community
- Convergence on the residences of wrongdoers and the sites of wrongdoing, as opposed to seats and symbols of public power
- Extensive use of authorized public celebrations and assemblies for the presentation of grievances and demands
- Common appearance of the participants as members or representatives of constituted corporate groups and communities rather than of special interests
- A tendency to act directly against local enemies but to appeal to powerful patrons for redress of wrongs beyond the reach of the local community and, especially, for representation vis-à-vis outside authorities

- Repeated adoption of rich, irreverent symbolism in the form of effigies, dumb show, and ritual objects to state grievances and demands
- Shaping of action to particular circumstances and localities

On the whole, these constitute parochial, particular, and bifurcated performances: parochial in concentrating on local targets, and basing themselves on local groupings rather than local segments of regional and national groupings; particular in having highly differentiated forms of action for different groups, situations, and localities; bifurcated in dividing between direct action with respect to nearby objects of claims and action mediated by dignitaries and powerful people with respect to distant objects of claims.

The "18th-century" repertoire reflected a politics in which many corporate groups and communities had established local rights; policing was relatively ineffectual in the absence of local consensus; authorities commonly used exemplary punishment and ordinary people sometimes followed their example; most people condoned direct action against moral offenders; rights of assembly faced stringent limits; all power holders and contenders employed elaborate, symbol-drenched stagecraft; and ridicule and shunning served as powerful punishments, while the distinction between private and public life remained quite blurred. Yet during the 18th century the capitalization of the economy and the expansion of the state were threatening many of the rights and local memberships that underlay such a politics. For that very reason, they generated widespread contention.

Remember the essential qualifications: "18th century" only offers a rough approximation of a more complex timetable; some episodes combined more than one of these forms; no single category of actors carried on all these performances; each performance linked at least two actors, at a minimum one of them taking the other as a target, and the other often riposting with a different performance; innovation and improvisation occurred incessantly within the broad limits set by each of these performances.

In London itself, furthermore, the distinction between local and national blurred, since king, parliament, financial magnates of the City, and national power holders such as the East India Company lay close at hand; some relatively ordinary people (London's tailors and Spitalfields's weavers, for example) intermittently laid claims directly on those who ruled the land. But even they adopted performances in the 18th-century mode. The number of standard forms remained strikingly limited, excluding a number of other performances – armed insurrection, the formation of popular political parties, ritual execution, mass meetings, and so on – that could, in principle, likewise have taken place. Indeed, in the 1760s and 1770s some new forms of contention did gain ground amid the 18th century's standard routines. Later, we will look closely at transformations within the 18th century. In retrospect, we discover seeds of the demonstration, the mass meeting, and the social movement.

By the 1830s, the "18th-century" performances had almost entirely disappeared. Schematically, 19th-century British popular collective action tended to match these patterns:

- Use of relatively autonomous means of action, of a kind rarely or never employed by authorities (authorities, for instance, never staged street demonstrations)
- Participation as members or representatives of special interests, constituted public bodies, and named associations
- Direct challenges to rivals or authorities, especially national authorities and their representatives
- Deliberate organization of assemblies for the articulation of claims
- Display of programs, slogans, and symbols of common membership such as flags, colors, and lettered banners
- Preference for previously planned action in visible public places
- Preference for forms of action that transferred easily from one circumstance or locality to another

The essential qualifications again apply. In contrast to the parochial, particular, and bifurcated character of 18th-century repertoires, these performances constitute a relatively cosmopolitan, modular, and autonomous set. Examples include turnouts, strikes, demonstrations, electoral rallies, public meetings, petition marches, planned insurrections, invasions of official assemblies, organized social movements, and electoral campaigns. Some of them occurred, of course, during the 18th century. But they only became the predominant forms of popular contention during the 19th. Much of this book's remainder documents how, when, and why the 19th-century repertoire displaced its 18th-century predecessor.

We should resist the temptation to label one of the two repertoires as more efficient, more political, or more "revolutionary" than the other. Nor does it help to call one repertoire "traditional" and the other "modern," any more than one can say that contemporary English is superior to that of Shakespeare, as if one were clearly more efficient or sophisticated than the other (for laudable skepticism on this score, see Archer 1990: 24, 251). We must recognize that repertoires of contention are sets of tools for the people involved. Backward/forward, pre-political/political and similar distinctions do not classify the tools, but particular circumstances for using them. The tools serve more than one end, and their relative efficacy depends on the match among tools, tasks, and users. A new repertoire emerged in the 19th century because new users took up new tasks and found the available tools inadequate to their problems and abilities. In the course of actual struggles, people making claims and counter-claims fashioned new means of claim making. They grouped complementary performances into repertoires.

Neither the new tasks nor the new forms of action were intrinsically revolutionary. After all, the English had managed two revolutions in the 17th century with repertoires similar to those that prevailed in the 18th century, but never managed to make one in the 19th or 20th century with their new repertoires. A larger share of performances in the older repertoire (such as Rough Music and the pulling down of poorhouses) involved direct action against adversaries, whereas a much greater proportion of the actions in the newer repertoire (such as the public meeting and the mass petition) took for granted the continued existence of the national structure of power. In these regards, the old repertoire was arguably more revolutionary than the new. Both repertoires reflected and interacted with the organization of power within their own historical contexts. The difference between them lay in the relations of repertoires and actors to their political settings.

Like most useful dichotomies, the reduction of many repertoires to just two simplifies radically for the sake of clarity. No actual group employed all the performances within either of the repertoires, no pair of actors shifted abruptly from one repertoire to the other, no sharp break in repertoires occurred in 1800 or at any other date. We are examining a history of continuous innovation and modulation. Yet surges of change in repertoires did occur, alterations in the contentious repertoires of one pair of actors induced alterations in adjacent pairs, broad conflicts produced more extensive repertoire changes than narrow ones, and some innovations caught on much more rapidly and durably than others. For these reasons, the exaggerated division of continuously changing multiple repertoires into 18th- and 19th-century sets serves as a useful guide to a complex history.

Steinberg's Weavers

Chapter 1 claimed that such arrays of contentious performances fall into strong repertoires, and that change and variation in repertoires result especially from causes at the level of performances, with secondary effects at the levels of actions, interactions, and repertoires. We can get a glimpse of repertoires at work in their settings by looking at a flourishing offshoot of the Great Britain Study. Marc Steinberg's work gives an idea of the promise and complexity of pinning down performances.

Steinberg worked on the Great Britain Study before going off on his own to become a superb analyst of British workers' struggles during the 19th century. Drawing on linguists' analyses of dialogue, he focused his attention on the place of discourse in performances and repertoires (Steinberg 1994, 1996, 1998, 1999a and b). His vivid book *Fighting Words* (1999a) digs deep into the working-class lives of silk weavers in London's Spitalfields and of cotton spinners in Lancashire's Ashton-Stalybridge complex from the late 18th century to the 1830s. We may already have encountered Steinberg's Spitalfields weavers in the unnamed authors of Lord Bute's mock execution at Mansion House in 1768.

Certainly in 1768 and 1769 silk weavers spearheaded workers' street politics in London. During that relatively prosperous time for the silk trade, indeed, Parliament yielded to their pressure by passing an act (1773) that mandated government-backed negotiation of piece rates between masters and men, with fines for anyone on either side who deviated from the price schedule. From that point on, silk weavers with grievances against the manufacturers regularly and righteously appealed to public authorities, including Parliament, for justice.

After the Napoleonic Wars, however, advocates of laissez-faire began dismantling the elaborate structure of industrial protection that Britain had erected during the 18th century. The Spitalfields Acts were among the last bricks to fall. But by the early 1820s both large silk manufacturers and advocates of Political Economy such as David Ricardo were attacking the laws as a drag on trade and therefore an obstacle to greater British prosperity. They won in 1824; Parliament repealed the Acts despite fierce weaver opposition. From that point on, competition from imported silk drove Spitalfields from depression to greater depression. Led by the largest firms, manufacturers dropped piece rates steadily. Weavers suffered from both unemployment and declining wages.

By 1826, silk weavers were mobilizing actively to counter their decline: staging public meetings, lobbying the government, appealing collectively to masters, striking, and petitioning Parliament. They rejected the manufacturers' version of free labor. As the *Trades' Free Press* newspaper summed up the indictment:

Is labour free? – Yes – for the rich capitalist to command it at his will and pleasure, and generally speaking, for what price he chooses ...

Is labour free? – Yes – to pay immense taxation, enormous pensions, and a standing army in time of peace, a great part of whose employment is to keep people in awe, which, if properly paid for their labour, would be loyal and obedient subjects.

Is labour free for the operative to fix the value of his labour? We answer, no; for though he is not compelled by the law of the land to work for what is not a living price, yet he is compelled by necessity – his poverty renders him dependent – his master's will is his law. (Steinberg 1999a: 112)

By 1829, Spitalfields's weavers added three very different performances to their repertoire: clandestine cutting of silk from the looms of manufacturers who were paying the lowest wages, general strikes of the trade, and (for manufacturers who failed to abide by strike settlements) sealing looms that were running at wages below the agreed-upon level. For the year, Steinberg catalogs thirty distinct episodes of Spitalfields weavers' collective action (Steinberg 1999a: 245–246). Manufacturers replied by calling in the government's armed force. The weavers lost an 1829 strike involving about 13 thousand men. They never recovered from that loss. Little by little, they drifted off to Australia, to America, or to local work outside their ruined trade.

Steinberg's analysis of the May performances provides a precious opportunity to combine two analytical activities: to identify contrasts between the violent and non-violent performances in the silk weavers' repertoire, and to show how we can systematize the evidence concerning those performances to make it available for comparison and synthesis. Let us single out two very different performances: silk cutting and meeting to discuss the masters' terms. At a general meeting of weavers late in April 1829, the 11th resolution adopted had offered a veiled threat to use force if masters continued to cut wages. "On the evening of May 3," reports Steinberg,

the type of action ominously portended by resolution XI commenced. Groups of "cutters" stealthily moved about the district destroying the partially finished fabrics of several manufacturers as they lay in their weavers' looms. The practice continued unabated for the next two days, with the goods of at least twenty-five looms being destroyed in the process. (Steinberg 1999a: 119)

My research team found multiple accounts of these attacks in 1829's *Times of London*. Here is how we transcribed and classified the major actions within a cutting incident on May 4th:

Transcription	Verb	Broad Verb Category
certain evil-disposed persons riotously assembled	assemble	move
entered the dwellings of the journeymen silk weavers	enter	move
and maliciously cut and destroyed the silk in the looms	destroy	attack
#end	#end	end
a reward of 200L is hereby offered	offer	bargain

The left-hand verb presents our simplified transcription of the phrase's central action. The right-hand column shows our placement of that action in one of eight extremely broad categories of verbs: attack, control, end, meet, move, bargain, support, and other. (More on verb categories in a moment.)

The CG's machine-readable transcription does not include the *Times'* full text, but it does include the excerpts, not to mention separate information on the episode's location, sources, actors, and much more. We inferred the cutters' dispersal from the account, which doesn't mention how the miscreants got away; hence the indication #end. The "#end" appears before the "offer" because Home Secretary Robert Peel only announced a reward (underwritten by the manufacturers) after the cutters had ceased their cutting.

Two days later, on the 6th, a weavers' delegation went to meet with masters, asking for restoration of 1824's prices and threatening to strike if the masters did not agree. The masters appointed a committee of twelve to negotiate with the weavers' delegates the next day. The masters' committee proposed concessions, but far less than the 1824 prices. That evening (the 7th) a huge weavers' meeting at the Crown and Anchor Tavern rejected the masters' terms. Here is the account we excerpted from the *Morning Chronicle*:

Transcription	Verb	Broad Verb Category
yesterday afternoon ... deputation of ... weavers, appointed by their committee	appoint	bargain
the deputation ... assembled	assemble	move
to meet and confer with the committee of masters	meet	meet
last night ... 12 or 14 thousand weavers were assembled	assemble	move
the deputation ... arrived	arrive	move
received by the meeting with loud cheers	cheer	support
read the report of the masters' committee ... submitted to the journeymen for their approval or rejection	submit	support
the meeting was uproarious, nothing but noise, clamour, and loud hisses	#cry out	bargain
resolved not to accept the terms proposed by the masters	refuse	control
#end	#end	end

This transcription treated the meeting of workers' deputies with masters (the first three verbs) as happening before the CG at hand. We started the CG's action with the assembly of 12 to 14 thousand weavers outside the Crown and Anchor. Once again, we drew some verbs directly from the account and inferred others, with "cry out" no doubt making the farthest stretch from the original text.

Systematic Features of Performances and Repertoires

The available reports do not tell us whether any of the same weavers who cut silk from looms also met with masters or addressed the huge 7 May meeting. That seems unlikely. But they do tell us that Spitalfields's well-organized weavers were capable both of violent direct action and of non-violent collective deliberation on a large scale. Both belonged to the repertoire of weaver-master interaction. The transcriptions also tell us that it is possible to extract simple verb-based descriptions of the sequence within each performance: assemble-enter-destroy-end versus assemble-arrive-cheer-submit–cry out–refuse-end. These examples do not incorporate our information on participating formations, locations, issues, sources, subjects of claims, and objects of claims. With that information, the machine-readable files occupy a middle ground between two irreconcilable extremes: action-by-action narratives on one side, abstract event counts on the other. They occupy the middle ground between narrative and epidemiology.

Take the actions in our CGs, represented as verbs. Our transcriptions included 1,584 different verbs. Using a combination of frequency, linguistic similarity, co-occurrence, general knowledge of British contention, and sheer intuition, I grouped them into forty-six more general categories. (The eight categories mentioned earlier simply collapse the forty-six categories even more radically.) My collaborator Takeshi Wada then performed a factor analysis relating these forty-six verb categories to broad types of event. Figure 2-3 reports locations of the most prominent and meaningful thirty-one verb categories on the first two dimensions drawn from the factor analysis.[1] The closer any two verb categories to each other in the diagram, the more frequently they appear together within the same types of events.

In the figure, verbs that appear frequently in indoor settings – especially public meetings – cluster toward the bottom, whereas the top contains many more verbs recurring in out-of-doors episodes. On the left we find verbs associated with disagreement, including violent disagreement; on the right, verbs associated with agreement. That leaves a central area full of verbs describing the collective taking of positions whether indoors or outdoors and whether leading to agreement or disagreement. The graph provides a remarkable description of the space within which Britain's performances and repertoires operated.

Notice the clustering of verbs within the space. On the left center, closely packed, we see control, resist, attack, block, attempt, and fight. The packing results from the verbs' appearing together in various forms of

---

[1] Wada performed a principal components analysis with a varimax solution, eliminating "End," "Other," and categories accounting for less than 2 percent of all verbs. The first two factors exhausted 57.5 percent of the variance. In this case, the data represent the proportion of all CGs in each of our crude event categories containing at least one verb in the verb category. The event categories run as follows: 1) authorized celebrations, 2) delegations, 3) parades, demonstrations, and rallies, 4) pre-planned meetings of named associations, 5) pre-planned meetings of public assemblies, 6) other pre-planned meetings, 7) strikes and turnouts, 8) attacks on blacklegs, 9) brawls in drinking places, 10) market conflicts, 11) poachers vs. gamekeepers, 12) smugglers vs. customs, 13) other violent gatherings, and 14) other unplanned gatherings.

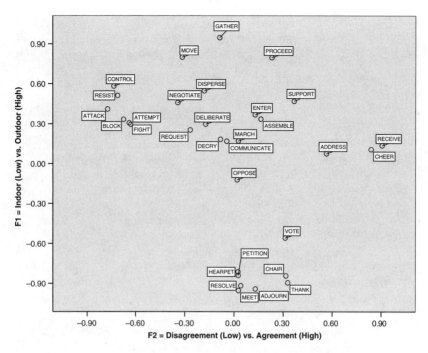

Figure 2-3 Locations of Action Verbs in Two-Factor Space

physical struggle. On the right we observe a somewhat looser cluster of address, receive, cheer, and support; they belong especially to occasions on which a delegation or a crowd addressed supplications or expressions of support to some dignitary. At the diagram's bottom we notice the large cluster of petition, hear petition, resolve, meet, adjourn, thank, chair, and vote, all of which belong particularly to public meetings. Vote stands at a certain distance from the other public meeting verbs. It does so because although voting did happen within meetings, it also occurred in contested elections in which the polling took place out of doors, often in the company of processions and of extensive interplay among candidates, electors, supporters, and spectators.

We can get some insight into how these verbs work by examining their connection with the crude types of performances my group used in its preliminary sorting of CGs: authorized celebrations, delegations, and so on. For each crude type, Box 2-1 lists the verb categories in the factor analysis that accounts of events employed with significantly more than average frequency. Very strong differences appear among the types. Pre-planned

Box 2-1: Over-Represented Verb Categories* by Broad Type of Gathering, Great Britain, 1758–1834

Authorized celebrations (78 CGs): bracket, celebrate, cheer, dine, enter, gather, observe, proceed, receive

Parades, demonstrations, rallies (142): attempt, block, bracket, celebrate, cheer, decry, dine, enter, gather, march, negotiate, observe, oppose, other, proceed, receive, support, vote

Delegations (79): address, bracket, deliberate, gather, negotiate, proceed, receive, support

Pre-planned meetings of named associations (985): dine, hear petition, meet, petition

Pre-planned meetings of public assemblies (3197): none

Other pre-planned meetings (1672): dine, meet

Strikes, turnouts (76): attack, attempt, block, control, deliberate, donkey, gather, hear march, move, negotiate, petition, observe, other, proceed, resist, turnout

Attacks on blacklegs (27): attack, block, control, decry, die, enter, fight, gather, move, observe, turnout

Brawls in drinking places (24): attack, attempt, block, bracket, celebrate, control, deliberate, dine, enter, fight, gather, give, move, negotiate, request, resist, turnout

Market conflicts (12): address, block, gather, negotiate, oppose, other, proceed, request, support

Poachers vs. gamekeepers (71): attack, attempt, block, bracket, control, deliberate, die, disperse, enter, fight, gather, hunt, move, negotiate, observe, other, proceed

Smugglers vs. customs (49): attack, attempt, block, bracket, celebrate, control, die, fight, gather, give, move, observe, other, proceed, resist, smuggle

Other violent gatherings (1156): attack, attempt, block, bracket, control, decry, enter, fight, gather, give, march, move, negotiate, observe, petition, proceed, resist

Other unplanned gatherings (520): block, celebrate, cheer, control, decry, demonstrate, enter, gather, march, move, negotiate, observe, other, proceed

* Over-represented = two or more times the proportion in all gatherings or (in the case of end and meet, which appear in 73 and 54 percent of all gatherings, respectively) 20% (or more) more than their general proportions.

meetings of named associations, for example, over-use verbs in the categories "dine," "hear petition," "meet," and "petition." All of these categories cluster in the meeting zone at the bottom of our two-dimensional space.

Pre-planned meetings of public assemblies (in which the verb categories assemble, chair, end, hear petitions, meet, petition, and resolve appear most frequently) weigh so heavily in the statistics that none of their verb categories qualify as "over-represented." Struggles between poachers and gamekeepers, in contrast, feature the verb categories "attack," "attempt," "block," "bracket," "control," "deliberate," "die," "disperse," "enter," "fight," "gather," "hunt," "move," "negotiate," "observe," "other," and "proceed." These verb categories cluster disproportionately in the upper left-hand quadrant – the outdoor disagreement and struggle zone – of the factor analysis.

In a sense, of course, the list of correspondences simply confirms that we did our initial sorting of events reasonably well. We were, after all, classifying narratives in which the verbs figured prominently. Nevertheless, it is reassuring to find that the actions and interactions comprising our CGs differ so significantly that we can almost tell a typical story about each type from the verb categories alone. Look, for instance, at the event type "market conflicts": contrary to their reputation as "food riots," the verbs "address," "block," "gather," "negotiate," "oppose," "other," "proceed," "request," and "support" differentiate them from other violent gatherings despite their occasional violence. Instead, they reveal a process of popular collective bargaining over the supply and price of food (Tilly 1975, Tilly 1995: 175–178). Similarly, the verb category "donkey" appears exclusively in strikes and turnouts. It describes the routine in which workers placed a strikebreaker on a donkey or a rail, pelting him with refuse and abuse as they drove him out of town.

In retrospect, the list of correspondences also tells us that my categories of event types exaggerated some distinctions. Drawing on general knowledge of change and variation in European contention, for instance, I had introduced a division between authorized celebrations, on one side, and parades, demonstrations, and rallies, on the other. For the first, I had in mind the way Europeans had frequently taken advantage of holidays such as Mardi Gras to voice complaints and jeer at their enemies. For the second, I was thinking of disciplined processions involving military units, religious groups, fraternal orders, and political supporters.

Each of those distinctive forms did appear somewhere among the 8,088 CGs. When they appeared, furthermore, they took on unmistakably

different looks. Pure instances of authorized celebrations involved tributes
to dignitaries, including royalty. Pure instances of parades, demonstrations, and rallies, in contrast, involved assertions of strength on the part of
distinctive organized groups. But I failed to anticipate two important
features of the evidence. First, groups of supporters for one cause or
another often took advantage of public holidays or other authorized celebrations by marching or demonstrating. Second, as street meetings and
demonstrations became common claim-making performances, they often
adopted routines already known from authorized celebrations. The
numbers show the result: every verb category that appeared disproportionately in authorized celebrations also appeared disproportionately in
parades, demonstrations, and rallies.[2]

Sheer numbers of CGs made the division of pre-planned meetings into
three types – named associations, public assemblies, and other – convenient. For some purposes we certainly needed distinctions among meetings involving 1) associations such as the anti-Catholic organizations that
multiplied during the later 1820s, 2) local parishes' or freeholders'
assemblies, and 3) heterogeneous followers of some leader, candidate, or
cause who joined an organized public discussion. Yet the distributions of
verb categories make clear that by the 19th century British people had
learned a basic style for conducting meetings, regardless of whether they
involved specialized associations, public assemblies, or varied groups of
supporters.

The same verb categories reappear: "assemble," "meet," "dine,"
"chair," "end," "hear petition," "petition," and "resolve." (If "dine" seems
to be keeping strange company, remember the importance of banquets,
drinks, and toasts in the political rituals of 1758–1834.) The rise of the
public meeting as a vehicle for voicing collective claims constituted one of
the main elements in the move from parochial, particular, and bifurcated
to cosmopolitan, modular, and autonomous performances.

Our two-dimensional space – disagreement-agreement by outdoor-
indoor – offers another way of thinking about changes in British performances and repertoires from the 1750s to the 1830s. On the average,

---

[2] The data also show significant overlap between delegations, on one side, and parades,
demonstrations, and rallies, on the other; delegations differ, as we might expect, by more
often including the verbs "address" and "deliberate," which nicely capture the connection
of collective voice with assembly and locomotion.

episodes in our sample moved within the space from the upper left toward the lower right: from a relatively high share of violent disagreement out of doors toward a much higher share of peaceful indoor action that could in principle reach agreement. At the back end of the arrow, we see public vengeance and shaming; at the arrow's front end, collective negotiation of agreement and support. The massive rise of public meetings (with their recurrent "meet," "chair," "resolve," "vote," "hear petition," "petition," "thank," and "adjourn") produced much of the movement along the arrow.

We have a subject-object pair when one actor does something to another actor. In the CG data, we represent that relation by subject, verb, and object. As we might expect, prevailing verbs vary enormously by paired categories of subjects and objects. Local people treat members of Parliament differently from their neighbors. Figure 2-4 displays some of that variation by identifying the most frequent subject-object pairs for three large categories of verbs: attack, bargain, and support. It lumps together the four counties of the London region – Kent, Middlesex, Surrey, and Sussex – over the whole period from 1758 to 1834, but excludes the rest of Great Britain.

We have already noticed the concentration of attack verbs to the middle left of our factor space, bargain verbs in the central zone, and support verbs to the right. In Figure 2-4 we learn more: we find that different pairs of actors predominate in different parts of the space. Attack verbs most often align a mob (our sources' word, not ours) against any number of antagonists, including single named individuals. In addition troops (who generally represent higher authorities, but sometimes act independently) attack local constables frequently in clashes of jurisdiction, unnamed persons sometimes attack crowds, named individuals attack each other, and – in a separate array – hunters attack game-keepers.

Bargain verbs form a very different pattern: instead of a "mob," constituted groups of local inhabitants regularly deal with a wide variety of officials as well as named individuals. But we also find electors negotiating with MPs, mobs and named individuals negotiating with each other, and (again) named individuals negotiating on their own. In the Support panel, we discover a much more national orientation. Both constituted societies and local assemblies regularly voice support for MPs, but so do crowds and distinguished gentlemen. Parliament as a whole also often receives support from electors, gentlemen, and

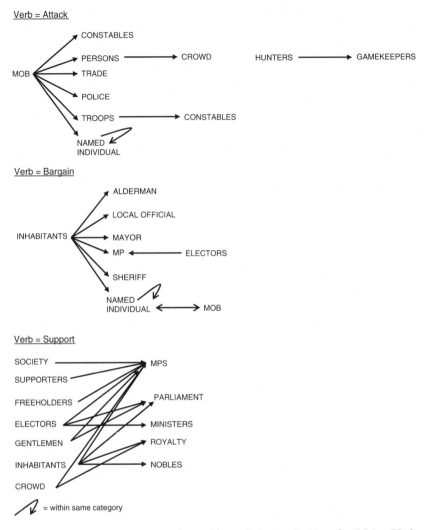

"Most frequent" = 1% or more of all appearances for verbs in the category

Verb = Attack

Verb = Bargain

Verb = Support

= within same category

Figure 2-4 Most Frequent Subject-Object Pairs in Actions, by Major Verb Category, London Region, 1758–1834

inhabitants, as ministers, royalty, and nobles gain cheers from electors, inhabitants, and/or crowds.

The three verb categories distinguish sharply different sorts of political relations. Two conclusions obviously follow: in general, the rise of public meetings and related settings for claim making moved contention away from attack toward bargaining and support, and the increasing salience of Parliament in public affairs figures as both cause and effect of that shift (Tilly 1997, Tilly and Wood 2003).

Changes in the mix of verbs between 1758 and 1834 amplify those two conclusions. Trends in the London region and in the rest of Great Britain did not differ significantly despite the consistent tendency of London to host more meetings than the rest of country. Figure 2-5 therefore lumps data from the London region alone (Kent, Middlesex, Surrey, and Sussex) for 1758 to 1820 with data from all of Great Britain for 1828 to 1834. Among our broad categories of verbs, some did not fluctuate much from year to year, and displayed no trend.

The verbs we classified together as Support, for example, included the subcategories "address," "cheer," "receive," and "support" in Figure 2-3, which in turn included such individual verbs as "admire," "aid," "applaud," "approve," "assent," "assist," "avow," "bear," "carry," and "cheer." Support verbs generally appeared in about a third of a given year's CGs. The minimum of 10 percent arrived in the oppositional tumult of 1768 and the maximum of 44 percent in 1820, when many anti-establishment Londoners thronged the streets to cheer beleaguered Queen Caroline, estranged wife of the new King George IV.

Figure 2-5 traces the four broad categories with the strongest trends: Attack, Control, Meet, and Other. Attack includes such individual verbs as "abuse," "accuse," "arm," "assail," and "assault." In Control we find "abduct," "acquit," "apprehend," and "arouse," not to mention "donkey," "mutiny," and "protest" – basically efforts to channel and repress. Meet includes the verb categories at the bottom of Figure 2-3, which individually contain such actions as "adopt," "amend," "answer," "appoint," and "argue." By definition, Other spans a wider range: "bracket," "celebrate," "die," "dine," "hunt," "observe," "smuggle," "turnout," and more.

The graph displays four important trends. First, on the whole Attack and Control moved together closely; they involved, after all, two sides of open struggle. Second, both of them declined unsteadily from great frequency in the CGs of the 1750s and 1760s to low levels after 1801. Third, Other declined rather regularly across the years, from a high in 1759 (when every single CG included at least one Other verb) to a low in 1832 (when only 51 percent of CGs included Other verbs). At the start of our period, food seizures, disciplining of strikebreakers, and attacks varied in detail from one parish to the next. By the end, meetings and marches

58

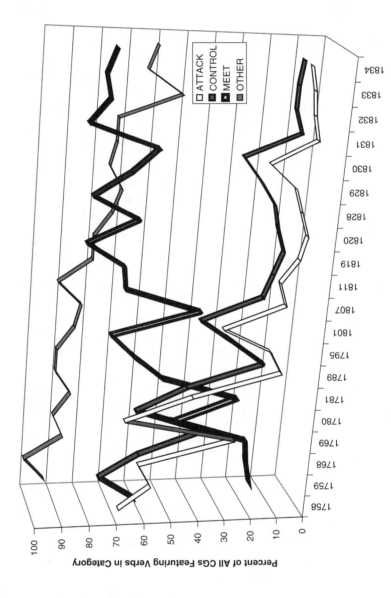

Figure 2-5 Major Categories of Verbs in British Contentious Gatherings, 1758–1834

looked much more similar from one end of Great Britain to the other. In the terms I used earlier, the decline of Other indicates that more modular performances were taking over.

That brings us to the fourth, and opposite, trend. Meet climbed more regularly than Attack and Control declined, despite dips in 1789 (widespread street violence), 1801 (more street violence, including resistance to military recruitment), and 1830 (the famous Swing Rebellion in the rural Southeast). By the 1820s, Meet verbs were typically showing up in three quarters or more of a year's CGs. Meet was displacing Attack, Control, and Other. The age of the relatively decorous public meeting with appeals to national authorities had arrived.

Earlier I summarized that movement as a shift from parochial, particular, and bifurcated performances to cosmopolitan, modular, and autonomous performances. Concrete descriptions of our thousands of episodes add that the shift occurred at the expense of popular direct action against malefactors and enemies. Actions like cutting silk from looms became rarer and less effective. Meanwhile, organized workers, inhabitants, and other local actors directed more and more of their claims toward national authorities, especially Parliament. As a consequence, popular contention became much more contained, and much more closely integrated into national political processes. The silk weavers of 1829 stood at the cusp of a massive change in contentious politics.

Strong Repertoires?

The material we have reviewed so far makes a good case for the coherence of contentious performances. We see that (as represented by verbs) actions and interactions within performances display systematic patterns of variation and change. Mixes of actions and interactions identify large differences among broad types of performance such as public meetings, collective seizures of food, and poacher-gamekeeper struggles. They also make it possible to pinpoint large shifts in the overall character of contention.

The evidence examined up to this point, however, falls far short of clinching the case for strong repertoires. As distinguished from no repertoire, weak repertoire, or rigid repertoire, the strong-repertoire hypothesis claims that in something like the style of theatrical performers, participants in contention are enacting available scripts. Within those scripts they innovate, mostly in small ways and incrementally. As a result, repertoires acquire both causal and symbolic coherence. What's more, they exercise constraint: one round of contention and its outcomes shape the next round of contention.

Whether in general or in the specific experience of Great Britain, the hypothesis of strong repertoires has significant empirical implications. Let me expand the strong-repertoire criteria laid out in Chapter 1:

- In particular times and places, performances cluster into a limited number of recurrent, well-defined types.
- Within the range defined by all contentious actions that a given set of actors carry on, substantial blanks appear; combinations of actions clearly lying within the technical reach of participants never occur. As a result, performance types have visible boundaries rather than distributing continuously over the space of technically possible performances.
- For a given set of actors and issues, those performances change relatively little from one round of action to the next; what happens in one round of action, furthermore, detectibly constrains what happens in the next round.
- Participants in contention give evidence that they are aware of those performances by giving names to them, referring to previous actions of the same kind, giving each other instructions, adopting divisions of labor that require prior consultation or experience, anticipating each other's actions, and/or terminating actions more or less simultaneously.
- Within a set of connected actors, each significant pair of actors has its own repertoire. In the pair, claim-making actors make choices within the existing repertoire. In the case of Great Britain, for example, great differences exist between the repertoires of worker-master relations and of citizen-Parliament relations.
- The more connected the histories of actors outside of contention, the more similar their repertoires. Hence a process of increasing connection tends to homogenize performances – that is, make them more modular.
- New performances arise chiefly through innovation within existing performances, but tend to crystallize, stabilize, and acquire visible boundaries once they exist.

Overall, the strong-repertoire hypothesis implies that most changes in performances and repertoires occur incrementally, bit-by-bit, in response to interaction between environmental change and innovations that develop in the course of struggle. In times of massive struggle and rapid change, to be sure, innovations appear more rapidly and dramatically. We have already seen signs that the 1760s, a time of mass mobilization in Great Britain and in its American colonies, new performances developed thick and fast. Most of the time, however, strong repertoires imply incremental change in available ways of making claims.

Some of these implications require Steinberg-style close observation of particular settings and populations. Compare donkeying with the organization of public meetings: the more particular the performances, the more we need close local observation to determine whether and how participants acquire and share knowledge of the available routines. On the other hand, tracing the influence of such changes as the rise of Parliament and the formation of national-level social movements can only work on the large scale. To the extent that performances and repertoires become national in scope, we need national-level observations. Chapters to come therefore combine local evidence with the examination of patterns across substantial expanses of time and space.

3

How Performances Form, Change, and Disappear

On 24 May 1768, local people staged a vivid contentious performance in Hastings, Sussex. As we transcribed reports of the performance for GBS:

The mob have already risen by the beat of a drum and insisted upon having wheat at 5s. per bushel. They then went to the house of Mr. White, a farmer, dragged him out to the middle of one of his own fields, [and] forced him to stay there while they broke open his granary and destroyed all his wheat. After this they returned and paraded it about the town. The mayor being afraid to oppose them, John Nicoll Esq., a Justice of the Peace, caused the ringleader to be brought before him and charged an officer with him, with a mittimus to convey him to Horsham Gaol. But the mob soon rescued their captain and then proceeded to Mr. Nicoll's house, whom they probably would have killed, if he had not made his escape through the back door.

As often happened in such reports, the phrase "destroyed all his wheat" actually meant that the attackers loaded it into carts and carried it away; they destroyed its value to Mr. White, but increased its value to local consumers. Our story came from very similar reports in *Gentleman's Magazine*, the *Annual Register*, and the *London Chronicle*. As was happening widely in England during that year of dearth, local people responded to shortage and high prices by taking collective control over the local food supply. Early in June:

Near 200 persons assembled, with clubs and other offensive weapons, at Boston, in Lincolnshire, and insisted that butchers meat should be sold at three pence a pound, which, for the sake of peace, was complied with, and they all dispersed quietly. (*Annual Register* 1768: 118)

Reports of this sort were coming in from all over England in that season of dearth and high prices.

In London itself on the 1st of July, according to the *Chronicle*:

Yesterday a great number of weavers assembled in Bunhill Row and Chiswell Street, where the country farmers were selling pease [peas] at 10d. a peck. The weavers got up in seven carts and sold them at 6d. a peck. One cart had eighty bushels.

Authorities called such events "disturbances" and "riots." Ordinary people called them doing justice. For our purposes, the events qualify as contentious gatherings featuring certain kinds of distinctive performances. Food seizures, we can call the performances.

This chapter unpacks contentious performances at three different levels. First, it scrutinizes real events closely enough to show that they evolved continuously, and sometimes rapidly. Second, it examines how and why the experiences of participants in contentious performances caused them to modify the scripts they followed. Third, it sketches how changes in national political and economic contexts influenced the viability of different kinds of performances, and thus contributed to longer-term transformations of performances. But we begin with old-fashioned food seizures.

In 1971, E. P. Thompson published the still-dominant theory of how such 18th-century performances unfolded (1971). Thompson deployed the talent of a great theorist, combining powerful general ideas with rich, concrete examples. He reported that he wrote his widely influential article, "The Moral Economy of the English Crowd in the Eighteenth Century," while waiting for proofs of his masterpiece, *The Making of the English Working Class* (1963). He based his telling analysis of English food struggles on nearly ten years of archival work. Thompson later described the subject of the "Moral Economy" as

the mentalité, or, as I would prefer, the political culture, the expectations, traditions, and, indeed, superstitions of the working population most frequently involved in actions in the market; and the relations – sometimes negotiations – between crowd and rulers which go under the unsatisfactory term of "riot." (Thompson 1991: 260)

Thompson claimed that England's local people saw their priority over local food supplies as a matter of right. They intervened in the market, he argued, to restore and protect that right. Thompson's article launched a strenuous debate on the generality and uniformity of the moral economy. Positions on the question ranged from attribution of similar moral economies to peasants across the world, at one extreme, to fine distinctions within 18th-century England, at the other (Randall and Charlesworth 1996, 2000).

Thompson himself made no claims for universality. He said clearly that his theory of the moral economy operated in a historical middle ground. The ground lay somewhere between the specific details of England's 18th-century food struggles and the general field of ruler-ruled relations. As in most of his historical work, Thompson sought to specify how England worked and changed from around 1700 into the early 19th century. He recognized that the English moral economy borrowed ideas from the 16th-century government's paternalist model of control over the food supply. Yet he insisted that conceptions of moral economy had acquired deep roots in English popular culture.

Thompson also recognized that, toward the 18th century's end, population growth, proletarianization, and industrialization were moving Britain from a net exporter to a net importer of grain. The wage-earning population was therefore becoming increasingly vulnerable to the price-wage scissors in times of shortage. But he railed against the "spasmodic" view of food struggles as automatic responses to hardship. For him, culture and social organization determined the intersection between hunger and contention.

Except for pointing out the general connection between subsistence crises and activation of the moral economy, Thompson's formulation made little effort to specify which kinds of struggles occurred in which sorts of localities under what circumstances. It referred instead to English class relations over the broad 18th century. It helped explain popular resistance to the "political economy" of free markets. That resistance, Thompson declared, employed "robust direct action, protective market-control and the regulation of prices, sometimes claiming a legitimacy derived from the paternalist model" (Thompson 1991: 261).

Thompson deployed an incomparable flair for mocking ideas he rejected. This chapter nevertheless seeks to capture the Thompsonian genius for a purpose that Thompson might well have scorned. Consonant with Thompson's analysis, it shows that England's contentious performances formed, changed, and disappeared through a process of innovation and adaptation from episode to episode. Innovation and adaptation responded strongly to specific alterations in England's economic, political, and cultural environment. But it also shows – or at least claims – that strong repertoires gain much of their strength from the interaction of local learning with large-scale change in the social environment of potential claim makers. The chapter begins by comparing the evolution of food struggles with that of street demonstrations in Great Britain during the GBS period, 1758–1834. It then goes on to a sketchier comparison of demonstrations and their evolution in Great Britain and France as a proxy for the more general history of the social movement in the two regimes.

Over the years, many a personal encounter with E. P. Thompson made me painfully aware of Thompson's deep suspicion when it came to the sort of social scientific formalization this book advocates. But (as Thompson reassured me not long before his death) at least we agreed on the necessity for solid evidence concerning popular contention as a bulwark against postmodern skepticism. My effort to document the operation of performances and repertoires follows a double Thompsonian inspiration: to identify common properties and principles of contention at the level of existing regimes and to avoid the obfuscation produced by such authorities' terms as "riot" and "disorder." Yet it breaks with Thompson by hewing to a middle ground between Thompson's supple literary narratives and the stiff numbers of classified event counts.

As Thompson was well aware, high prices and food shortages often figured in very different struggles from Hastings's grain seizure of May 1768 and London's forced sale of peas in July 1768. Two weeks before the Hastings event, on 7 May:

On Saturday a great body of sailors met in St. George's Fields in the East. They divided themselves into two parties. One went over London Bridge, the other marched thro' the City and went to St. James, with colours flying, drums beating and fifes playing, and presented a petition to His Majesty, setting forth the hardships they at present labour under, on account of the smallness of their wages, the high price of provisions &c. and praying for relief. (*Gentleman's Magazine* 1768: 262)

Two days later, London again heard from massed workers about the high price of provisions. In our transcription from eight different articles in *Gentleman's Magazine*, the *Annual Register*, and the *London Chronicle*:

Last night a large mob gathered. [It] came down Cornhill about 150 in number [with] a gibbet, a boot and a green petticoat on it, carried before the mob. [It] halted at the Mansion-House, complaining of the high price of provisions etc. and broke several of the lamps and windows. The Lord Mayor ordered his servants to bring back the gibbet. Philip Pyle gave it a shake, which obliged the mob to quit it. He was pulling it along when a man, who he believed was the prisoner, catched a flambeau out of his hand and broke his head with it in several places, dropping the gibbet. There were now two or three striking him. He recovered his flambeau, made a stroke at the assailants and was endeavouring to retreat for fear of falling, in which case, he said, he must undoubtedly have been murdered, Hawkins laying about him with a stick stuck with nails. [He] saw him strike two or three people who proved to be his Lordship's servants. [He saw] a stick stuck full of nails, which happily flew out of the prisoner's hand, and his fellow servant snatched it up. The prisoner then endeavoured to defend himself with his hands.

They had seized the prisoner Hawkins and were dragging him towards the Mansion-House. But when [they] had got him within ten yards of the Mansion House, the mob rescued him and he was making off when Mr. Way collared him and with the assistance of the wounded servants secured him in the Mansion-House. The Lord Mayor went out among them in the most complaisant manner with Mr. Cook the City Marshal intreating them to desist from any acts of violence notwithstanding which, some of them cried out, "Knock him dead." The Lord Mayor himself with Mr. Cook the City Marshal secured some of the ringleaders who were carried to the Poultry compter. The mob then dispersed. [We saw a truncated report of the same episode from *Gentleman's Magazine* in Chapter 1.]

In July, William Hawkins (by then "the prisoner" in the testimony just quoted) and Joseph Wild received convictions at Old Bailey for assault and disturbing the peace; they were to pay fines of a shilling each and spend a year in Newgate Jail. In London, high prices or not, you didn't attack the Lord Mayor's servants with impunity.

Nevertheless, among workers, high provision prices provided an occasion for complaining more generally about the corruption and incompetence of the British ruling classes. The boot, petticoat, and gibbet then on display in London advertised that popular critique of governmental corruption. (The petticoat reflected the popular belief that the Princess Dowager was Lord Bute's mistress.) But they did so in an idiom far removed from the market negotiations Thompson analyzed in his "moral economy" essay. We must therefore take great care to separate the issue – dearth and high prices – from the performances by which English people made claims.

So-Called Food Riots

During the 18th century, market conflicts in the Hastings, Sussex, style occurred much more often than parades with gibbets, boots, and petti-coats. Their study has inspired a small academic industry, including the talented historian Roger Wells. Like most other British students of "food riots," Wells ignores Thompson's warnings concerning terminology, but heeds his injunction to look at what people actually do when they make claims. Seeking to ground collective claims closely in local circumstances and in the full range of contentious practices, Wells explicitly rejects my "inadequate conceptualisation" of popular contention in terms of contentious gatherings and repertoires (Wells 2000: 210). Nevertheless, his massive compilation of "disturbances" and "riots" concerning food across England from 1795 to 1801 provides substantial evidence of strong repertoires. It falls into the broad tradition of analyzing contention by assembling classified event catalogs.

Wells's catalog of almost four hundred events distinguishes three main sorts of action: 1) collective price setting (which he calls taxation populaire, following the standard French term), 2) blocking the shipment of food and retaining it for local consumption, and 3) touring farms to identify and often to commandeer hoarded supplies (Wells 1988: 418; cf. Tilly 1986: 156–159, 190–192). The Hastings, Sussex, episode with which this chapter began falls into the third category – touring and commandeering. In passing, Wells also documents two other forms of direct action: 4) posting of threats by letter, poster, or graffiti and 5) parading with symbols of dearth such as bread loaves on pikes or bayonets. Type 1, price setting, predominated. In price setting, consumers confronted a food merchant – most often a grain seller or a baker – and either forced him to lower his prices or seized his stock and sold it below the merchant's asking price, turning the money over to the merchant.

Wells reports widespread price setting in 1795:

The first major set of disturbances in 1795 commenced with a massive mobilisation of miners and canal-diggers near Leicester at the end of March. The Volunteers' shortcomings were symbolized by their inability to take prisoners, while markets at Leicester, Ashby-de-la-Zouch and Shackerstone bore the initial brunt of popular fury. More serious troubles developed in mid-April, with repeated descents on market towns, including Bedworth, Nuneaton and Hinckley, by south Warwickshire miners. Simultaneously rioting started to the east at Nottingham. Coventry was engulfed by prolonged disorders when invading colliers were joined by urban workers; arrests served only to galvanise attacks on the town jail, and the restoration of peace necessitated concessions by the Corporation. By this time most of the region was disturbed, with the army, narrowly containing a huge exodus from Warwickshire towns and industrial villages, targetted on the key mart at Burton-on-Trent. Toward the end of April, further riots occurred at Nuneaton, Solihull, Kidderminster, Bewdley, Hinckley and Lichfield. The sole recorded divergence from the imposition of price controls involved the roughing-up of hucksters attempting to make bulk purchases at Lichfield. (Wells 1988: 97)

Behind Wells's language of "disturbances" and "riots," then, we see clearly a limited number of claim-making routines, especially the one he calls "taxation populaire." We see a contentious repertoire in action.

Remember the criteria for strong repertoires:

- In particular times and places, performances cluster into a limited number of recurrent, well-defined types.

- Within the range defined by all contentious actions that a given set of actors carry on, substantial blanks appear; combinations of actions clearly lying within the technical reach of participants never occur. As a result, performance types have visible boundaries rather than distributing continuously over the space of technically possible performances.
- For a given set of actors and issues, those performances change relatively little from one round of action to the next; what happens in one round of action, furthermore, detectibly constrains what happens in the next round.
- Participants in contention provide evidence that they are aware of those performances by assigning names to them, referring to previous actions of the same kind, giving each other instructions, adopting divisions of labor that require prior consultation or experience, anticipating each other's actions, and/or terminating actions more or less simultaneously.
- Within a set of connected actors, each significant pair of actors has its own repertoire. In the pair, claim-making actors make choices within the existing repertoire.
- The more connected the histories of actors outside of contention, the more similar their repertoires. Hence increasing connection tends to homogenize performances – that is, make them more modular.
- New performances arise chiefly through innovation within existing performances, but tend to crystallize, stabilize, and acquire visible boundaries once they exist.

Even Wells's detailed accounts rarely catch participants consulting with each other about what to do next. Yet in general they demonstrate clear awareness of the available routines for price setting, blocking, touring, threatening, and parading. Although participants sometimes combine these performances, they don't confuse them. Wells's accounts establish that objects of claims, such as farmers, bakers, grain merchants, millers, and local authorities, know which performance is unfolding, however angrily they resist the claims. They also demonstrate the expected combination of scripted interactions with local improvisation.

British experience during the latter half of the 18th century shows us the presence of a limited number of food-controlling performances by local consumers, clustering of those performances into a repertoire connecting consumers with suppliers, and innovation in response to changing economic and political situations. To that extent, accounts by Wells and other close students of England's food struggles confirm the presence of strong repertoires. They likewise establish that important mutations were occurring during the 1790s.

As compared with such classic subsistence crises as that of 1766, the wartime struggles of 1795–1801 revealed two kinds of shifts: toward a greater proportion of demands on public authorities rather than on farmers, millers, bakers, or grain merchants and toward a combination of demands concerning prices, wages, and public assistance. "The 1790s," comments Wells, "did not witness a simple resort to food rioting on the traditional model; food prices, wages and – crucially – poor relief levels were increasingly juxtaposed" (Wells 1990: 157).

Not that the old forms of contention over the food supply simply vanished. In 1794–1796, harvest failure, industrial recession, and large requisitions of food for military forces produced what might have been the largest wave of struggles over food England ever saw. The struggles involved all five of Wells's forms of action: taxation populaire, blockage of shipments, touring and commandeering, posting of threats, and displaying symbols of dearth (Bohstedt 1983, Booth 1977, Charlesworth 1983, Wells 1988). Yet demonstrations, public meetings, and takeovers of local markets by the military also multiplied. For 1795, indeed, eleven of the nineteen food-connected CGs in GBS files involved meetings in which participants demanded or offered help for the hungry. The remaining eight consisted of:

- Three incursions of the militia – this was, after all, wartime – into the markets of Chichester, Blatchington, and Wells, where they forced the sale of food at reduced prices
- An attack on the dwelling of a cheating baker in Westminster (London)
- A march of two hundred women and girls in Brighthelmstone, with bread and beef impaled on sticks
- In Wells, blockage of flour shipments to London
- A crowd at St. James that surrounded nobles and the king on the way to Parliament, carrying tiny loaves of bread wrapped in black crepe as they called for bread and peace
- A similar crowd that made the same demands of chief minister William Pitt two months later

At most three of the nineteen food-related 1795 episodes in GBS files, then, belonged to the five classic types of "food riot" cataloged by Roger Wells. Food shortages and high prices continued to stimulate popular contention into the 20th century. But price setting, blocking, touring, threatening, and parading soon disappeared in favor of public meetings, petitions, and demonstrations.

By 1812, food seizures and forced sales in Lancashire mingled with machine-breaking and demands for parliamentary reform (Bohstedt 1983: 157–164, Charlesworth, Gilbert, Randall, Southall, and Wrigley 1996: 42–46). The crowds of disfranchised workers who supported radical Henry Hunt in the Bristol by-election of 1812 "marched in huge crowds to the cry 'Hunt and Peace' behind a loaf of bread on a pole and a Cap of Liberty" (Prothero 1979: 82). Increasingly, food shortages and high prices became evidence of political wrongdoing rather than the malfeasance of farmers, millers, and bakers.

Commenting on East Anglia's food struggles of 1816, Thompson noted that they shared some features with their 18th-century pre-decessors, but "in other features – the demand for a minimum wage, the sporadic expression of social and political demands, the inchoate reaching out towards organization – they anticipate the 'last labourers' revolt' of 1830, and even the trade unionism and radicalism of later years, in which East Anglia has always played so prominent a part" (Thompson 1965: 10).

Here is a crude indication of the shift. We coded the major issue for 117 of our 8,088 CGs as either "food prices" or "distress." (As Wells's catalog of 400 episodes for 1795–1801 alone indicates, our 117 CGs greatly under-counted the frequency of food and price events between 1758 and 1834.) They split between 85 formal public meetings and 32 other gatherings, 16 of them involving violence. Figure 3-1 displays their trends. The informal gatherings are labeled "Nonviolent" and "Violent."

The dramatic increase in numbers of CGs after 1820 mainly reflects the fact that our data up to 1820 come from the London region alone, while the 1828–1834 data cover the whole of Great Britain. But the numbers show a clear shift away from the informal gathering (violent or not) toward the public meeting as the standard site of contention over dearth. Meetings accounted for 52 percent of the CGs from 1758 to 1820, 79 percent of them from 1828 to 1834. The so-called food riot was on its way out.

While it survived, however, the performance Wells calls "taxation populaire" formed a crucial part of a strong repertoire. The repertoire connected local consumers to local farmers, merchants, millers, shop-keepers, and authorities. For decades, ordinary people buffeted by dearth and high food prices chose mainly among 1) price setting, 2) blockage of food shipments, 3) touring farms, mills, and merchants' storehouses, 4) posting of threats, and 5) parading with symbols of want. They sometimes

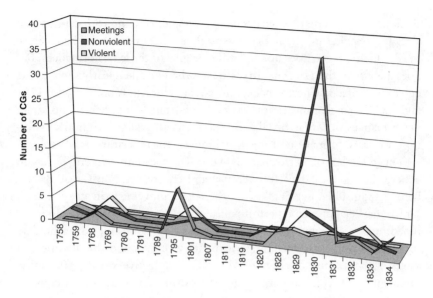

Figure 3-1   Food-Related CGs, Great Britain, 1758–1834

mixed two or more of those performances in the same episode. In details, of course, these performances varied from locality to locality and circumstance to circumstance. Nor did they become modular: they never generalized to other issues than food shortages, hoarding, and prices or to other actors than participants in local markets. Nevertheless, the repertoire as a whole displayed remarkable uniformity across Great Britain.

In this sense, Great Britain's struggles over food conformed to the strong repertoire model from the 17th century up to the 1790s. From that point on, we notice a striking fact: individual performances changed little, but a major shift occurred in the composition of the food-oriented repertoire. Temporarily, market takeovers by military units joined the repertoire. For a longer term, a visible shift toward public meetings and street demonstrations occurred. Individual instances of food seizures recurred locally into the 1830s, but the repertoire as a whole mutated toward the modular forms of national political claim making.

Demonstrations

If E. P. Thompson's association of popular food struggles with Tudor subsistence policy holds, the basic performances of seizing food and

shaming hoarders that we have seen operating during the 18th century had
already prevailed in Great Britain for about a century and a half before
1758. Our evidence does not cover the origins of those performances, but
does document their decline. In contrast, GBS episodes clearly show us the
emergence of a new performance: the street demonstration. Between 1758
and 1834, the demonstration crystallized from a number of disparate
performances in Great Britain. By following the demonstration's evolution, we trace formation of the social movement repertoire as a whole.

The complex of performances we call a social movement began to
cohere during the later 18th century and consolidated in Great Britain
before 1850. (Chapter 5 takes up the social movement in great detail.)
Unlike earlier popular repertoires, the social movement effectively combined three elements: 1) sustained campaigns of claims on power holders
to advance programs such as parliamentary reform and the abolition of
slavery, 2) repeated displays of WUNC – collective worthiness, unity,
numbers, and commitment – in the form not only of disciplined
demonstrations but also of wearing colors, singing songs, chanting slogans, and displaying shared symbols, and 3) employment of a distinctive
repertoire. The social movement repertoire included not only the demonstration but also the public meeting, the petition drive, the press
statement, widely displayed symbols of personal affiliation, and the formation of specialized associations devoted to pursuit of a cause. John
Wilkes's supporters pioneered a number of these performances in the
1760s, for example, by converting themselves from friends of Wilkes into
the Society of Supporters of the Bill of Rights.

Performances in the social movement repertoire, as we have already
seen, had 18th-century precedents. But in Western Europe and the
Americas the social movement consolidated during the 19th century.
Starting then, it eventually spread to a wide range of democratic and semi-
democratic regimes across the world (Tilly 2004b).

The demonstration soon became a multi-purpose tool rather than an
instrument oriented to some single goal or political inclination. The
demonstration's history intersected with British demands for parliamentary reform. Yet its trajectory did not resemble that of parliamentary
reform, which took off slowly during the 1760s, grew intermittently
during the later 18th century, surged after the Napoleonic Wars, and
achieved a negotiated settlement in the Reform Act of 1832. Unlike
reform, the street demonstration as such lacked a name, a program, and an
organized set of advocates. Yet by the 1830s British activists – including

advocates of parliamentary reform – had learned to mount all three variants of the street demonstration that are still familiar today: the disciplined march through public streets, the organized occupation of a public space, and the combination of the two in a march to or from a public meeting.

Well before the 1750s, many of Britain's publicly recognized groups had the right and the practice of marching or assembling collectively in public space under specified conditions and with the assent of local authorities. Frequent marchers included military units, religious congregations, funeral parties, craft associations, and fraternal orders. (At that point, the word "demonstrate" in this sense referred chiefly to displays of military power and discipline.) In addition, authorities tolerated or even encouraged public participation in official ceremonies, holidays, punishments, and elections.

Finally, orderly delegations from constituted bodies such as a parish or a recognized craft to authorities such as a lord mayor, the Parliament, the king, or assembled masters of a craft generally had the right to proceed ceremoniously through the streets before presenting their petitions, resolutions, or respectful demands. In times of intense political and industrial conflict authorities kept magistrates, troops, constables, and the Riot Act ready to contain marches and assemblies they deemed to threaten public order. In the absence of a threat, however, constituted bodies of Britons enjoyed partial rights to assemble and march so long as they informed the appropriate officials.

What happened between the 1750s and the 1830s? Four important changes occurred. First, rights to assemble and march expanded from constituted bodies to ad hoc collections of citizens. Second, delegations swelled from a few representatives in their Sunday best to massed marchers, often bearing or wearing symbols of their affiliations and demands. Third, election campaigns and elections themselves became occasions for vast displays of support and opposition by partisans who lacked the vote. Fourth, routines for marching and assembling standardized; participants, observers, authorities, and objects of claims all learned their parts. A new modular performance emerged.

The emergence of the demonstration signaled a profound change in British politics. Well into the 19th century, British rulers insisted that parliamentary representation, however restricted its franchise, provided the sole legitimate channel for popular voice. No electorate, much less any popular assembly, had the right to instruct members of Parliament in their specific duties. Virtual, not direct, representation prevailed. From the later 18th century onward, however, British radicals claimed the people's right to address their rulers directly, even to instruct them. Radicals even formed the project of assembling a popular Parliament to deliberate popular welfare, since the existing Parliament resisted doing so (Parssinen 1973). The street demonstration, initiated without the mediation or consent of national authorities, enacted that right to popular voice.

The demonstration acquired a remarkable capacity to signal the presence of weighty political actors. It advertised their WUNC (Tilly 2006). It broadcast an implicit claim to popular sovereignty – the right of ordinary people to voice their preferences and thereby shape the system of rule. In the hands of able political entrepreneurs, it became a significant means of popular power. Major mobilizations, organized by able entrepreneurs, marked the history of the demonstration in Great Britain.

Wilkes's friends, for example, promoted the establishment of the gala street march as a way of broadcasting a political program. Those marches often featured shouts of "Wilkes and Liberty," which became a rallying cry of democrats on both sides of the Atlantic. They likewise made multiple references to the number forty-five in honor of issue number forty-five of Wilkes's paper *The North Briton*, which carried Wilkes's famous critique of the king's 1763 speech defending the government's policy in the American colonies. While in jail, Wilkes won election to Parliament from suburban Brentford. After a victory march, Wilkes's supporters controlled the streets and demanded recognition of their hero, breaking windows of houses whose inhabitants failed to illuminate in honor of the victor.

As our transcription of a report from election day described the scene: "A prodigious concourse of people assembled at Brentford who would suffer no coaches to enter the town without No. 45 and the words 'Wilkes and Liberty Pro' on them. Several flags were flying with the motto more meat and fewer cooks."

In central London a more violent episode unfolded:

The mob proceeded from Fleet-Street, through St. Paul's Churchyard, Cheapside & the Poultry, where the inhabitants immediately illuminated their houses. The mob demolished the windows of Lord Bute, Lord Egmont, Sir Samson Gideon, William Mayne & many other gentlemen and tradesmen in most of the public streets of London & Westminster. [At] Charing-Cross, at the Duke of Northumberland's, the mob also broke a few panes, but the ladies had the address to get rid of them, by ordering up lights immediately into his windows and opening the Ship Ale-house, which soon drew them off.

But when they came to the Mansion House, there being no proper persons authorized to obey their commands, they began to be outrageous, and broke all the windows to pieces all around the house which they could reach; and in the great room facing Charlott-Street, they broke the large chandelier that cost upwards of 100£ and a large pier glass in another room that cost 50£, after which two companies of soldiers were sent for from the Tower, who came beating their drums, and playing on their fifes as loudly as possible, and surrounded the Mansion-House.

But a worthy Alderman ordered them away to Cornhill, and to stay there with their backs to the Mansion-House, to wait for his orders, which was according observed. He then came out of the Mansion-House great door, with a candle in each hand, placed them on the balustrades, pulled off his hat, and huzza'd "Wilkes for ever," and then addressed the mob on the impropriety of their zeal for Mr. Wilkes's success, and ordered what candles could be procured to be set out. He then represented to them that their present conduct, instead of serving Mr. Wilkes, would imitate his enemies, and greatly prejudice his cause.

In short, his prudent, resolute, sensible and affable behavior, effectually quieted the mob, after which he quitted his station with a huzza for Wilkes and Liberty, which was re-echoed by the mob, who were as much pleased with his conduct on the success of Mr. Wilkes, and joined their names together, with repeated huzzas of applause. [Of course, in our machine-readable transcription, each new verb started a separate line; I have grouped the lines together for easier reading.]

London's Wilkite demonstrations of 1768 and 1769 incorporated elements from older public celebrations of momentous events such as coronations and military victories, non-voters' participation in contested elections, and workers' marches on behalf of threatened rights. But their attachment to a program of popular rights and their identification of a formidable popular force distinguished them as a new sort of performance.

Parliament itself rejected Wilkes's 1768 election. He remained in prison, and he continued to run for the Brentford seat. When Wilkes won his third re-election while still serving his prison term in April 1769, according to the *Middlesex Journal*:

At a little after ten o'clock 200 of Mr. Wilkes's friends, preceded by music, and a flag with the words – FREEDOM. LIBERTY! entered Brentford. This procession was closed by Mr. John Swan, carrying a white wand. Five minutes after this came a coach and six, the horses sumptuously adorned with blue ribbons; and persons were on the roof, bearing flags, inscribed BILL OF RIGHTS. MAGNA CHARTA. At half past ten 300 sons of liberty entered Brentford on horseback, preceded by six French horns, and four silk flags, with the above inscription in letters of gold ... Many ladies (freeholders) were among the friends of freedom, and [were] distinguished by breastknots of blue and silver, with the motto abovementioned. (Brewer 1976: 181)

The Brentford demonstration of 1769 took place as an election celebration, but it borrowed heavily from the pomp of celebrations for victories in the Seven Years' War, which had ended only six years earlier. A new synthesis was emerging.

Elections became favored sites for demonstrations. In 1812 the great radical Henry Hunt ran a spectacular, if losing, campaign for a parliamentary seat in Bristol. He attracted mass support from partisans who lacked the vote. Hunt staged his entry into Bristol in a carriage bearing a long pole to which his followers had attached a large loaf of bread inscribed "Hunt and Peace" (Belchem 1985: 37). The *Bristol Gazette* set the scene:

Mr. Henry Hunt entered this city (as previously announced by placards) on Saturday about three o'clock, in an open carriage, attended by Mr. John Allen and several other friends, from Bath, together with some of his Committee, in another carriage and on horseback, preceded by two large purple silk flags, bearing his name in gilt letters, and an arch raised up poles covered with laurel leaves, and surmounted with carved doves, on which and its appendages were inscribed 'Plenty and Peace. Minority of 235' etc. Arriving opposite the Exchange, Mr. Hunt stepped from the carriage over the shoulders of the populace to one of the brazen pillars, and addressed a very crowded auditory for about two hours and a quarter. (Harrison 1988: 216)

As the polls proceeded, Hunt's supporters attacked Tory properties and fought his enemies, including club-wielding Kingswood colliers hired to support Hunt's opponent, in Bristol's streets (Belchem 1985: 37–38). When the two weeks of polling ended with Hunt far behind his Tory opponent, however, the Tories staged victory demonstrations of their own.

British demonstrations kept their festival air into the 19th century, but expanded well outside the range of elections. Henry Hunt figured centrally in the so-called Peterloo Massacre of 16 August 1819. In that demonstration-meeting, about 60 thousand people (many of them marching in ranks through the streets on their way to the meeting) gathered in St. Peter's Fields, Manchester, to hear Hunt and other radicals speak on behalf of parliamentary reform. Local magistrates sent in first constables and then the mounted militia to arrest Hunt and other agitators. In the melee eleven people died and more than five hundred received injuries. Although the authorities succeeded in seizing and imprisoning Hunt and his companions, the incident embarrassed both the local authorities and the national government. By ricochet, it reinforced the right of citizens to march and assemble peaceably on behalf of such controversial programs as parliamentary reform. The demonstration was becoming available for a wide range of public claim making.

The huge popular mobilization of 1820 in support of the new king's estranged wife, Caroline of Brunswick, gave an enormous boost to the demonstration as a political device. (Chapter 5 returns to Queen Caroline in much greater detail.) In the Queen Caroline affair, processions went to the queen's residence day after day from all over London. In October 1820 London's shipwrights and caulkers borrowed from the pageantry of craft and benefit society processions as they marched six abreast, wearing sprigs of oak, sprigs of laurel, or white favors. Four bands accompanied them. This was their order of march:

Two men on white horses
A blue flag with the motto 'Address of the Ship-builders to the Queen.'
A model of Noah's ark, carried on a pole.
A blue flag, fringed with silver lace, motto 'Hearts of Oak.'
Blue flag with a portrait of the Queen, 'God protect the innocent C.R.'
Model of the head of a ship, inscription:
Long may our wooden walls defend our native land
May innocence and truth break the tyrants' band!
Blue flag, 'Hail! Hail! Star of Brunswick.'
Model of a first-rate ship of war.
White flag, high decorated, 'We maintain and protect the innocent.'
Union Jack, 'What we have we guard.'
White flag, four hands united.
Blue flag, side view of ship's keel, 'Let Justice guide the helm.'
Blue flag, 'The Wooden Walls of Old England.'
Blue flag, 'The ship-caulkers' Tribute of respect to insulted Majesty.'
Blue flag, 'Ship-caulkers of the Port of London.'
Two small blue flags like Persian standards, 'cheer up virtue.'
Large flag with picture of Noah's ark, 'Ezekiel, chapter 28, verse 4.'
Union Jack.
Flag, arms of the ship-caulkers, 'Sons of Freedom and Justice.' (Prothero
    1979: 141–142)

Mobilization on Caroline's behalf subsided as the year went on. But when the wronged queen died in August 1821, her funeral procession became one of the largest and most tumultuous demonstrations London had ever seen. Although royal authorities made every effort to block popular participation in the demonstration, they could not clear the streets or summon up a legal pretext for invoking the Riot Act (Prothero 1979: 147–151). The street demonstration had acquired both a coherent form and a grudgingly conceded legal standing.

In addition to manifestly political issues like the king's attempt to get rid of Queen Caroline, demonstrations also accompanied major labor disputes. When the cotton masters in Stalybridge, near Manchester, cut piece rates in 1830, labor organizers called a meeting in a meadow at the close of work on Saturday. As Marc Steinberg describes the scene:

At noon on that Saturday, the mills disgorged their workers, and the roads swelled with operatives. A procession formed in Stalybridge, with hundreds of boys leading the parade. A band of music displaying the tricolor and a sardonic banner with the words "Free Trade" marched several steps behind. Male workers, many openly armed, were arrayed ten to twelve abreast, with another tricolor at the rear ... Hundreds of women and children, many with tricolored ornaments, swelled the ranks ... At its height, the procession was said to have stretched more than a mile. (Steinberg 1999a: 215)

The recent French revolution of 1830 made the French tricolor a symbol of concerted popular resistance. More than 20 thousand people gathered in the meadow, heard fiery speeches, and approved a resolution condemning the masters.

By 1830, the street demonstration occupied a crucial place in Britain's repertoires of contention. In 1828 and 1829, demonstrations and public meetings had figured centrally in relatively successful social movements on behalf of rights, first of Protestant Dissenters and then of Catholics. In 1830 an unprecedented and partially successful movement for parliamentary reform swept Great Britain, culminating in the Reform Act of 1832. (I call the movement "partially successful" because the Act enfranchised the property-owning bourgeoisie but excluded most of the workers who had joined the mobilization in huge numbers. The worker-based Chartist movement of 1838–1848 held that exclusion from the 1832 enfranchisement as a major grievance.)

Yet, as we have just seen, labor movements had likewise appropriated the demonstration as a way of displaying worker power and determination. The demonstration had become doubly modular: not only available for a wide range of social movements, but also crucial to the somewhat separate labor movement repertoire of strikes, turnouts, and attacks on employers. Two strong repertoires had formed, with the street demonstration a valuable element of each one.

The food-controlling repertoire of price setting and related performances never acquired the modularity of the street demonstration. It stuck closely to the issues of food shortage, high prices, and hoarding. Its individual performances, furthermore, did not evolve significantly during

the period for which we have substantial evidence. Instead, a new repertoire began to displace the old one: public meetings, marches, and appeals
to national authorities gained prevalence as attacks on local farmers and
merchants declined. Indeed, issues of food prices did not disappear, but
moved into the modular social movement repertoire as the old repertoire
faded away. By the 1830s, agitation against the Corn Laws took the forms
of meetings, resolutions, and statements to the press. In that regard, it
drew on the same repertoire as parliamentary reform.

Performances and repertoires evolved in response to two interacting
but still distinguishable sets of causes. At the level of individual episodes,
innovations, successes, and failures in claim making affected subsequent
claim making with respect to similar issues. Wilkites' occupation of the
streets on behalf of not only a candidate but also a fresh political program, popular marches and assemblies on behalf of Queen Caroline, and
the relative success of campaigns for religious inclusion in 1828 and
1829 successively shaped and confirmed the social movement repertoire.
By the 1820s, the social movement repertoire had become widely
available for collective claim making. Parliamentary reformers and other
activists adopted it with unprecedented zeal and effectiveness from 1830
to 1832.

At the level of national political economy, however, changing opportunity structures strongly affected the viability of different performances
and repertoires. As food markets nationalized and authorities collaborated
increasingly with the policy of moving food to London and other major
population centers, the old repertoire of price setting, blocking, touring,
threatening, and parading gave way rapidly to meetings, demonstrations,
and appeals to national holders of power. As connections between local
and national politics strengthened, conversely, the social movement repertoire of meeting, demonstrating, petitioning, and forming specialized
associations gained effectiveness as a means of pursuing both local and
national claims.

Demonstrations in France and Great Britain

A glance across the English Channel will clarify how change and variation
in national political economies affects repertoire change. Because the
establishment of the demonstration occurred significantly later in France
than in Britain, my treatment of France will begin in the 19th century and
only end in the recent past. In France, despite momentous marches

and occupations during the early years of the French Revolution, neither the demonstration nor the social movement repertoire as a whole gained a regular political footing until late in the 19th century. Yet France's 19th-century alternation between revolutionary and reactionary regimes provided intermittent opportunities for demonstrations from the 1830s onward.

Consider Lyon. On 24 February 1848, Parisian revolutionaries had overthrown the royal administration and declared a republic. The news reached Lyon on the 25th. Several hundred weavers marched down into the city center from the silk-producing quarter of Croix-Rousse. Singing the Marseillaise, they proceeded along the Rhône River, then crossed the city's central island to the Place des Terreaux and the Lyon city hall. Overwhelmed by the crowd, the military on hand asked the acting mayor to announce the new republic from a city hall balcony. After he did so, members of the gathering entered the hall and chose an executive committee consisting of weavers plus a minority of bourgeois republicans.

During the preceding July Monarchy (1830–1848), organized silk weavers had missed few opportunities to show their strength by marching in funerals and on authorized holidays. During insurrections of 1831 and 1834, they had also marched. But outside of crises and authorized public assemblies they had until then generally avoided anything like the self-initiated parade of February 1848, if only because royal officials could take the very fact of their organized assembly as evidence that they were visibly violating the legal ban on workers' coalitions.

As the revolutionary regime settled into place, popular militias emerged from the organizations of workers and revolutionaries that had lurked in Lyon's political shadows. Political associations likewise multiplied; some of them formed anew and some of them simply transformed clandestine cells or informal drinking clubs into legal entities. They often staged patriotic ceremonies that included planting of liberty trees. Despite efforts of an increasingly conservative national government to restrain Lyon's radicals, militias and clubs assembled and marched through the city streets repeatedly between the February Revolution of 1848 and Louis Napoleon's coup d'état of December 1851.

In its issue of 14 March 1848, for example, Lyon's left-wing newspaper *Tribun du peuple* reported that

with four men carrying the liberty cap, a numerous troop of citizens crossed the city on the 12th. Following that holy emblem of our deliverance, the cortege marched in two files. Toward the middle, an equally significant emblem attracted great attention. It was a man bound with rough ropes held by citizens forming a square around him. He carried a pathetic faded flag hung with black crepe; it was the white flag, carried almost horizontally and poorly attached to its pole, resembling the coffin of a miserable criminal on his way out, to everyone's great satisfaction. (Robert 1996: 86)

The red cap stood for revolution, the white flag for Legitimacy, the claim of the elder Bourbon branch (which had returned to power after Napoleon's defeat, but lost out in the revolution of 1830) to rule France. Within two weeks of the Parisian revolution, Lyon's citizens were regularly mounting or watching street demonstrations. Using widely recognized national symbols, furthermore, demonstrators enacted the worthiness, unity, numbers, and commitment – the WUNC – of their cause.

As of March 1848, then, had Lyon and France installed the social movement as a regular vehicle of popular politics? The question turns out to be both interesting and controversial. We must look closely at 1848 to determine whether the combination of campaign, repertoire, and WUNC displays had become readily available to a wide range of claimants. The best answer is: yes, but only temporarily.

Speaking specifically of the demonstration rather than of the entire social movement apparatus, Pierre Favre declares that "the first unambiguous examples date from the 1830s, but only in 1848 did the demonstration become a specific, autonomous means of action, distinct from the riot" (Favre 1990: 16).

Lyon's historian Vincent Robert demurs. He argues that despite a flurry of demonstrations under the Second Republic (1848–1851), demonstrations did not really become readily available ways of pressing collective claims until the great May Day mobilizations of the 1890s put them on the map. (Warning: the word "*manifestation*," which both Favre and Robert employ and which I am translating as "demonstration," did not actually displace such words as "*cortège*," "*défilé*," "*démonstration*," and "*rassemblement*" in common French usage until after World War II; Pigenet and Tartakowsky 2003: 84.) Authorities themselves did not publicly recognize demonstrations as valid forms of political action, according to Robert, until just before World War I. At that point, Lyon's authorities began assigning police to protect and channel demonstrations instead of routinely breaking them up as illegal assemblies.

Yet Robert recognizes proto-demonstrations in Lyon as early as 1831. On 19 January of that year, some 1,400 workers assembled across the

Saône River from Lyon's center and marched to shouts of "work or bread"; the authorities eventually arrested fifteen participants (Rude 1969: 198–202). Further demonstrations occurred on 12 February (this time with a black flag of insurrection) and on 25 October (with about 6 thousand participants) before the full-scale insurrection that began with a massive demonstration, then took over the city from 21 to 24 November (Rude 1969: 208, 316, 357–596). In partial collaboration with Parisian rebels, Lyon's silk workers mounted another major insurrection in 1834. At least among Lyon's silk workers, demonstrations had already laid down a significant political history before the Revolution of 1848. From that point forward, they occurred more frequently in times of relaxed repression or democratization, but still receded when governmental repression tightened again.

At least eight demonstrations crossed Lyon during the first month of the 1848 revolution. During March and April the Central Democratic Club organized major demonstrations on behalf of radical democracy (Robert 1996: 94–100). Soon women's groups, political clubs, veterans of Napoleonic armies, schoolchildren, workers from the national workshops set up to combat unemployment, and strikers who actually had jobs were demonstrating in Lyon. Most of them demonstrated in displays of solidarity with the new regime combined with statements of particular demands.

Soon, however, popular street marches and assemblies ceased under the weight of repression; for about fifteen years, demonstrations disappeared. During the later years of Louis Napoleon's Second Empire, a time of rapid industrialization in France, the regime began to relax some of its controls over workers' organizations and actions. In 1864, the Empire granted a limited right to strike. In 1868, it became legal for workers to hold public meetings without prior authorization from the government. Later the same year an imperial edict permitted trade unions to organize, only so long as they had their rules approved by authorities, deposited minutes of their meetings with the authorities, and allowed police observers to attend.

Thus backed by partial legality, Lyon's workers' demonstrations reappeared in abundance during the Second Empire's crisis year, 1870. As the police agent in charge of the Jardin des Plantes station reported on 30 April:

Yesterday evening a band of about two hundred people came down from the Croix-Rousse into my quarter, led by an improvised master of ceremonies who carried a stave and who preceded four torch-bearers with a sixteen-year-old carrying a red flag ... Of these individuals, who seemed to range from fourteen to twenty-five years of age, two-thirds were carrying staves. They sang the

Marseillaise, the song of the Girondins, and then to the melody of the Lampions "Down with the Emperor! Long live the Republic!" On each side of the sidewalk, the band was followed by about thirty individuals thirty to forty-five years old who appeared to be workers and who seemed to be serving as protection. (Robert 1996: 168–169; the Lampion, literally a torch, comes from the name of an older revolutionary song including a three-beat chant on a single note)

Between then and the new revolution of 4 September 1870, authorities and demonstrators played cat and mouse in Lyon.

A red flag of revolution flew at the Lyon city hall from September into the spring. The city established its own version of a radical, autonomous commune, which government forces crushed brutally in April 1871 (Aminzade 1993, Gaillard 1971, Greenberg 1971).

Demonstrations reappeared during the new revolutionary interval, although at a slower pace than that of 1848. Once the Third Republic's authorities restored top-down order, nevertheless, for two more decades Lyon's demonstrations consisted chiefly of adaptations within other sorts of events: anticlerical funerals, local celebrations of Bastille Day, official ceremonies, religious processions, and workers' delegations to municipal or state authorities. Legalization of trade unions (1884) did not change the situation fundamentally. Only with the expansion of voluntary associations during the later 1880s did demonstrations again assume prominence in Lyon's public life.

As it did elsewhere in France (Tilly 1986: 313–319), May Day 1890 inaugurated a great series of annual workers' demonstrations in Lyon; perhaps 15 thousand workers came out for that first great international display of workers' solidarity (Robert 1996: 270). During the next two decades, far more than workers demonstrated in Lyon: Catholics, anti-Catholics, anti-Semites, and many more, increasingly in cadence and coordination with national social movements. As Robert puts it, by World War I

the demonstration had become a normal form of urban political life, and a significant element in political life at large; even though the organization of a march depended on official permission, by then the authorities knew that it would be more dangerous to forbid than to authorize and that barring accidents it would occur peacefully. (Robert 1996: 373)

Around the 1848 Revolution, many of the older forms of public claim making began a rapid decline across the country, while for a privileged year or so the demonstration became a standard way of supporting programs, projecting identities, and claiming political standing in France.

Danielle Tartakowsky picks up the history of French demonstrations where Robert leaves off, at World War I. She points out the blurred boundary between the politically initiated demonstration and the often politically tinged parades of May Day, Bastille Day, and Armistice Day, which she eventually excludes from her catalog. She also distinguishes the demonstration proper from the sorts of identity processions – for example, Catholics' Joan of Arc Day – that dissidents of the early Third Republic often mounted to advertise their political and moral presence.

Tartakowsky sums up the 19th-century background:

Most of these demonstrations, become everyday affairs, belong to the action repertoire that grew more solid at the start of the 20th century in the context of parliamentary democracy, differentiating themselves increasingly from old regime forms of action. Food riots, rural revolts, revolutionary "days," rebellious gatherings, insurrections, and revolutions disappeared one after another, giving way to new means of struggle and expression: the petition, the strike, and the demonstration. At first seen as illegitimate by the emerging parliamentary system, they gradually gained standing within that system as means of affecting its choices, sometimes to defend threatened democracy, and never more to launch frontal attacks on the system. (Tartakowsky 2004: 7–8)

With this context in mind, Tartakowsky inventoried demonstrations over France as a whole from 1919 to 1968. In addition, Olivier Fillieule has prepared event catalogs for Nantes from 1975 to 1990 and Marseille from 1980 to 1993, and Jan-Willem Duyvendak for France as a whole (but drawing events from just one newspaper issue per week) from 1975 to 1990.

Tartakowsky has also drawn counts of demonstrations for Paris alone from annual reports of the Police Prefecture, warning that police counts include "many very small mobilizations and festive gatherings that posed the same sorts of problems for the office of Order and Traffic as did more directly political mobilizations" (Tartakowsky 2004: 14). Figure 3-2 groups all the authors' findings together.

Tartakowsky's 15 thousand catalogued events and the smaller collections of Fillieule and Duyvendak establish that after World War I the demonstration became a major means of advertising political identities and programs in France. The police counts for Paris describe an enormous increase during the 1990s. Every major political controversy produced its own surge of demonstrators – and often of counter-demonstrators as well.

Both right-wing (e.g., Croix de Feu) and left-wing (e.g., communist) groups initiated disproportionate shares of demonstrations; more often than groups in the center of the right-left continuum, they were the

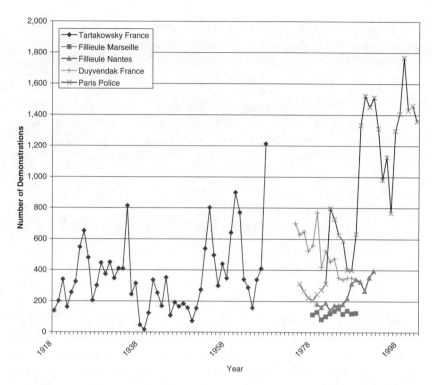

Figure 3-2 Number of Demonstrations in France and Selected French Cities, 1919–2002

political groupings that recurrently asserted their identities as significant actors and sought to place forbidden issues on local or national agendas. Demonstrations served both purposes in France. World War II and the German occupation, as we might expect, produced the low point of demonstration activity registered by these series. During that exceptional period, women complaining to authorities about food shortages and high prices became the most frequent initiators of the rare demonstrations.

Although differences in method and geographic scope forbid strict comparisons, the data also make clear that demonstrations became far more common after World War II than they had been before. Even the 814 demonstrations Tartakowsky identified during the great Popular Front mobilization of 1936 did not match the 899 of 1961 (massive conflict around the Algerian War) or the 1,213 of 1968 (immense movement activity mostly opposing the de Gaulle regime). As students of new social movements will not be surprised to learn, the all-time peak up to that point arrived in 1968.

Although the series of Fillieule, Duyvendak, and the police point in somewhat different directions, put together they indicate that the demonstration continued to thrive in France after 1968. In 2002 and 2003 alone, France mounted some huge demonstrations:

- 1 May 2002 (in Paris and elsewhere), 1.7 to 2.6 million people (depending on whether you believe the police or the organizers) marched against the presidential candidacy of right-winger Jean-Marie Le Pen.
- 15 February 2003 (in Paris), 100 to 250 thousand marched against the imminent American invasion of Iraq.
- 25 May 2003 (Paris), 150 to 600 thousand demonstrated against proposed retirement reforms.
- 10 June 2003 (France as a whole), 440 thousand to 1.5 million demonstrated against the same reforms. (Tartakowsky 2004: 15)

In terms of sheer numbers, the 21st century saw the street demonstration as live and well.

By 2003, two sorts of innovations in French demonstrations were occurring that might signal a more rapid change in the French social movement repertoire than had occurred since the late 19th century. First, organizers and participants were using electronic communication, compact discs, and other new technologies to organize and coordinate their occupations of the streets. Second, anti-war and anti-globalization activists were starting to stage multiple and simultaneous mass demonstrations at sites across the world as well as to create counter-summits to parallel and counter the meetings of financial and political elites in such protected places as Davos and Dubai (Agrikoliansky, Fillieule, and Mayer 2005). Tartakowsky herself expresses disquiet at the detachment of the French demonstration from the solid local and organizational bases that supported it for a century (Tartakowsky 2004, 2007). For our purposes, however, the innovations provide evidence of the demonstration's remarkable flexibility as a vehicle of political voice.

Like its British counterpart, the French demonstration has evolved in response to two interacting sets of causes: innovations that occurred within claim making itself and alterations of national political economy. Within claim making, for example, organized radicals and workers introduced May Day marches in 1890 as a way of asserting workers' WUNC – not only worthiness, but also emphatically unity, numbers, and commitment – and initiating the campaign for an eight-hour day. The first of May became a de facto holiday and a major occasion for demonstrations across the country. From the 1920s onward, it also provided an opportunity for the major labor federations to display their strength and compete with each other for public attention.

Just as clearly, general alterations of France's national political economy transformed the demonstration and the social movement repertoire. Although the National Assembly – France's parliament – acquired great influence with the revolution of 1789, 19th-century monarchs mitigated its influence; only with the definitive establishment of a republic in the 1870s did the National Assembly achieve the political centrality that its British counterpart acquired from the later 18th century onward. Just as British claimants responded to that parliamentarization by turning increasingly to Parliament and its members, once the National Assembly became France's dominant political institution, French claimants concentrated their claims on deputies and the Assembly. Within Paris, the march to the Assemblée Nationale became a standard feature of radical demands from left and right alike (Tilly 1986, chapter 10).

Economic change likewise shaped French contention. As France industrialized after World War I, workers became a more prominent urban presence, a substantial influence on government, and a threat to bourgeois, politically organized Catholics, and nationalists. The sharpening division between labor-backed left and authoritarian right during the early 1930s, for example, translated immediately into a surge of demonstrations. First left and (especially) right activists mounted separate shows of strength. But by 1936 the temporarily ascendant Popular Front and its right-wing enemies battled each other repeatedly in the streets as they deliberated mounted demonstrations and counter-demonstrations.

Alas, no one has done detailed catalogs of Britain's 20th-century demonstrations to match the great efforts invested in them by French researchers. Nevertheless, the available evidence makes one thing clear: differences between France and Britain in the paces of parliamentarization and industrialization translated into very different timetables of repertoire change. British activists had almost fully adopted the social movement repertoire, including the street demonstration, by the 1830s. Despite intermittent flourishing of demonstrations and other social movement performances during brief revolutionary periods, the new repertoire did not prevail in France until the closing decades of the 19th century. Once in place, nevertheless, that strong repertoire dominated the public making of claims in both countries. A new repertoire took over public politics. It remains familiar today (Reiss 2007a and b).

4

From Campaign to Campaign

In his panorama of Mexican popular collective action between 1968 and the 1990s, Sergio Tamayo shows how one national campaign shaped the next. The transformation of popular contention, he concludes,

was a cumulative process of citizens' actions that during the first five years of the 1990s reached a level of extensive participation, using every sort of resource, as much legal and formal as informal and violent ... As for Mexico City, the citizenry appeared with great strength, certainly a result of the city's special character as capital of the republic and urban center where regardless of its origin the national political debate concentrated. (Tamayo 1999: 353)

That "continuous process" produced a mutation, Tamayo tells us, from a turbulent 1968 in which students and workers alike agitated for various forms of socialism to a wide range of demands for citizen power during the 1990s. To some extent, violent visions of class confrontation gave way to democratic debate.

Tamayo sees five elements that transformed Mexican popular politics: 1) the Zapatista rising of 1994 and thereafter signaled a new phase of action at the national scale, 2) demonstrations, strikes, and union filing of complaints justifying strikes (*aplazamientos a huelga*) multiplied as vehicles of popular voice, 3) the contested elections of 1988 and 1994 weakened the hegemonic party, PRI, 4) civil society grew larger, more vocal, and more fragmented, and 5) old forms of participation – "performances" in this book's terms – used by the local citizens' committees of 1988 gave way to the national and international actions pioneered by the Zapatistas: "We can add that precisely because of the way that the [elections of 1988] ended, a cycle of participation and social movement development could close in Mexico, and with the Zapatista movement a new cycle could open" (Tamayo 1999: 355).

The (possibly fraudulent) loss of populist presidential candidate Cuauhtémoc Cárdenas to Carlos Salinas de Gortari in 1988 first stirred enormous protests. But that mobilization's failure, Tamayo observes, sounded the death knell for the time-honored performances of Mexican populist politics. A new kind of political campaign took shape.

Tamayo's rich account of popular contention in Mexico thus raises a question of general importance for the study of contentious politics: under what circumstances, to what extent, and how do claim-making campaigns transform the character of contention itself? At a smaller scale, how does one campaign influence what happens in the next campaign? Without a clear understanding of that influence, any account of repertoire change remains woefully incomplete. This chapter attempts to clarify our understanding of the impact of claim-making campaigns on subsequent claim-making campaigns.

A campaign is a sustained, coordinated series of episodes involving similar claims on similar or identical targets. In 1968, leftist students initiated a campaign for democratic rights on the eve of the Mexico City Olympic Games and suffered severe repression by the government of Gustavo Díaz Ordaz. As Tamayo says, the Zapatista campaign for indigenous rights launched in 1994 took a fundamentally different tack: guerrilla mobilization in the Chiapas backlands, control of ostensibly liberated zones, national and international broadcasts of critiques, and eventually peaceful mass marches from the jungle to the national capital.

Without for a moment pretending that Tamayo frames his analysis in these specific terms, we can schematize the argument as in Figure 4-1. Here a campaign transforms political opportunity structure (POS), changes the array of available models for contentious performances, and alters connections among potential actors. Among other ways, a campaign sometimes alters POS by bringing new actors into a regime, changing a regime's repressive policy, or establishing new alliances between challengers and established holders of power; all three happened in Mexico after 1968. Such alterations in POS almost inevitably alter the repertoire of subsequent campaigns.

A campaign sometimes produces changes in available models of performances, most directly by innovating as the Zapatistas did in 1994 and thereafter. Old models generally retain prestige and predictability, but at least occasionally repertoire change occurs because of innovative campaigns. Once an innovation has occurred and produced results for the

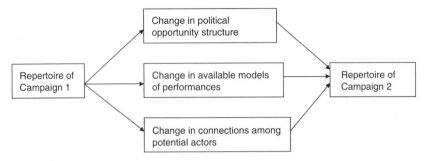

Figure 4-1 Campaign Transformation Schematized

innovators, others frequently try it. Tamayo tells us that the Zapatistas' national and international performances produced just such a change.

Finally, a campaign sometimes alters connections among potential actors. Tamayo describes new alliances within civil society as occurring in response to the crises of 1968 and, especially, 1988. New alliances brought about the possibility of broad citizens' fronts on behalf of democracy. Often the most durable impact of a relatively successful campaign appears less in POS and repertoire than in altered connections among actors who collaborate in subsequent campaigns.

To be sure, between campaigns POS, models, and connections interact. Shifts in POS affect the viability of different performances, new models foster fresh connections among potential claimants, and newly elaborated connections sometimes alter POS itself. In the case of Mexico, the Zapatista rising caused all three to happen at once, as international activists who supported the Zapatistas allied with domestic activists, promoted their models of claim making, and intervened with unprecedented force in the Mexican structure of power.

The three sets of changes, then, shape the next campaign. The relative weights of the three causal paths – POS, models, and connections – vary from regime to regime and time to time. Nor does the scheme exhaust likely causes. Most clearly, changes external to contention, such as international influences and transformations of political economy, often produce changes in POS. Here we follow Tamayo closely by concentrating on the effects of domestic Mexican campaigns on later Mexican campaigns.

Let us look more closely at each of the three paths of change: POS, repertoires, and connections. The idea of POS has come in for spirited attacks by knowledgeable students of contentious politics (notably

Goodwin and Jasper 1999). Most often, critics have lodged three complaints against the idea: that analysts have used it inconsistently, that it denies human agency, and that it remains unverifiable because it only applies after the fact. The charge of inconsistency is correct, but unfortunately applies to most concepts in the field of contentious politics; it takes time for codification to occur in a fast-moving field. The second and third complaints are false. POS can only shape contention through human agency. And it is perfectly possible to specify POS independently of the changes in contention it causes.

Figure 4-2 shows how and why. It points out that any full conception of POS includes both opportunity and threat. It also declares that the elementary theory of POS bundles predictions about effects of changes in six features of political environments: openness of the regime, coherence of its elite, stability of political alignments, availability of allies for potential actors, repression or facilitation, and pace of change in all these regards. Change in one direction constitutes opportunity, change in the other direction, threat. On the whole, increased opportunity predicts to greater extensiveness and effectiveness of contention, increased threat to declining extensiveness and effectiveness of contention.

Examined closely, to be sure, the effects of opportunity and threat are asymmetrical and somewhat more subtle. For example, rising threats to collective survival tend to incite increases in collective action by well-connected groups, at least in the short run (Davenport 2007, Goldstone and Tilly 2001). For the moment, however, it matters most that campaigns often affect all six features of POS: openness of the regime, coherence of its elite, stability of political alignments, availability of allies for potential actors, repression or facilitation, and pace of change. In the case of Mexico from 1968 to the 1990s, Tamayo provides evidence that the radical and populist campaigns of the 1970s and 1980s increased the opportunity for new challenges. They did so by increasing divisions within the elite, promoting instability, and helping install new allies for challengers.

What about change in available models of performances? Tamayo provides rich documentation concerning this set of effects. The Zapatistas offer the most dramatic examples. Their guerrilla activity actually followed extensive models from elsewhere in rural Mexico from the 1960s through the 1980s (Turbiville 1997). But after initial bloody encounters with the Mexican army, they shifted their focus from clandestine attacks on government forces to ingenious publicity for their demands, extensive outreach to potential allies both within and outside of Mexico, and public

Shifts in opportunity = Changes in the environment of political actors (in this case, an idealized single challenger) that signal shifts in likely consequences of different interactions with other actors

Category	Increasing Opportunity	Increasing Threat
Openness of regime	Regime becoming increasingly open	Regime closing down
Coherence of elite	Increasing divisions within elite	Increasing solidarity of elite
Stability of political alignments	Rising instability	Increasing stability
Availability of allies	New allies in regime available to challengers	Potential allies disappear or lose power
Repression/facilitation	Increasing facilitation, declining repression	Decreasing facilitation, rising repression
Pace of change	Acceleration in any of the above	Deceleration in any of the above

This also applies cross-sectionally: if regime A is more open, its elites more divided, more generally unstable, richer in potential allies, and less repressive than regime B, similar challengers will contend more extensively and effectively in regime A.

Figure 4-2 Political Opportunity, Political Threat, and Their Impacts on Contention

displays of WUNC through rallies and marches (Olesen 2005). Clifford Bob describes one Zapatista performance:

On March 11, 2001, 24 leaders of Mexico's Zapatista Army of National Liberation (EZLN) trooped into the Zócalo, Mexico City's huge central square. Seven years after their armed uprising, the Zapatistas arrived with government blessing, the group's spokesman, Subcomandante Marcos, proclaiming "We are here" to an audience of more than 100,000. Days later, Comandanta Esther addressed the Mexican Congress, urging adoption of a law granting significant new rights to the country's indigenous population. Throughout the Zapatistas' multiweek stay in the capital and their triumphal bus journey from remote bases in the southern state of Chiapas, foreign supporters accompanied the rebels. Conspicuous among them, dressed in white overalls and acting incongruously as security guards, strode dozens of monos blancos, or white monkeys, Italian activists prominent at European antiglobalization protests. In the Zócalo to greet the Zapatistas stood a host of left-wing luminaries: France's ex–first lady Danielle Mitterrand, film producer Oliver Stone, and McDonald's "dismantler" José Bové. Around the world, thousands of Zapatista followers monitored the March for Indigenous Dignity, the "Zapatour," on the Internet. To pay for the event, the Zapatistas solicited donations from national and transnational civil society and opened a bank account accessible to depositors around the world. (Bob 2005: 117)

Obviously, the Zapatistas had gone far beyond the Ché Guevara–style focus of the 1960s.

Just as obviously, our third element – change in connection among potential actors – was occurring in Mexico, and strongly affecting the new round of campaigns. Thomas Olesen distinguishes three levels of organization in the Zapatista mobilization: the Zapatista organization (EZLN) as such, the transnational solidarity network that grew up in immediate support of the Zapatistas, and the "transnational justice and solidarity network" that dealt with a wide variety of leftist causes, including the Zapatistas. The third level, according to Olesen,

barely existed at the time of the EZLN uprising in 1994, when the left was still finding its feet after the end of the Cold War. It began to take shape in the second half of the 1990s, and made its first strong impression in Seattle in November 1999. The EZLN, and especially the intercontinental encounters in Chiapas in 1996, have played an important role in this development. The prospects for the left have, accordingly, undergone significant change during the 1990s, and the EZLN has seen many of its political ideas and visions echoed in the activities of the transnational justice and solidarity movement. (Olesen 2005: 209)

The EZLN, Olesen speculates, may be fading from the international scene, but leaving behind it crucial transnational connections among activists. From the late 1990s, those connections shaped the transnational politics of anti-globalization.

Parallel processes occurred within Mexican politics. Tamayo stresses how Mexican feminists allied themselves with activists on other issues than women's rights:

Feminist activists who were also political party militants added a major component to internal party dynamics between electoral campaigns. It might be surprising but appears clearly that after the elections of July 1988 and with the new emergence of a movement against electoral fraud women participated actively and collectively ... Thus as the period of transition closed various women's organizations called for the National Assembly to combat institutionalized electoral fraud, creating the Benita Galeana Women's Alliance with working class clusters, political parties, activists, and nongovernmental organizations. (Tamayo 1999: 320)

A major double transition was occurring in Mexican popular politics: from clients of populist leaders to self-starting activists, from single-issue mobilizations to broad coalitions for democratic reform. Claim-making campaigns themselves played major parts in the two transitions. They did so by altering POS, available models, and connections among potential actors.

Mexico was not unique. On the contrary, Mexico from 1968 to the 1990s illustrates two extremely general patterns in contentious politics. First, much of the change in performances and repertoires that occurs anywhere results from the influence of one campaign – successful or not – on the next. Second, that influence operates through interacting alterations in three channels: POS, available models, and connections among potential actors.

Here we begin to see clearly the analytic advantages of treating collective claim making as a series of learned performances that group into repertoires. The three elements – POS, available models, and connections – identify three different aspects of the situations faced by potential makers of claims. POS identifies the likely political outcomes of different collective actions claimants might undertake together. Available models identify the known routines among which claimants can choose. And connections indicate who is likely to participate, as well as how. The three together produce a matrix of choice for potential participants in contention. But they also produce a matrix of explanation for us observers of contentious politics.

Relevant explanations operate at two different levels: local and national. Locally, we analyze the situations of particular sets of potential claimants in terms of their involvement with POS, models, and interpersonal connections. That should help us anticipate the forms and intensities of their collective claim making – and, in many cases, their inaction. ("Local" is of course a relative term, because potential claimants often connect across the boundaries of villages or even metropolitan areas.)

Nationally, we examine how all the actors in a regime respond to shifts in POS, available models, and connections. As the rest of this chapter and later chapters will show forcefully, because central governments play exceptional parts in the monitoring, channeling, and repression of contentious politics, performances and repertoires become more uniform within whole regimes than the variety of local cultures might lead us to expect. When national political institutions such as parliaments become more prominent and powerful, furthermore, their increasing influence promotes greater national uniformity in performances and repertoires. Just such a political transformation underlay the British shift of repertoires from particular, parochial, and bifurcated to modular, cosmopolitan, and autonomous between the 18th and 19th centuries. The increasing centrality of Parliament to British national politics, as we will see in exquisite detail, spearheaded the transformation of contention. It acted on contentious politics through changes in POS, available models, and connections among political claimants.

Drawing on the incomparably detailed evidence from Great Britain, let us examine the three change channels separately before putting them back together: first, a look at how campaigns alter POS, which in turn shapes subsequent campaigns; second, a similar examination of the sequence of campaign shifts – new models of action – in later campaigns; and third, a review of the bridge from campaign to changing connections among actors to altered coordination in the next campaign. In each case, a comparison of successive campaigns will serve us well.

Political Opportunity Structure

For POS, we have a colorful pair of London campaigns: the mass popular support for John Wilkes in 1768 and 1769 plus Lord George Gordon's mobilization of his Protestant Association in 1780. We met Wilkes fleetingly on the very first page of this book's first chapter, then watched him and his supporters act in Chapter 3. But we did not see him in political context. Although he had entered Parliament in 1757, Wilkes did not attract national attention until 1762. He then founded an opposition political newspaper, *The North Briton*. Wilkes's paper competed with a regime-supporting paper, *The Briton*, recently established by Scottish pamphleteer and novelist Tobias Smollett. *The Briton* favored, and *The North Briton* opposed, Scottish Lord Bute, the king's minister and object of the charades with Scots bonnet, boot, petticoat, and gallows we also encountered in Chapter 1.

In 1763, notorious issue number forty-five of *The North Briton* published Wilkes's critique of the king's speech defending the crown's American policy. Wilkes implied that the king had lied. For that libelous offense, Wilkes suffered a seizure of his papers on a general warrant and spent time in the Tower of London. Daringly, he challenged his arrest in court, and eventually won compensation from the government. He then pushed his luck, both re-publishing number forty-five and producing a pornographic pamphlet. The courts again prosecuted, instructing the London sheriff and the hangman to burn the newspaper's offending issue publicly. At that occasion, the crowd seized the newspaper from its executioners and assaulted them. Soon after, Wilkes escaped to France, Parliament expelled him, and the courts pronounced him an outlaw. Meanwhile, Wilkes became a transatlantic icon of opposition to arbitrary rule and the number forty-five a potent symbol of liberty. The cry "Wilkes and Liberty" resounded from London to Boston, Massachusetts.

Mass support for Wilkes revived early in 1768, when he sneaked back into England, failed in an appeal for a pardon, stood for Parliament again, lost one poll, won another, entered jail voluntarily, and received a rebuff from Parliament. On 10 May, as the *Annual Register* reported it,

a great body of people assembled about the king's-bench prison, in expectation, as it is said, that Mr. Wilkes was to go from thence to the parliament-house, and designing to convey him thither. They demanded him at the prison, and grew very tumultuous; whereupon the riot-act was begun to be read, but they threw stones and brickbats while it was reading, when William Allen, son of Mr. Allen, master of the Horse-shoe inn and livery tables in Blackman-street, Southwark, being singled out, was pursued by one of the soldiers, and shot dead on the spot. Soon after this, the crowd increasing, an additional number of the guards was sent for, who marched thither, and also a party of horse-grenadiers; when, the riot continuing, the mob were fired upon by the soldiers, and five or six were killed on the spot, and about 15 wounded. (*Annual Register* 1768: 108)

In Wilkite legend, the confrontation became famous as the Massacre of St. George's Fields. During 1768 and 1769, Wilkes repeatedly ran for

Parliament from his jail cell, repeatedly received rejections from Parliament, and repeatedly attracted great crowds of supporters both at the jail, in London's streets, and at the polls, where his agents managed his candidacies. While still imprisoned in 1769, Wilkes won election as a London alderman. After leaving jail in 1770, he became sheriff, lord mayor and, after multiple rejections, again a member of Parliament (1774). His fame only spread.

Meanwhile, Wilkes's elite supporters organized as well. In February 1769 Wilkes's defenders (notably the clergyman John Horne, later known as Horne Tooke) began meeting at the London Tavern as the Friends of Mr. Wilkes and the Constitution. They then reorganized as the Society of Supporters of the Bill of Rights. The Society combined electoral support for Wilkes with more general agitation for constitutional rights (Goodwin 1979). For example, they helped organize popular petitions to the king for the seating of Wilkes in Parliament, thus defying the Common Council's previous monopoly of petition rights. Creation of an electoral association with a constitutional program defied the British ban on public political consultation outside the scope of Parliament. It did more: it established what came to be known as an anti-Parliament, and it formed the nucleus of an eventually overwhelming popular program for parliamentary reform.

Popular vengeance and mass expressions of support for popular heroes had occurred many times before in British history. But three features of the 1768–1769 Wilkes campaigns counted as powerful innovations. First, Wilkes's mostly disfranchised supporters converted tolerated electoral rallies into mass marches – shows of strength not only for the candidate but also against arbitrary rule. Second, legal battles by Wilkes and his attorneys overturned general warrants, broadened rights to publish criticism of the government, and established Wilkes himself as one of Britain's most stalwart defenders of American rights. Third, the formation of an association and a public program on behalf of constitutional rights at large set a precedent for public, popular, association-based making of claims (Tilly 1995: 150–162). In POS terms, Wilkes's campaigns of 1768 and 1769 pried open the regime, exacerbated divisions within the national elite, destabilized political alignments, installed new allies for challengers, and to some small degree diminished regime repression.

We can detect the POS-mediated consequences of the Wilkes campaign in a struggle over Catholic rights that began only a few years later. When Great Britain defeated France in the Seven Years' War (1756–1763), it added Québec's large Catholic population to its already restive Catholics of Scotland, England, and especially Ireland. In the Québec Act of 1774, Québec's Catholics received more extensive political rights in the colony than their co-religionists enjoyed in the British Isles. During the 1770s, war with the thirteen colonies south of Québec made the British government eager to solicit support among Catholics and to recruit Catholic soldiers (previously barred from service by the requirement that they abjure the Pope). Parliament made modest concessions to Catholic rights in the Catholic Relief Act of 1778. John Wilkes, for one, saw those concessions as minor and acceptable (Rogers 1998: 157). Nevertheless, the government's proposal to extend those concessions to Scotland excited a vigorous anti-Catholic mobilization.

Anti-Catholicism had attracted plenty of support – and Catholics had suffered serious restrictions of their political rights – in Great Britain since the Glorious Revolution of 1688–1689 had dethroned a Catholic king. But the Protestant Association, formed in 1779, produced something new. It gave anti-Catholicism an organizational base and a mass following on the model of Wilkes's supporters. Unlike the reform associations that were starting to spring up across Great Britain, it adopted "radical forms to press for appeal, holding monthly general meetings, distributing handbills, advocating instructions to MPs, and embarking on mass petitioning" (Rogers 1998: 158). All of these innovations built on precedents supplied by the Wilkes campaign. Scottish Lord George Gordon's speeches against the Catholic Relief Act and its extension to Scotland catapulted Gordon into the presidency of the London-based Association. In bringing the Association's campaign to Parliament the following year, Gordon precipitated one of Britain's bloodiest domestic struggles in decades.

In partial collaboration with London's Common Council, the Association initiated a petition to Parliament for repeal of the Catholic Relief Act (Rudé 1971: 178–179). Over some resistance within the Association, Gordon called a mass meeting for 2 June 1780 in St. George's Fields. Up to this point, British petitioners had sometimes held public meetings or circulated their petitions for signature at already authorized meetings of constituted assemblies, but then ordinarily sent a small delegation to present their petition to Parliament or the king. This time, something like 50 thousand supporters assembled and marched across the Thames to Parliament for presentation of the petition. Many carried banners saying "No popery." An estimated 17 thousand remained outside of Parliament to hear the result (Rogers 1998: 159). Some entered the lobby and harassed their petition's opponents, including members of the House of Lords. Members of the crowd roughed up MPs and fought the troops sent to guard the legislature. After the House of Commons overwhelmingly rejected the repeal petition, the Association's supporters left the grounds of Parliament.

That was only the beginning. During the night, Association activists started lighting bonfires in the streets and sacked the Catholic chapels of the Sardinian and Bavarian ambassadors. Over the next five nights groups smashed, looted, and burned more chapels, homes of Catholic dignitaries, and jails that held those arrested in the first rounds of governmental repression. Although for the first few days Association supporters confined their attacks almost exclusively to Catholic properties, when a reconvened Parliament renewed its opposition to their pleas on 6 June their targets multiplied:

After a crowd had dragged Lord George Gordon's chariot through the streets in popular triumph, protesters broadened their jurisdiction to include not only Catholics but members of the establishment. Lambeth Palace was threatened; so, too, were the residences of the Archbishops of Canterbury and York. Crowds also directed their anger upon leading members of the government and the Opposition who were known to be sympathetic to the Act, a departure from their earlier strategy outside parliament. (Rogers 1998: 161)

Troops sent to quell the attacks eventually killed about 450 people. The government arrested Gordon on a charge of high treason. He spent six months in the Tower, but finally received an acquittal. After a bizarre series of adventures in Europe and Africa and after conversion to Judaism in 1787, he died in Newgate Prison in 1793 at the age of 42. By that time, the mass petition march and confrontation he pioneered had become common practice in British contention, including the mass campaign against slavery that began during the 1780s.

GBS makes it possible to compare shapes of the Wilkes and Gordon campaigns in hopes of detecting shifts mediated by alterations of POS. Figures 4-3 and 4-4 present the elementary comparisons for the 23 CGs and 131 actions with objects of the Wilkes campaign, plus the 21 CGs and 232 actions with objects of the Gordon campaign. The rise from the 5.7 actions per CG of Wilkes to the 11.1 actions per CG of Gordon already conveys the greater street mobility of participants in the Gordon campaign. Figure 4-3 confirms that impression: in Gordon, verbs of "control," "move," and especially "attack" outshadow their equivalents in Wilkes. Fundamentally, the distributions of verbs in the two campaigns, with

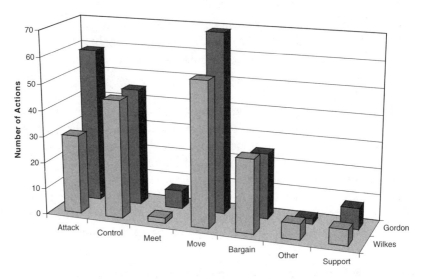

Figure 4-3   Verbs in Wilkes and Gordon CGs, 1768–1780

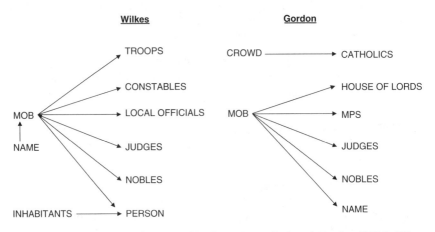

Figure 4-4   Structures of Claims in Wilkes (1768–1769) and Gordon (1780) CGs

their domination by "attack," "control," and "move," identify them with
Britain's 18th-century out-of-doors confrontational politics. Yet we
notice some hints of change in Gordon's greater frequency of "meet" and
"support" verbs. The 1780 meeting in St. George's Fields, the march to
Parliament, and the presentation of a mass petition all became possible in

part because of POS changes caused by the earlier confrontations between Wilkites and the establishment.

The structures of claims in the two campaigns point timidly in the same directions. In each case, the diagrams identify each subject-object pair that involved four or more actions of any kind. In Figure 4-4, the two diagrams resemble each other greatly and convey a very 18th-century image. At the center, actors for which our sources use terms such as "mob" make aggressive claims on members of the establishment. In Wilkes, those objects of claims remain largely local and include repressive forces sent to face them down. In Gordon, two channels of claim making appear. "Crowds" attack Catholics, as we might expect. But "mobs" make claims not only on judges and nobles (as in Wilkes) but also on MPs and the House of Lords. Perhaps relying excessively on hindsight, we can infer that the Wilkes campaign opened up the national opportunity structure at least a chink.

In the first transforming channel, then, an influential campaign reshapes POS through one or more of its six elements: general openness of the regime, coherence of the elite, stability of political arrangements, availability of allies, repression and facilitation, and/or pace of change in these regards. The reshaping occurs because members of the previously existing regime join the contention by making concessions, establishing alliances, polarizing, or otherwise responding to the campaign of claims. They, too, participate in contentious politics.

Models of Action

The second channel need not involve power holders so directly. Innovation by claimants, especially successful claimants, makes new models of performances available to other potential actors. Most such innovation occurs incrementally and on the small scale, but it occurs. During the 1820s and 1830s, Great Britain experienced a great many performance innovations that stuck. A comparison of two overlapping campaigns in the 1820s will make the point. Seen from the pinnacle of parliamentary politics, repeal of the Test and Corporation Acts (1828) and passage of Catholic Emancipation (1829) look like feats of elite maneuvering that then transformed public opinion. As John Stuart Mill summed it up in a letter to Gustave d'Eichthal in March 1829: "The alteration of so important and so old a law as that which excludes Catholics from political privileges, has given a shake to men's minds which has weakened all old prejudices, and will render them far more accessible to new ideas and to rational innovations on all other parts of our institutions" (Hinde 1992: 187).

Seen from the valleys of popular politics, however, these abolitions of religious restrictions on political participation rested on extensive contention. What's more, they fortified models of performance that shook the British establishment over the next few years. They contributed significantly to the forms of activism that developed during the great parliamentary reform campaign of 1830–1832.

The stories of the Test and Corporation repeal and of Catholic Emancipation go back to the era of Wilkes and Gordon. Even farther back, they touch 17th-century exclusions of non-Anglicans from public office in Great Britain and Ireland. Since the 18th century, special legislation had allowed individual Protestant Dissenters to enter Parliament and to hold other national offices. But the law still stigmatized non-Anglicans, especially Catholics. From the time of Lord George Gordon, British reformers often advocated the relaxation of religious restrictions on office holding. In 1787 and 1789, for example, London's Revolution Society (formed to commemorate 1688's Glorious Revolution) conducted unsuccessful campaigns for repeal of Test and Corporation. From that time onward, reformers and religious associations regularly supported a program of combining Test and Corporation repeal with Catholic Emancipation – removal of political bars on Catholics in general.

During the years of the French Revolution and Napoleon, the British state, radicals, and reformers had struggled over rights to associate. The government prosecuted both what it defined as subversion and as infringements on Parliament's sole right to represent the British people. Under the Seditious Societies Act of 1799, for example, the government allowed formally organized local groups to discuss public affairs for their own benefit and even to initiate petitions for Parliament or the king, but not to create national organizations. After the end of the Napoleonic Wars, however, reformers and radicals pushed formal associations beyond their previous limits by such devices as creating correspondence committees and capturing already authorized assemblies of local authorities, elections, trades, and religious congregations. The years from 1815 to 1830 became a golden age of organizing.

From 1816 onward, association-based organizers tried repeatedly to push Catholic Emancipation through Parliament, but they failed. Although political unions and trade associations led the way within Great Britain, the most powerful organizing effort went on in Ireland. There barrister

Daniel O'Connell (who had collaborated extensively with British reformers in the failed attempts to engineer an act of Parliament) organized the Catholic Association. With cooperation from local Catholic clergy and with dues (the "Catholic rent") of a penny per month, the Association became the most effective special-purpose association the British Isles had ever seen. Despite the British government's attempts to outlaw the association, it revived as the New Catholic Association, undergirding Irish mobilization on behalf of Emancipation and acquiring a substantial following among British Catholics and non-Catholic reformers as well. It had such great organizing success, indeed, that Britain's anti-Catholic organizers paid Emancipation's organizers the grudging tribute of emulating them. They created their own Protestant-based Brunswick Clubs to oppose Emancipation.

O'Connell precipitated a major crisis for anti-Catholics when he decided to run for Parliament from County Clare, Ireland in June 1828. He became the first Catholic to stand for a parliamentary seat since the 17th century. Although he was competing for what had been an uncontested Tory seat, with support of his Catholic Association, major Catholic churchmen, and impressive local organization, O'Connell won a great victory. In fact, he defeated a Tory who already favored Catholic Emancipation. So doing, he also vanquished a landlord class that had never before faced such an electoral rebellion. His victory set the stage for the successful mobilization of 1829. "Such is the power of the agitators," wrote the (Anglican) Lord Lieutenant of Ireland, Anglesey, "that I am quite certain they could lead on the people to open rebellion at a moment's notice ... I believe their success inevitable – that no power under heaven can arrest its progress" (O'Farrell 1981: 200).

Yet Catholic Emancipation only won after massive resistance within Great Britain. The campaigns of 1828 and 1829 occurred in three over-lapping phases: a first successful attempt to repeal the Test and Corpo-ration Acts, which ended with acceptance by the House of Lords in April 1828; a failed attempt to pass Catholic Emancipation in 1828; and a tumultuous and ultimately successful campaign in 1829.

From October 1828 onward, the Brunswick Clubs and anti-Catholic activists mounted their own counter-campaign, with an organization ironically and significantly modeled directly on the Catholic Association (Jupp 1998: 367–376). In 1829, their meetings and petitions outnumbered the efforts of Emancipation's supporters within Great Britain. But mass mobilization at the edge of insurrection in Ireland combined with pres-sure from reformers within Britain to persuade prime minister the Duke of Wellington and home secretary Robert Peel to push Emancipation past a reluctant king and House of Lords. The legislation that granted Emancipation signaled as much; it also dissolved the Catholic Association and greatly increased the property qualifications for voting in Ireland.

Obviously a great deal more was going on in 1828 and 1829 than the influence of one campaign on another. Nevertheless two analyses parallel to those of Wilkes and Gordon reveal some likely campaign-to-campaign impacts. In particular, campaign dynamics produced a dramatically increased concentration of Emancipation's supporters on Parliament (that is, individual MPs, the House of Commons, the House of Lords, or Parliament as a whole). The proportions of actions in CGs with MPs or Parliament as their objects varied as follows:

	Test and Corporation	Emancipation 1828	Emancipation 1829
MP	11.3%	11.1%	10.1%
Parliament	66.1%	12.3%	50.0%

The Test and Corporation repeal campaign consisted very largely of public meetings with petitions to Parliament as their outcomes. A much smaller share of 1828's Emancipation CGs involved that format. But by 1829, the focus on Parliament had greatly sharpened: half of all reported actions in Catholic Emancipation CGs for 1829 selected Parliament itself as their object, and another 10 percent aimed at MPs.

Figure 4-5 shows the impact of that shift on the forms of contentious gatherings. The first row dramatizes the concentration of Test and Corporation mobilization on public meetings: the formula was basically "Meet." In the second row, the 1828 Emancipation CGs include plenty of meeting, but they also involved much more moving, bargaining, and pledging support than did Test and Corporation gatherings. By 1829, in contrast, Catholic Emancipation actions centered almost as much on "Meet" as had their Test and Corporation predecessors of the previous year. Rights advocates and their opponents alike were learning to concentrate their attention on local assemblies that displayed popular support for parliamentary action.

The detail on structures of claims amplifies this account. Figure 4-6 shows clearly how much Test and Corporation supporters concentrated

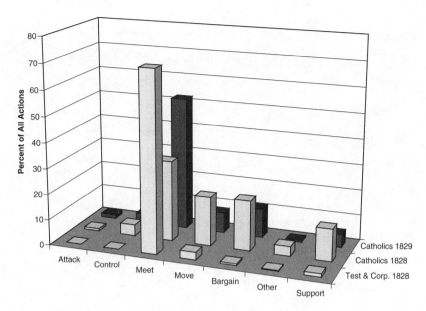

Figure 4-5   Verb Distributions in Religious Campaigns, Great Britain, 1828–1829

on Parliament and individual MPs. The claimants were either Protestants at large or societies organized to press public claims. The Catholic Emancipation campaign of 1828 certainly included claims on Parliament and MPs. But a great many other claims occupied the year's gatherings. In 1829, other things continued to happen in CGs concerning Catholic Emancipation. Attacks of persons (not otherwise identified) on Irish reflected the counter-mobilization against the drive for Emancipation. Still, the system of claims as a whole centers more directly on Parliament than it did in 1828. Meetings in which citizens assembled to petition Parliament came to dominate the Emancipation campaign.

In retrospect, of course, we can interpret the movement toward public meetings and Parliament as the inevitable outcome of a long-term trend. On the hard ground of political struggle, nevertheless, participants in contention were incessantly making tactical decisions. After all, the advocates of Catholic Emancipation failed repeatedly before the partial success of 1829. Anti-Catholics, furthermore, did not give up until the bitter end. They treated the government's reluctant sponsorship of Emancipation as betrayal. It took the threat of insurrection in Ireland to

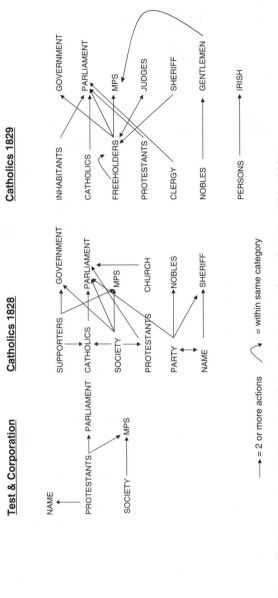

Figure 4-6 Structures of Claims in Religious Campaigns, Great Britain, 1828–1829

persuade the ministry and Parliament that concessions to Catholic rights were necessary to maintain the peace.

Connections among Potential Actors

Ironically, the disappointment of anti-Catholic activists contributed to their support for parliamentary reform. They were right to think that if a much more popular franchise had existed in 1828 and 1829, MPs who wanted to stay in office would have been much less willing to grant Catholics concessions; their constituencies would have turned them out.

The Emancipation Act had an immense effect in advancing the cause of reform. It carried the disruption of the Tory party a stage further and thus weakened and divided the anti-reformers' forces. It drove a wedge between the country gentlemen and the "ministerial interest," and so shattered the precious link on which the Tories' supremacy depended. It naturally started a rumor that Wellington and Peel might "rat" on the unreformed system as they had ratted on Protestantism (Brock 1973: 55; see also Jupp 1998: 259–261).

Those changes took place chiefly in POS. Modeling also played its part: like Thomas Attwood's Birmingham Political Union, many a reform organization emulated the structure of the Catholic Association (O'Farrell 1981: 271–272). But at the same time the campaigns for religious rights produced new connections among potential actors. Within Ireland, for example, the Liberal Clubs that formed to support Emancipation soon became the bases of organized support for parliamentary reform (O'Farrell 1981: 274–277). In London, the successful Emancipation campaign energized and brought together a wide variety of radicals and reformers (Prothero 1979: 272). Those connections figured mightily in the struggles over reform that shook Great Britain from 1830 to 1832.

British 19th-century historians in search of topics take note! Ideally, the evidence for influence of the religious rights campaigns on the new campaigns for parliamentary reform would consist of tracing successive activist networks from the 1820s through the passage of reform in 1832. Such an investigation would show us, for example, radicals Henry Hunt and William Cobbett occasionally teaming up to advocate religious rights, then reappearing in testy competition and intermittent collaboration during the reform mobilization. In different combinations and locations, the networks would also include Sir Francis Burdett, Henry Brougham, Daniel O'Connell, and the ever-present Francis Place.

In principle, two kinds of evidence would establish the creation of new connections: co-presence at the same events and communication among activists. Among other occasions, for instance, Hunt and Cobbett both spoke for the minority pro-Catholics at a huge Brunswick Club meeting on Penenden Heath, Kent, on 24 October 1828. But so much of the organizing took place outside of such public gatherings that it would take a whole new research project to pin down the changing network connections. As a weaker alternative, I will simply offer anecdotal evidence of interpersonal ties among activists, then reason mainly from similarities in the patterns of contentious gatherings from 1828 through 1832.

The reform mobilizations of 1830–1832 drew on substantial precedents going back to the times of Wilkes and Gordon. From that time, reformers called for a more representative Parliament based on a more extensive franchise. Meanwhile, radicals proposed manhood suffrage, annually elected parliaments, and abolition of property requirements for public office. In the wake of religious reform, parliamentary reform became the order of the day for reformers and radicals. Daniel O'Connell, now a Catholic MP by grace of Emancipation, became a major proponent of parliamentary reform.

Seen as a series of governmental and parliamentary actions, the rough chronology of reform extends from 1830 to 1832. Even with no more than a hint of the popular contentious politics that accompanied and to some extent impelled governmental action, the timetable in Box 4-1 describes a tumultuous transition. Direct or indirect struggles over reform brought down three governments between November 1830 and May 1832. The House of Lords resisted for almost two years. It only conceded in May and June 1832, when King William IV agreed to name new peers and thus create the needed majority in the Lords if necessary.

In the face of that threat, a reluctant House of Lords accepted a truncated reform. The Reform Act of 1832 gave greater representation to cities and eliminated a number of constituencies that had essentially remained in the pockets of patrons – hence the term "pocket boroughs." The reform bill that finally passed fell far short of radicals' demands and produced only a modest expansion of the national electorate. But it did produce two major outcomes: it increased the power of the commercial and industrial bourgeoisie as it advanced the principle of representation at least roughly proportionate to population.

Box 4-1: A Chronology of Governmental Action on Parliamentary
Reform, 1830–1832

1830

June	King George IV dies; William IV becomes king
July–September	General election, Tory government under Duke of Wellington forms with difficulty
October–November	Whigs begin to propose bill for parliamentary reform, as Wellington declares against reform
November	Tory government resigns after defeat on Civil List; Whig Earl Grey forms government

1831

January–March	Whigs present reform proposals to king, then House of Commons; bill passes by one vote
April	Opposition to reform defeats government; new general election April–June
June–September	Whig government introduces revised reform bill, which eventually passes Commons
October	House of Lords rejects reform bill
November	Government proclamation against military organization of political unions
December	Government introduces new reform bill, which passes Commons

1832

January	King agrees to create new peers if House of Lords again rejects the reform bill
March	Final passage of bill by Commons
April–May	Lords first passes bills, but then passes amendments that cause ministry to resign
May	Tories fail to form new ministry under Wellington; king recalls Grey ministry and gives Grey authority to create new peers
June	Under that threat, Lords passes bill; king signs
July–August	Parallel reform acts for Scotland and Ireland

Contentious gatherings conformed to the reform struggle's timetable, with peaks of popular activity in:

- March to May 1831: Commons debate and passage of the Reform Bill, rejection by the Lords, and a general election
- October 1831: Second rejection by the Lords, followed by violent demonstrations in Derby, Nottingham, Bristol, and elsewhere
- May 1832: Defeat of Whig government in Lords, failure to form Tory government, king's agreement to create new peers favorable to reform, return of Grey ministry, all against a background of furious local political activity throughout Great Britain

In that background, contingent and constantly changing coalitions were forming among advocates of reform. The range ran from popular radical leaders such as Henry Hunt and William Cobbett to moderate but effective MPs such as Sir Francis Burdett and Joseph Hume. Many of them had already collaborated in the drive for Catholic Emancipation.

An organization named the National Political Union (NPU) brought together reformers and a network of local political unions from Birmingham, London, and elsewhere. A more proletarian National Union of the Working Classes (NUWC) became the site of constant struggle between direct action radicals and those who were willing to compromise with the parliamentary path. At a meeting of April 1831, resolutions passed by the NUWC included the following proposal:

To obtain for the nation an effectual reform in the Commons House of the British parliament; the basis of which reform shall be annual parliaments, extensions of the suffrage to every adult male, vote by ballot, and, especially, NO PROPERTY QUALIFICATION for members of parliament; this Union being convinced, that until intelligent men from the productive and useful classes of society possess the right of sitting in the Commons House of Parliament, to represent the interests of the working people, justice in legislation will never be rendered unto them. (Hollis 1973: 130)

Yet, in the opinion of knowledgeable D. J. Rowe, "a general impression is that the NUWC was rather more opposed than indifferent to the Bill but that at times when the Bill was in danger it swung towards grudging support" (Rowe 1977: 160).

Political entrepreneurs faced the task of bringing together not only organizations such as the NPU and NUWC but also their constituencies and individual leaders who had their own networks. Take the consummate political entrepreneur Francis Place. After he retired from the tailoring business in 1817, Place devoted himself energetically to agitation for workers' rights and political reform. He supported Catholic Emancipation among a great many other causes. But he greatly distrusted calls for direct action and formation of national workers' unions. In October 1831 (a time of violent struggle over reform in a number of English cities), labor leader John Doherty declared that the people themselves must seize reform by force. Place replied that

it was absurd to expect such a combination among the working people as would enable them to defeat the army and others who would not quietly submit to be plundered. That the working people unaided by the middle class never had accomplished any national movement, and that it was insane in him to suppose that they could effect any change by force. (Wallas 1898: 266)

Place left behind him a huge collection of clippings, correspondence, and (tendentious) memoirs on the era of reform (Rowe 1970). One fascinating section of his British Museum archive bears the title "Political Narratives 1830–1835" (British Museum, Additional MS 27789–27797). The narratives cover a great deal of other material, but return over and over to Place's brokerage of connections among radicals and reformers on behalf of parliamentary reform.

The word "brokerage" makes Place's work seem easier and less coercive than the reality. Inside the National Political Union, Place found himself occupying a middle position between MP Francis Burdett (an insider on the Reform Bill) and the radical William Lovett. He maneuvered, for example, to make sure that authentic working-class activists joined the council of the NPU, but worked hard against any inclusion of the hard-liners who preached insurrection at Southwark's Rotunda (BM Add. MS 27791: 71–72).

In the end, however, he served as more of a bridge than a crevasse. In a letter to his parliamentary ally John Cam Hobhouse on 8 November 1830, Place described Thomas Attwood, founder of the Birmingham Political Union, as "the most influential man in England" and current advocate of withholding taxes to bring down the government (BM Add. MS 27789). Place himself helped found the National Political Union on the Birmingham model and supported the proposal for tax withholding if necessary. Place exemplified the continuity and influence from one campaign to the next.

Not that Place always knew, much less planned, what happened next. As of March 1832, when the Commons again passed a modified reform bill and passed it on to the Lords, Place thought all four of these scenarios possible:

1. The Lords pass the bill on their own initiative.
2. The Lords resist, but the king names enough peers to produce a majority for the bill.
3. The Lords reject the bill, and a successful general strike of the working classes ensues.
4. The Lords reject the bill, a general strike occurs, but Wellington and the army put it down. (BM Add. MS 27792)

What happened, of course, was none of the above: the Lords passed blocking amendments, the Grey ministry resigned, the king and Wellington failed to form a Tory alternative, the king recalled Grey, and the threat of #2 (above) finally brought the House of Lords to heel in June.

The evidence from CGs of 1830–1832 shows the influence of connections forged during previous campaigns no more than indirectly (see Figure 4-7). Still it is consistent with a significant carryover of connections. If we compare the succession of reform mobilizations in 1830, 1831,

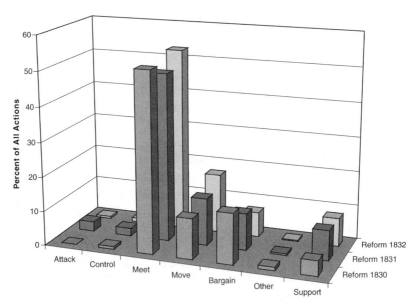

Figure 4-7 Verb Distributions in Reform CGs, Great Britain, 1830–1832

and 1832 with religious rights mobilizations of 1828 and 1829, we notice striking resemblances. As we might expect, the violent struggles of October 1831 introduce a greater frequency of Attack and Control verbs into that year's CGs than appeared in either 1830 or 1832. But otherwise the Meet dominance of Test and Corporation (1828) and Catholic Emancipation (1829) reappears in the reform campaigns. POS, modeling, and previous connections combined to promote a standard pattern of addressing Parliament from local assemblies.

The structures of claims in successive years (Figure 4-8) not only confirm that standard pattern, but show it consolidating between 1830 and 1832. In the CGs of 1830, Parliament and MPs certainly get the bulk of attention, but a number of local actors are making claims on each other: inhabitants on named individuals, mayors on inhabitants, inhabitants on sheriffs, and so on. Reflecting the violent incidents of the fall, the 1831 diagram identifies some local interactions, including attacks of "mobs" on named individuals. But the 1831 system of claims centers even more decisively on relations between inhabitants and the national government, including Parliament. By 1832, we observe a set of claims emanating almost entirely from groups of inhabitants and addressing national authorities almost exclusively.

In short, campaigns certainly influenced subsequent campaigns. As summarized in Figure 4-1, however, my initial formulation oversimplifies. Instead of identifying three neatly segregated causal channels – POS, models, and connections – the evidence reviewed in this chapter makes a strong case for cross-flow among the three. Yes, the Wilkes campaign altered British political opportunity structure and thus opened up unexpected possibilities for Lord George Gordon's own challenge to Wilkite radicalism. But it affected POS in part by making available new models of performance, notably the mass march to make claims on public authorities.

Again, campaigns for religious rights of the later 1820s certainly wove new connections among activists, but those new connections in themselves made a difference to POS. After all, it wasn't every day that collaborative political ventures extended from street radicals and ex-convicts such as Henry Hunt and William Cobbett to pillars of the establishment such as Henry Brougham. In the move from religious rights to parliamentary reform, political opportunity structure, available models of performances, and connections among potential political actors changed continuously, in constant connection with each other. They did, in any case, transmit the influence of one contentious campaign to the next.

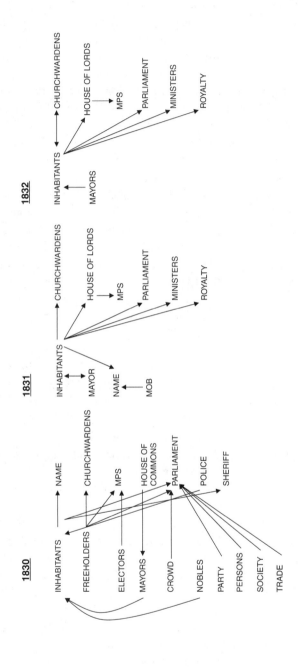

Includes all actions with objects accounting for 2% or more of total for year.

Figure 4-8 Structures of Claims in Reform Campaigns, Great Britain, 1830–1832

We encounter a nice paradox. On one side, particular features of campaigns – innovations and outcomes that distinguish them from other campaigns – link them to subsequent campaigns through POS, models, connections, and interactions among the three. Yet those particular causal paths create general transformations of repertoires. In 18th- and 19th-century Britain, the succession of campaigns from Wilkes to Gordon, from one religious rights mobilization to the next, and from unsuccessful to successful bids for parliamentary reform involved specific learning, but also advanced the cosmopolitan, modular, and autonomous repertoire that prevailed in Great Britain from the 1830s onward. The same combination of incremental, particular changes and general transformation occurs widely in popular contention. The next chapter shows it occurring in the invention of the social movement.

5

Invention of the Social Movement

On 19 August 1765, the *Boston Gazette* published a colorful account of recent doings in central Boston:

Early on Wednesday morning last the Effigy of a Gentleman sustaining a very unpopular office, viz. that of St – p Master, was found hanging on a Tree in the most public Part of the Town, together with a Boot, wherein was concealed a young Imp of the D – l represented as peeping out of the Top – On the Breast of the Effigy was a Label in Praise of Liberty, and denouncing Vengeance on the Subverters of it – and underneath was the following Words, HE THAT TAKES THIS DOWN IS AN ENEMY TO HIS COUNTRY. – The Owner of the Tree finding a Crowd of People to assemble, tho' at 5 o'Clock in the Morning, endeavored to take it down; but being advised to the contrary by the Populace, lest it should occasion the Demolition of his Windows, if nothing worse, desisted from the Attempt.

The effigy-bearing tree became famous as the Liberty Tree. It served first as a rallying-point for Boston's patriots, then as a model for other colonial cities, and finally as a symbol of revolution in Western Europe, including the Netherlands, France, and Great Britain. Boston's early-morning tableau mingled visions of violence and of disciplined patriotism.

Effigies, their parading, and their ultimate destruction often figured in Boston's popular celebrations. They appeared notably in the anti-Catholic Pope's Day festivities organized by rival groups from the North and South Ends.[1] In this case, a number of small merchants known as the Loyal Nine had brought North and South Enders together in organizing

---

[1] Pope's Day was 5 November, anniversary of the Catholic-inspired Gunpowder Plot in 1605, for which Guy Fawkes, caught in tunnels beneath Parliament with barrels of gunpowder, was hanged, drawn, and quartered; in British parlance, a "guy" is an effigy meant for the flames.

the display and recruiting the crowds who witnessed it. (Benjamin Edes, a member of the Loyal Nine, co-published the *Boston Gazette*.) This time the effigy represented Andrew Oliver, who had received the commission as Massachusetts' distributor of revenue-raising stamps for the British crown. On the effigy's breast someone fixed this verse: "A goodlier sight who e'er did see? / A Stamp-Man hanging on a tree!" The boot punned on the king's favorite, Lord Bute, and bore a new "green vile" sole, referring to royal minister George Grenville (Hoerder 1977: 90–101).

Lieutenant Governor Thomas Hutchinson ordered the sheriff to cut down the effigy, but the crowd kept the sheriff's men from reaching it. That evening members of the crowd themselves cut the dummy from the tree, placed it on a bier, paraded it to Oliver's recently built warehouse, tore down the building, used the planks to burn the effigy, then went off to attack Oliver's house. As earlier chapters have shown, executing effigies and tearing down dishonored buildings occurred regularly as avenging actions in Great Britain during the 1760s. Massachusetts and other American colonies used much the same idioms of vengeance as their British cousins of the time.

Oliver soon resigned as stamp tax collector. The Boston episode spurred open resistance to the Stamp Act in the American colonies. Passed by Parliament in March 1765, the Stamp Act was supposed to help pay for the cost of the Seven Years' War (1756–1763) and the additional expense of maintaining troops in a set of colonies greatly expanded by Britain's seizure of Canada from France in the war. The Act called for purchase of tax stamps for a wide range of public transactions, newspapers, pamphlets, almanacs, playing cards, and dice to become compulsory in November 1765. In fact, the Stamp Act galvanized resistance across the lower colonies from New Hampshire to Georgia. Colonial leaders argued that Parliament had no right to tax colonies without receiving their consent. Activists hounded designated stamp sellers until they resigned their commissions. In every colony but Georgia, attacks and threats almost completely prevented the revenue stamps from being sold.

Resistance began with intimidation of stamp agents, but soon extended to a wider range of actions: public meetings to protest the Act and coordinate resistance across the colonies; formation of associations, congresses, and committees of correspondence linking the colonies; petitions to provincial governors, provincial assemblies, and Parliament; unstamped trade in defiance of the law; and boycotts of British goods. (At the 1765 commencement of Princeton University, BA candidates "appeared on their own accord dressed in plain homespun and homewoven clothes"; Conser 1986: 39). Resisters regularly formed political associations, which they often called Sons of Liberty (Maier 1972: 81–87). Despite the best efforts of royal officials, the Stamp Act remained a dead letter in the colonies until its repeal in March 1766. Prime Minister William Pitt led the campaign for repeal.

News of the repeal finally reached Charleston, South Carolina, on 5 May 1766. At this point, the *South Carolina Gazette* published its notice, quoting a letter that had taken months to cross the ocean:

"This serves just to tell you that the STAMP-ACT was REPEALED this Day. I send this after Captain Lee, in the Downs, as I am persuaded it will be an AGREEABLE Piece of News."

As soon as the foregoing very agreeable and important INTELLIGENCE was known, a general Joy appeared in the Countenance of every Well-wisher to his Country, and the glorious cause of LIBERTY. At Four o'Clock in the Afternoon, the Artillery Company, commanded by Christopher Gadsden, Esq. and the Company of Light Infantry, commanded by Thomas Savage, Esq., appeared under Arms, and went through their Exercise, Firing &c. In the Evening the Town was handsomely illuminated, and the Day ended with Loyalty and Mirth, echoing with loyal Toasts to his Majesty King GEORGE the Third ... the great Patriot, Mr. PITT ... and other worthy Friends in England ... The Town was also handsomely illuminated last Night.

Gadsden and Savage were substantial Charleston merchants. Although Savage eventually sided with Great Britain, Gadsden first served as the most visible leader of Charleston's Sons of Liberty and then went on to become a military chief in the Revolutionary War.

In 1766, Gadsden, Savage, and other opponents of the Stamp Act were taking risky steps that would cumulate into open warfare after nine years and victory over Great Britain after seventeen years. Did those steps amount to a social movement? Not yet. This chapter argues that social movements did not yet exist anywhere in the world during the 1760s, but were then in the making. In Western Europe and North America, participants in contentious politics were fashioning new ways of making collective claims. They were inventing the social movement.

What Are Social Movements?

People often use the term "social movement" to mean any sort of popular struggle, especially a popular struggle of which they approve. In this book, however, we have good reasons for using the term more narrowly. Between the 1760s and the 1830s, a distinctive new form of popular politics came into being on both sides of the North Atlantic, became a vehicle for a wide variety of claims, and brought the term "social movement" itself into widespread use (Tilly 2004b: chapter 2). During the 19th and 20th centuries, the social movement spread through the world in the wake of (and sometimes in the vanguard of) democratization. It involved not only new performances such as the street demonstration, but a whole new repertoire. Previous chapters have repeatedly described different aspects of social movements. Now it is time to put them together and to ask where they came from.

Anyone who studies social movements needs a deep distinction between social movement bases and social movements as such (Tilly and Tarrow 2006: chapter 5). Every social movement depends on a base of connections among potential participants in the collective claims forwarded by the movement. Those connections include interpersonal networks, shared previous experiences, and formal organizations. Some of the relevant formal organizations specialize in preparation for the making of collective claims, but others – for example, workers' mutual benefit societies and religious congregations – carry on a great many other activities. Students of social movements often call the specialized ones social movement organizations (SMOs). Social movements rarely issue from a single SMO. When they do, in fact, we commonly think of them as anomalies rather than full-fledged, coalition-based movements.

In examining how one campaign affects the next (Chapter 4), we have of course already seen social movement bases at work. For example, a large network of workers' and reformers' organizations that formed during the 1820s played an enormous part in the mobilization for parliamentary reform in Britain from 1830 to 1832. Such political entrepreneurs as Francis Place devoted much of their effort to shaping and knitting together the social movement bases for reform. More generally, two of the three critical links between successive campaigns – change in available models of performances and change in connections among potential actors – operate within the social movement base. Even the third (change in political opportunity structure) either consists of or exerts influence on changes in the social movement base. This chapter repeatedly identifies shifts of social movement bases, not only in the American colonies but also in Great Britain itself, as the social movement took shape between the 1760s and the 1830s.

In the run-up to the American Revolution, such newly formed organizations as the Sons of Liberty specialized in the making of claims, while a great many previously existing organizations (for example, local fire companies) joined the revolutionary effort. The American Revolution does not qualify as a full-fledged social movement. Yet there, too, we need a distinction between base and movement. In the American colonies, organizations specializing in the preparation of claim making, other organizations, interpersonal networks of all potential participants in contention, and shared previous experiences formed an essential base for the struggles of 1765–1783.

Nevertheless, as Chapter 1 said, we should remain clear about this book's object of explanation. It is thin rather than thick. We are seeking explanations of change and variation in contentious performances, using variable social bases of contention as part of our explanations. In this chapter we seek an explanation of the social movement's emergence. Changes in the base help explain the emergence of social movements. The question for this chapter is how the complex of contentious performances we call social movements came into being.

Social movements join three elements: campaigns, a repertoire, and WUNC displays (public enactments of worthiness, unity, numbers, and commitment). Box 5-1 sums up the three. A campaign includes repeated, coordinated collective claims concerning the same issues and targets. Although social movements often include petitions, declarations, and mass meetings, unlike a one-time petition, declaration, or mass meeting, a campaign extends beyond any single event. Campaigns center on identity, standing, and program claims: claims for recognition of the claimants' existence, claims for ratification of their standing as specific kinds of political actors such as indigenous peoples or registered voters, and/or claims for the adoption or abolition of public programs.

A campaign always links at least three parties: a group of self-designated claimants, some object(s) of claims, and a public of some kind. The claims may target governmental officials, but the "authorities" in question can also include owners of property, religious functionaries, and others whose actions (or failures to act) significantly affect the welfare of many people. The public includes potential participants in future campaigns, citizens whose interests the campaign's outcome will affect, and spectators who learn something about the politics of their regime from the struggle, even if they do not participate. Not the solo actions of claimants, object(s), or public, but interactions among the three, constitute a social movement campaign.

Chapter 2 began by describing Mark Beissinger's analysis of campaigns for political autonomy or independence by groups representing many of the Soviet Union's officially designated nationalities – Armenians, Estonians,

Box 5-1: Elements of Social Movements

1. *Campaign:* a sustained, coordinated series of episodes involving similar collective claims on similar or identical targets. Claims come in three varieties: identity, standing, and program claims.
   - Identity: we exist and demand you recognize our collective existence
   - Standing: we belong to an existing and legitimate political category (e.g., political party, association, local community) within the regime
   - Program: we ask that you act to promote a certain outcome or set of outcomes

2. *Repertoire:* participants in campaigns regularly use two or more of these performances to make collective claims:
   - Formation of special-purpose associations and coalitions devoted to a campaign's identity, standing, and/or program claims
   - Public meetings
   - Petition drives, coordinated letter writing, sending of signed addresses
   - Street demonstrations, vigils, rallies
   - Public statements of claims, both oral and written
   - Lobbying

3. *WUNC displays:* collective enactments of worthiness, unity, numbers, and commitment:
   - Worthiness: dignity, decorum, presence of mothers with children, clergy, military veterans, etc.
   - Unity: common colors, clothing, badges, or symbols, marching in ranks, singing, chanting, etc.
   - Numbers: filling spaces, headcounts, messages from constituents, signatures on petitions, etc.
   - Commitment: braving bad weather, visible participation by the old and handicapped, resistance to repression and opposition, ostentatious sacrifice, subscription, and/or benefaction

Moldavians, and more. The groups repeatedly made three kinds of claims: identity claims for recognition of their distinctive, coherent existence; standing claims asserting that they qualified as bona fide nations; and program claims demanding political autonomy. Most of the campaigns failed, but fifteen of them produced independent states.

The social movement repertoire overlaps with the repertoires of other political phenomena such as trade union activity and electoral campaigns. The social movement repertoire includes an array of claim-making performances that activists usually employ in sets of two or more: formation of special-purpose claim-making associations and coalitions, public meetings, petition drives, street demonstrations, vigils, rallies, public statements, and lobbying of political authorities.

Chapter 4 started with Sergio Tamayo's chronicle of Mexican political change between 1968 and the mid-1990s. Tamayo identifies all of the social movement performances as becoming common during the 1980s after being relatively rare in the old days of patron-client politics. Some of these performances also occur in other sorts of campaigns – for example, electoral campaigns – than social movements. During the 20th century, special-purpose associations and crosscutting coalitions in particular began to do an enormous variety of political work across the world well outside of social movements. But the integration of most or all of these performances into sustained campaigns marks off social movements from other varieties of politics.

WUNC displays usually occur within collective performances. People march, sing, chant, and fill public spaces with their acting out of collective value. WUNC displays also sometimes spill over into individual action, as activists wear badges or colors to signal their affiliations. John Wilkes's supporters wore blue ribbons during the Brentford election of 1769, for instance, even when they were not marching or demonstrating.

WUNC displays have three distinctive features that lend them power and flexibility. First, their components cumulate – effective organizers maximize signs of worthiness, unity, numbers, and commitment to the extent that they can. Second, up to a limit their components compensate for each other; a group few in numbers can bulk up by emphasizing displays of worthiness, unity, and commitment, whereas very large numbers make up to some extent for lack of perfect unity. Third, if any of the non-numerical traits fall to a very low value, the display loses its impact: an obviously unworthy rabble becomes a mob, a mass of people who lack unity become no more than a crowd. As a result of these three features, rivals and authorities often disparage WUNC displays by disputing the organizers' claimed number of participants, singling out the presence of unworthy persons, underlining evidence of disunity, or claiming that supposed participants are actually uncommitted spectators.

Unlike much of the 18th century's direct action repertoire, the combination of campaign, repertoire, and WUNC displays gains strength from its largely nonviolent character. It conveys the message that a substantial number of people back a specific set of claims and connect sufficiently well that they could back up those claims with further coordinated action. Unlike the common 18th-century recruitment of distinguished intermediaries for communication of ordinary people's claims on the powerful, furthermore, the social movement speaks directly to its targeted objects, its rivals, and its own constituency. In addition to its specific identity, standing, and program claims, it asserts the right of ordinary people to public voice. It signals that people united around a set of claims have the capacity to act together consequentially.

Social movement voice comes at a price. Avenging actions such as pulling down a dishonored person's house directly damaged the object of claims. Donkeying a strikebreaker, seizing and selling overpriced food, pelting an enemy with garbage, or rescuing a popular figure from the hangman – all common 18th-century performances – had the advantages of getting immediate results and relying on readily available local connections among the performers. The array of campaign, repertoire, and WUNC displays depended on broader and longer-term coordination. Almost never could social movement supporters hope to accomplish their shared objectives in a single outing. Indeed, social movements could not survive without political entrepreneurs who know how to organize meetings, bring out throngs of supporters, and draft public statements. Social movement activists sacrifice the advantages of direct action in favor of making statements to larger audiences and asserting a continued presence on the public scene. Hence the increased importance of identity and standing claims in social movement campaigns.

Campaigns and WUNC displays existed separately well before makers of claims created a new repertoire and then combined campaign, repertoire, and displays into a distinctive, effective package. We can reasonably consider the mobilization of 1768–1769 in support of John Wilkes to constitute a coordinated campaign, but not yet a full-fledged social movement. Individual performances in the social movement repertoire likewise had plenty of precedents. Processions of religious congregations, military units, fraternal orders, and political candidates' supporters, for example, supplied some of the form and precedent for street demonstrations (Tilly 2003: 120–127). During the Stamp Act campaigns of 1765 and 1766, activists in Boston, Charleston, and elsewhere had not yet combined campaigns, performances, and WUNC displays into social movements. Their burning of effigies and formation of patriotic societies had the spark but not the full flame of social movement activism. The longer colonials resisted Great Britain's arbitrary rule, however, the closer they came to social movements.

Why did social movements emerge and displace older forms of claim making? They resulted from the increasingly direct involvement of ordinary people in national politics. Three great changes contributed to the nationalization of popular participation during the later 18th century: commercial expansion, proliferation of communications, and parliamentarization. Commercial expansion meant that markets connected people more closely to regional and national capitals as increasing dependence on wages sensitized workers to fluctuations in the national economy. Proliferation of turnpikes, canals, newspapers, and other print media circulated information more rapidly and extensively. As a result, connections greatly increased among sets of people that might share an identity, standing, or program.

Parliamentarization takes a bit more unpacking. As wars became larger and more expensive, rulers called increasingly on national assemblies, however unrepresentative, to authorize rising taxation. Members of those assemblies bargained with their monarchs, and thus acquired power. They also typically represented territorial units – counties, provinces, and the like – regardless of whether the residents of those territories had much control over their actions. As a result, parliamentarization built on a previously existing set of connections between localities and the central government. Although Great Britain provides the obvious example of parliamentarization, after 1760 Americans were also contributing to the process both by transforming their own provincial assemblies into bases of popular power and by linking provincial political networks into what would become a national system and an alternative to the royal authority previously exercised by governors and their councils.

The process had two momentous effects: partial displacement of hereditary rulers from centers of national power and increasing involvement of parliaments in the broad range of governmental affairs. Ordinary people responded by forming further-reaching connections with like-minded others and directing more and more of their demands to national centers of power, including parliaments. Eventually they even demanded representation in parliaments. Together, commercialization, expanded communications, and parliamentarization promoted coordination of popular claims at a national scale. Social movements formed as by-products of the great changes.

As the convergence of commercialization, communications, and parliamentarization suggests, full flourishing of social movements depends on the substantial presence of political rights. Rights to associate, assemble, and speak collectively all undergird the conduct of campaigns, the use of the social movement repertoire, and the staging of WUNC displays. Christian Koller's crisp, informative review of rallies and street demonstrations in Zurich from 1830 to 1940 shows that social movement gatherings built on the precedent of public processions and guild marches, but came into their own as ways of making collective claims during Switzerland's partial democratization of the 1830s and 1840s (Koller 2007: 196–198; see also Tilly 2007: 66–72). Bourgeois establishment of the right to assemble publicly at a movement's own initiative then opened the way for organized workers to fill the streets on May Day and other days of proletarian display:

The bourgeois rallies and the proletarian marches have an explicit message, namely that a large number of citizens supported the claims of the respective movements. The marches of the labour movement, however, also had other, less explicit messages. They were intended to show that the workers were not a rebellious mob, but a disciplined class, fighting for its rights by peaceful means. (Koller 2007: 210)

In this book's terms, the marches displayed WUNC. By the 1890s, both democratic rights and social movements had come of age in Switzerland.

When can we reasonably say that social movements exist in a given regime? In order to sort out priority claims as well as to trace the subsequent spread of the social movement, it helps to break the central question into four parts. Observing popular collective action in any particular regime, we can ask separately about resemblance, combination, availability, and spread:

1. Resemblance: does this particular campaign, performance, or WUNC display resemble those that commonly occur in full-fledged social movements?
2. Combination: does this particular campaign combine performances and WUNC displays in a recognizably similar manner to social movements elsewhere?

3. Availability: in this setting, is the characteristic combination of campaigns, performances, and WUNC displays now widely available for different issues, claimants, and objects of claims?
4. Spread: did this regime's available combination of campaigns, performances, and WUNC displays provide influential immediate models for social movement activity outside the regime?

If we ask only the resemblance question, we can no doubt trace back social movements for centuries before the 1760s. After all, such characteristic social movement performances as marches and public meetings have long, long genealogies, and such episodes as the Protestant Reformation surely included sustained campaigns. The combination question bites harder. It narrows us to a few candidates: the American colonies, Great Britain, the Netherlands, France, and perhaps the Nordic countries.

Adding the questions of availability and spread, however, tips the balance toward Great Britain, where, from antislavery campaigns during the late Napoleonic Wars onward, the combination of campaign, repertoire, and WUNC displays not only characterized popular politics continuously, but also provided significant models for social movement activity elsewhere. Even in the new United States the social movement complex did not become a readily available and imitable model of public politics until early in the 19th century. British-initiated antislavery provided a major stimulus to that American political transformation.

Revolutions and Social Movements

The social movement gained much of its form and rationale from 18th-century revolutionary mobilizations. Revolutions occurred long before social movements emerged, and occurred in places untouched by social movements (Tilly 1993). Revolutions are not social movements, although sometimes the two overlap and stimulate each other. A full revolution combines two elements: a revolutionary situation and a revolutionary outcome. In a revolutionary situation, at least two centers of power emerge, each of them commanding significant coercive force and each of them claiming exclusive control over the state. In a revolutionary outcome, a transfer of power over the state occurs such that a largely new group of people begins to rule. Revolutionary situations and social movements overlap when movement-based mobilization goes so far as to split the regime into at least two armed factions, each claiming the unique right to rule. That happened widely, for example, during Europe's revolutionary mobilizations of 1848 (Tilly, Tilly, and Tilly 1975).

Although full-fledged social movements had not yet come into being, we can see a similar overlap and mutual stimulation of popular mobilization and revolutionary schism in the revolutions, both failed and successful, of the later 18th century. The American Revolution provides a case in point. In Great Britain's American colonies, popular mobilization against the crown began to edge into a revolutionary split during the 1760s.

In December 1766, Boston patriotic leader Samuel Adams wrote to Charleston's Christopher Gadsden, proposing regular communication among patriotic merchants from all the colonies (Alexander 2002: 45). In response to the 1767 Townshend Acts, which imposed a wide range of levies on the colonies, Adams drafted a circular letter of protest in hopes of collecting endorsements from Massachusetts and the other colonies. Late that year, a meeting of Boston inhabitants organized by the expanding web of patriotic associations resolved to encourage American manufacturing and reduce reliance on British imports.

In January 1768, the Massachusetts legislature itself petitioned the king, stating provincial objections to taxation in muted, respectful terms. After initial rejection, in February the same legislature endorsed a strong version of the Adams-initiated circular letter to the other colonies. By this time Massachusetts patriots were insisting that Parliament had no right to pass bills solely for the purpose of raising revenue from the colonies.

"These resolutions," reported the *Annual Register*, distancing itself prudently from the American claims,

> were adopted, or similar ones entered into, by all the old Colonies on the continent. In some time after, a circular letter was sent by the Assembly of Massachuset's Bay, signed by the Speaker, to all the other Assemblies in North America. The design of this letter was to shew the evil tendency of the late Acts of Parliament, to represent them as unconstitutional, and to propose a common union between the Colonies, in the pursuit of all legal measures to prevent their effect, and a harmony in their applications to Government for a repeal of them. It also expatiated largely on their natural rights as men, and their constitutional ones as English subjects; all of which, it was pretended, were infringed by these laws. (*AR* 1768: 68)

Despite an explicit demand from King George, the Massachusetts legislature voted ninety-two to seventeen not to rescind its assent to the circular letter. To rescind would, the majority declared, "have left us but a vain Semblance of Liberty" (Alexander 2002: 55).

While leading merchants pursued their program by means of deliberate legal action, Boston sailors and artisans frequently took the law into their own hands. They forcefully resisted press gangs, blocked the quartering of soldiers, attacked customs agents, and hung effigies of British officials or their collaborators on the Liberty Tree. They often doubled mercantile and official resistance with direct action.

When negotiations with the governor (representative of the crown in Massachusetts) and with the British government grew rancorous, the populace of Boston joined in. In May 1768, British customs officers seized wealthy Boston merchant (and smuggler) John Hancock's ship *Liberty* for its failure to pay duties. Bostonians manned another ship, cut loose the impounded vessel, and took it away:

The populace having assembled in great crowds upon this occasion, they pelted the Commissioners of the Customs with stones, broke one of their swords, and treated them in every respect with the greatest outrage; after which, they attacked their houses, broke the windows, and hauled the Collector's boat to the common, where they burnt it to ashes. (*AR* 1768: 71)

The customs officers fled first to a royal warship and then to Castle William in Boston Harbor. Town meetings of protest convened without official authorization throughout the Boston area. When word reached Boston (12 September) that two regiments were coming from Ireland and another body of military assembling in Halifax (Nova Scotia) to restore order in Boston, members of the Massachusetts Bay assembly began organizing resistance committees throughout the colony.

Massachusetts patriots quickly gathered allies throughout the other colonies. Mostly the allies began by using the established forms of elite public politics: resolutions, petitions, and solemn meetings. Innovative forms of contentious gatherings elsewhere in America, furthermore, regularly adapted the forms of previously tolerated assemblies.

In the fall 1768 elections to the South Carolina colonial assembly, for example, "mechanicks and other inhabitants of Charles Town" met at Liberty Point to choose candidates:

This matter being settled, without the least animosity or irregularity, the company partook of a plain and hearty entertainment, that had been provided by some on which this assembly will reflect lasting honour. About 5 o'clock, they all removed to a most noble LIVE-OAK tree, in Mr. Mazyck's pasture, which they formally dedicated to LIBERTY, where many loyal, patriotic, and constitutional toasts were drank, beginning with the glorious NINETY-TWO Anti-Rescinders of Massachusetts Bay, and ending with Unanimity among the Members of our ensuing Assembly not to rescind from the said resolutions, each succeeded by three huzzas. In the evening, the tree was decorated with 45 lights, and 45 sky-rockets were fired. About 8 o'clock, the whole company, preceded by 45 of their number, carrying as many lights, marched in regular procession to town, down King Street and Broad Street, to Mr. Robert Dillon's tavern; where the 45 lights being placed upon the table, with 45 bowls of punch, 45 bottles of wine, and 92 glasses, they spent a few hours in a new round of toasts, among which, scarce a celebrated Patriot of Britain or America was omitted; and preserving the same good order and regularity as had been observed throughout the day, at 10 they retired. (*South Carolina Gazette*, 3 October 1768: 2)

In addition to its impressive capacity for alcohol, the Charleston electoral assembly's blend of political ingredients boggles the mind. Charleston's Liberty Tree directly emulated its Boston model. The toast to ninety-two anti-rescinders (those members of the Massachusetts assembly who voted against withdrawing Samuel Adams's circular letter) identified the South Carolinians with Massachusetts patriots. The number forty-five, obviously, signaled the relevance of John Wilkes. Lighting up (in this case the procession rather than the city's windows) likewise enacted a public declaration of allegiance and solidarity.

As of 1768, neither in London, Boston, or Charleston had opponents of arbitrary rule already invented social movements. Nevertheless, their innovations moved popular public politics toward social movement forms. They enlisted ordinary citizens such as artisans and sailors in campaigns of sustained opposition to royal policies. (In contrast to Boston's small merchants, Charleston's Sons of Liberty expanded from a volunteer fire company composed largely of artisans; Maier 1972: 85.) They combined special-purpose associations, public meetings, marches, petitions, pamphleteering, and statements widely reported in the public media. To some extent, they even adopted displays of WUNC: wor-thiness, unity, numbers, and commitment. The *South Carolina Gazette* remarked on "the same good order and regularity as had been observed throughout the day."

Although the "mechanicks and other inhabitants" of Charleston remained quite capable of attacking royal officials, resisting customs agents, and sacking the houses of their designated enemies, at least on ceremonial occasions they abandoned direct action in favor of program, identity, and standing claims: we are upright people, we deserve a voice, and we oppose arbitrary rule with determination. In fact, Charleston's artisans "spearheaded" the city's anti-importation agreements in alliance with merchant-patriot Christopher Gadsden (Maier 1972: 116).

Integration of popular forces into elite opposition campaigns split the ruling classes, but took an important step toward the creation of the social movement as a distinct form of public politics.

Other Revolutions

Other western revolutions also accelerated the basic processes that promoted development of social movements: commercialization, communications, and parliamentarization. Chronologically, the American Revolution came first, but Western Europeans did not lag far behind. In what Dutch historians call the Fourth English War (1780–1784), for example, Dutch forces joined indirectly in the wars of the American Revolution, taking a severe beating from superior British naval power. As the disastrous naval engagements continued, a sort of pamphlet war broke out within the Netherlands. Supporters of the Prince of Orange attacked the leaders of Amsterdam and its province, Holland, as the opposing Patriots (based especially in Holland) replied in kind; each blamed the other for the country's parlous condition.

Drawing explicitly on the American example, Patriots called for a (preferably peaceful) revolution. Earlier claim making in the Low Countries conformed to local variants of the older repertoire we have already seen operating in England and America (Dekker 1982, 1987, van Honacker 1994, 2000). But during the 1780s petition campaigns began in earnest: first demanding recognition of John Adams as a legal representative of that contested entity, the United States of America, then proposing remedies to a whole series of domestic political problems.

Citizen's committees (possibly modeled on American committees of correspondence) soon began to form, along with citizens' militias across Holland's towns. In a highly segmented political system, their incessant pressure on local and regional authorities actually worked. Between 1784 and 1787, Patriot factions managed to install new, less aristocratic constitutions in a number of Dutch cities, and even in a whole province, Overijssel. The Prince of Orange and his followers, however, still disposed of two crucial advantages: British financial support and military backing from the Prince's brother-in-law, King Frederick William of Prussia. Late in 1787, a Prussian invasion broke the Netherlands' Patriot Revolution (te Brake 1989, 1990, Poell 2007, Schama 1977).

As the French Revolution opened up nearby, those Dutch Patriots who had not fled their country hoped, conspired, and even (late in 1794) made a poorly coordinated attempt at a coup. The next invading army arrived in January 1795, when French revolutionary forces established a Batavian Republic with active support from revived Patriots. (Liberty Trees went up in Leiden and Amsterdam; Schama 1977: 194.) Despite governmental alterations on a French model, the new Republic soon deadlocked between advocates of centralizing reforms in the French style and the customary federalism of the Netherlands. From 1798 to 1805, a quartet of faction-backed coups – unaccompanied by widespread popular mobilization – produced major political changes. The Republic gave way to a French satellite Kingdom of Holland (1806), then to direct incorporation into France (1810–1813).

The post-Napoleonic settlement created a bifurcated kingdom that until 1839 nominally included both the Netherlands and what became Belgium. From the French takeover onward, the Dutch state assumed a much more centralized administrative structure than had prevailed in the heyday of autonomous provinces. With the Batavian Republic of 1795, committees, militias, and Patriots returned temporarily to power, only to be integrated rapidly into the new sort of regime, with French overseers never far away. Recognizable social movements did not start occurring widely in the Netherlands until after Napoleon's fall. In newly independent Belgium, social movements did not enter their heyday until after the Revolution of 1848 (Tilly 2004b: chapter 3).

France likewise approached creation of social movements after 1780. As the Revolution of 1789 proceeded, French activists formed politically oriented associations at a feverish pace, made concerted claims by means of those associations, held public meetings, marched through the streets, adopted slogans and badges, produced pamphlets, and implemented local revolutions through most of the country (Hunt 1978, 1984, Jones 2003, Markoff 1996a, 1996b, McPhee 1988, Woloch 1970, 1994). If such mobilizations had continued past 1795 and if they had become available for a wide variety of claims thereafter, we might hail the French as inventors of the social movement. As it happened, however, the full array of social movement claim making did not acquire durable political standing in France for another half-century, around the Revolution of 1848 (Tilly 1986: chapter 9). Even then, repression under Louis Napoleon's Second Empire delayed the full implementation of social movement politics through much of the country for another two decades.

Great Britain experienced its 18th-century revolutions indirectly, but powerfully. As we have seen, British radicals took up the American cause during the 1760s. Leaders such as Thomas Paine participated directly in the American and French Revolutions. During the early 1790s, the French Revolution became a model for British reformers, despite royal attempts to snuff them out as subversives. The London Revolution Society claimed to have met annually from the Glorious Revolution of 1688, but welcomed new revolutionary principles from across the Atlantic and across the Channel.

In 1789 the Reverend Richard Price addressed the Revolution Society in a fiery speech that prompted Edmund Burke to pen his anti-revolutionary *Reflections on the Revolution in France* (1986). The Society also promoted formation of corresponding societies on the American model, not least because they evaded the legal ban on national associations that could compete with Parliament as representatives of the people. As in America, these mobilizations against the crown's arbitrary power came close to combining all three elements of the social movement: campaign, repertoire, and WUNC displays. Commercialization, communications expansion, and parliamentarization joined to push British popular politics toward the creation of social movements.

Religious activists bolstered Great Britain's claim to have invented the social movement. The drive against Atlantic slavery began with Anglican and (especially) Quaker congregations and became the first full-fledged international social movement anywhere (Hochschild 2005). Opposition to slavery joined with opposition to empire, including British hegemony in North America (Brown 2006). During the 1770s and 1780s, jurists in both Great Britain and North America began to deliver rulings that challenged the legality of slavery. The Vermont constitution of 1777 banned slavery, while between 1780 and 1784 Pennsylvania, Massachusetts, Rhode Island, and Connecticut took legal steps toward general emancipation. In both Great Britain and the American colonies, organized Quakers were creating antislavery associations during the 1770s. In fact, Friends congregations on both sides of Atlantic were then expelling members who refused to free their own slaves.

In 1783, English Quakers sent Parliament its first (but by no means its last) petition for abolition of the slave trade. Britain's nationwide campaigns against the slave trade began, however, in 1787, with mass petitioning and formation of the Society for the Abolition of the Slave Trade. At that point, antislavery organizers worked chiefly within Quaker and Evangelical congregations; church services therefore overlapped with petition-generating meetings (Davis 1987, Drescher 1982, 1986, 1994, Temperley 1981, Walvin 1980, 1981).

The initiative did not come from London, but from the industrial North, especially Manchester. The 11 thousand signatures on the Manchester petition of December 1787 represented something like two-thirds of all the city's men who were eligible to sign (Drescher 1986: 70). Echoing the non-importation agreements that had proven so effective in the American colonies' campaigns against Great Britain, antislavery activists also introduced another weighty innovation: a general boycott of sugar grown with the labor of slaves, with perhaps 300 thousand families participating in 1791 and 1792 (Drescher 1986: 79).

During the years of war with France, British governmental repression tamped down all performances in the social movement repertoire: associations, meetings, petitions, and more. Nevertheless, the 1791 slave revolt in the French colony of St. Domingue (today's Haiti) eventually and surprisingly promoted a revival of antislavery mobilization. By the time Haiti became independent in 1804, French forces had found that they could not put down the determined rebellion of St. Domingue's black population, British forces had found that they could neither drive out the French nor conquer the colony, and Britain's chief sugar-producing rival lay in ruins. The pro-slavery argument that freeing slaves on sugar plantations would leave the French in control of the industry thus lost its force.

In 1807, Great Britain (or, rather, the United Kingdom, which had formally joined Ireland with England, Wales, and Scotland in 1801) abolished the slave trade. In 1808, the United States followed suit. In 1833, after multiple mobilizations, Parliament finally passed an emancipation act applicable throughout its colonies. The United States remained fiercely divided on the issue and eventually fought a civil war over it. Yet by the 1830s abolition had become the crux of a vast American social movement as well.

When Social Movements Became Politically Available

The smashing success of antislavery mobilization made the social movement campaign a model for pursuit of an astonishing range of claims. From 1789 to 1795, the early surge of antislavery action accompanied and encouraged proliferation of associational activity around other issues, including parliamentary reform. Then wartime repression shut down most large-scale public claim making in Great Britain. Revolutionary conspiracies and workers' combinations went underground, and only parliamentary elections provided significant occasions for expressions of collective dissent. The Treasonable Practices Act and the Seditious Meetings Act (1795), the Act against Unlawful Oaths (1797), the Act for the Defence of the Realm (1798), and the Combination Laws and Unlawful Societies Act (1799, 1800) all upped the penalties for subversive organization. Antislavery succeeded in 1807 without anything like the mass mobilizations of the late 1780s or of 1830–1833.

The United Kingdom's governmental repression relaxed with the end of the Napoleonic Wars. As repression declined, both organized workers and advocates of parliamentary reform renewed the efforts that repression had subdued from the later 1790s. The chronology of Box 5-2 (compiled from a wide variety of sources, including the CGs of 1819 and 1820) shows the result. Contention of 1816–1827 reveals the social movement's coming of age in Great Britain.

As frequent landless laborers' attacks on farmers, industrial workers' attacks on machinery, and insurrections reveal, social movements did not immediately sweep the field. Yet the energetic creation of national workers' associations and coalitions and the revival of reform campaigns brought social movement–style mobilization to unprecedented intensities. The government tried desperately to stem the new tide with the Coercion Acts and a Seditious Meetings Act (1817), the Six (coercive) Acts (1819), and the Unlawful Drilling Act (1820). But by then campaigns, claim-making performances, and WUNC displays were occurring month after month.

The pivotal Peterloo Massacre of 1819, indeed, grew from initially peaceful social movement activity. In Britain's industrial regions, workers had been performing military drills and occasionally attempting insurrection for two years, so regional authorities were on their guard against mass meetings that might turn into attacks on employers or public authorities. When reformers announced a great assembly in St. Peter's Fields, Manchester, for 16 August 1819, magistrates and military commanders called up three hundred to four hundred troops of various units, including the Manchester Yeomanry. (The central government, however, raised doubts whether the gathering would turn violent without provocation; Palmer 1988: 187.)

On the big day, something like 60 thousand participants proceeded to St. Peter's Fields, many of them marching in ranks. Some wore liberty caps, by then signals of revolution. Local authorities sent in cavalry to arrest the main speaker, radical reformer Henry Hunt. They captured

Box 5-2: Major Issues of Contentious Gatherings in Great Britain, 1816–1827

1816   Farmworkers' attacks on farmers, landlords, and enclosures; industrial workers' attacks on machinery; struggles over food supply; reform meetings

1817   Workers' strikes, assemblies, processions, marches, and insurrections; reform meetings

1818   Reform meetings and demonstrations; major strikes, processions, workers' meetings; attacks on agricultural and industrial machinery

1819   Reform meetings and demonstrations, including responses to yeomanry's massacre of meeting participants in Manchester (Peterloo) and radical Henry Hunt's arrest at that meeting; electoral gatherings and fights

1820   Electoral gatherings; meetings, processions, delegations, forced illuminations, and street gatherings in support of Queen Caroline; reform meetings, processions, and demonstrations; attempted insurrections; major strikes

1821   Processions and demonstrations (including a vast funeral procession) in support of the queen; reform meetings; coronation celebrations

1822   Workers' gatherings, attacks on agricultural and industrial machinery

1823   Workers' gatherings, strikes, including agitation of Spitalfields weavers against repeal of the Protective Act

1824   Workers' meetings, strikes

1825   Strikes, attacks on industrial machinery; organizing meetings of workers

1826   Workers' meetings, strikes, attacks on industrial machinery; meetings against the Corn Law; reform meetings; contested electoral assemblies

1827   Workers' meetings

Hunt, but they also killed eleven people and wounded hundreds more. Fellow reformer Sir Francis Burdett (who did not attend the Manchester meeting) wrote a letter to the newspapers calling for protest meetings led by gentlemen across the country. For that impertinence, the government charged him with seditious libel. Both he and Hunt received prison terms at their trials in 1820.

Radical reformers played incessant cat-and-mouse games with the law. Because they commonly pressed their rights to organize at the edges of existing legal boundaries, they shifted tactics as repressive laws changed, but, when successful, pushed out those boundaries little by little. After the failure of a series of radical efforts, for example, T. J. Wooler, editor of the *Black Dwarf*, organized a fund for political prisoners in 1820:

> Wooler's aim was quite clear, to provide, as in 1817, a means of organization and communication under the cover of relief funds and so defeat the blows delivered to public meetings, the press and political associations by the six acts. There were to be a managing committee and monthly meetings of subscribers; it urged the formation of provincial societies, and had a committee of correspondence. The idea spread. The ultras tried in March to start their own fund at the Spotted Dog, but probably merged with Wooler's, and in the provinces, where similar moves had already begun, permanent patriotic funds were set up at such places as Manchester, Birmingham, Glasgow, and Nottingham. These efforts at recreating radical organisation had some success, and by the autumn there were travelling delegates again in the north and a conference took place at Manchester. (Prothero 1979: 132–133)

Wooler and his allies were working toward something like a revolution, but were using social movement means to advance it.

This sort of negotiation with the law has two powerful implications for the lives of social movements. First, over the longer run social movements depend on some minimum of rights to assemble, speak, and associate. That dependency accounts in part for the broad association of social movements with democratization and for their disappearance when authoritarian regimes take over, as in Fascist Italy or Nazi Germany. Second, in the short run authorities and social movement activists negotiate constantly over the limits of acceptable claim making. Fine fluctuations in political opportunity structures make a difference as to how social movement organizers behave, but innovations in social movement organization or strategy also affect governmental responses to them.

The Age of Queen Caroline

The year 1820 looks like a pivot in the shift of British repertoires toward social movements. A year after Peterloo, workers and reformers were still organizing despite heightened state repression. But the vast campaign around Queen Caroline dominated the year's contention; we coded

"royalty" as the principal issue for 144 of the year's 274 CGs. Mobilization in the Queen Caroline affair, as historians call it, combined a recognizable core of social movement activism with a substantial periphery of
performances in the 18th-century style: forced illuminations, attacks on
public figures, overflowing of public ceremonies, and so on. It involved a
remarkable, if temporary, coalition of radicals and reformers against the
government. For the most part, it proceeded rambunctiously but without
much physical damage to persons and property.

In 1795, the rakish Prince of Wales (future George IV) married
his cousin Princess Caroline of Brunswick – he was thirty-two, she
was twenty-six. He had long since secretly married the Catholic Maria
Fitzherbert, but the marriage had no legal standing in Anglican Britain.
He then acquired notoriety as a carouser and womanizer. But his debts
and the royal family's preference for public propriety persuaded him to
marry again. Caroline bore a daughter, Charlotte, exactly nine months
after the wedding. Soon after Princess Charlotte's birth, George and
Caroline essentially separated bed and board forever. Both kept lively
company with members of the opposite sex, although his adulteries always
remained more visible than hers.

In 1806, the government carried on an inquiry into Caroline's affairs
called the "Delicate Investigation"; its scandalous accusations shadowed
her for the rest of her life. From that point on, the Whig leader Henry
Brougham (no admirer of hers) became a major defender of her case and
used it repeatedly to needle the government. When George III's insanity
made Caroline's husband Prince Regent in 1811, life in England became
more uncomfortable for her. In 1814, she fled into continental exile. The
death of Princess Charlotte in childbirth (1817) broke the last substantial
tie between George and Caroline. It also eliminated Caroline's claim to
be mother of a future queen. Caroline spent most of the next three years
in Italy, again accumulating rumors of illicit liaisons.

Box 5-3 says what happened next. In January 1820, George III died,
after a reign of fifty-two years. The Prince Regent became heir to the
throne, and Caroline the legal queen-elect. The new king-to-be took
every possible step to disbar her from the title. When she returned to
England in June for a re-assertion of her rights, two momentous things
happened. First, George initiated formal proceedings of censure and
divorce against Caroline, setting off a momentous parliamentary inquiry.
Second, under the initial guidance of Brougham and of London alderman Matthew Wood, a huge campaign to defend Caroline began.

Box 5-3: A Brief Chronology of the Queen Caroline Campaign,
        1820–1821

1820

January	George III dies, Caroline of Brunswick, new king's estranged wife, becomes Queen Consort
June	Caroline arrives in Dover from Calais, makes triumphal procession to London; king initiates divorce proceedings against the queen; parliamentary debate begins, secret parliamentary committees formed to investigate the affair (Matthew Wood and Henry Brougham advising Caroline)
June–August	Frequent public appearances of queen in London, to cheers of crowds; public political campaigns on her behalf by William Cobbett, William Hone, and other radicals
August–November	"Trial" by parliamentary bill of Caroline in House of Lords, huge crowds attending arrival and departure of Caroline and others
September	During three-week parliamentary break, flood of meetings, marches, delegations, and addresses, overwhelmingly in favor of Caroline
November	House of Lords passes bill by small (and diminishing) majority; government drops the case; simultaneous celebrations and attacks on pro-government persons and newspapers across much of Britain

1821

January–February	Parliament rejects bills to restore Caroline's name to the Anglican liturgy
July	Caroline turned away from George IV's coronation, despite large supporting crowds
August	Caroline dies; during funeral procession through London on the way back to Brunswick, Queenite crowds disrupt the line of march, clash with troops, carry on one last huge demonstration on Caroline's behalf; massive funeral ceremony for two workers killed in the demonstration

The campaign soon attracted support from a wide range of radicals and reformers both inside and outside of Parliament. Francis Place (a republican, and therefore no great friend of royalty) brought his incomparable entrepreneurial skills to the campaign. Among notable radicals, William Cobbett and William Hone organized an extensive print campaign, as Cobbett drafted the queen's replies to addresses of support that came in from across the country.

From June to August 1820, every public appearance of the queen attracted cheering crowds. Benefit societies and organized trades took to staging meetings and marches on her behalf, often ending in the presentation of supportive addresses, signed by thousands of artisans, at her residence. On 15 August, a great procession of artisans followed the script:

It was well organised, and exemplified the trade societies' liking for show and pageantry. They assembled at 11 am at St. Clements' Church in the City, marshaled into groups by men with white wands. The address was borne between two people genteelly dressed in mourning, but wearing white silk rosettes. These white ribands, symbolising innocence and purity, were [radical artisan John] Gast's idea. Behind the address walked in pairs about a hundred men dressed in the same way, and then another hundred dressed in coloured clothes, some with aprons, others with silk coloured handkerchiefs and, like the rest of the procession, many wearing sprigs or leaves of laurel. These were nearly all clean and "the better class of journeyman mechanic." Their numbers swelled as they marched. In Knightsbridge they caught up with the Middlesex cavalcade and were then themselves caught up with by the Hammersmith and Shoreditch processions, to make one continuous line from Hyde Park to Hammersmith. Only fifty went up to the drawing-room behind Gast, who made a long speech before reading the address, all then kissed her hand and she appeared at the window to cheers from the rest outside. (Prothero 1979: 139–140)

Once the House of Lords took up the accusations against Caroline on 17 August, the mobilization only multiplied. As the principals, including Caroline, proceeded to and from Parliament, cheering and jeering crowds lined the London streets, held back by troops and constables.

The movement reached its peak during a three-week parliamentary break in September 1820. Addresses arrived from all over Great Britain, with thousands of signatures from Bristol, Nottingham, Newcastle upon Tyne, Birmingham, Edinburgh, Paisley, Manchester, Glasgow, Monmouth, Portsmouth, Warwick, and Bury St. Edmonds, many of them signed exclusively by the queen's female supporters (Robins 2006: 237). In November, the government dropped its case against Caroline in response to a narrow and diminishing majority for it in the House of Lords and the prospect of defeat in the Commons. At that point, a new burst of support for the queen occurred:

On 10 November 1820 ... the nation was focused not on what might have been, but on the reality of the Queen's triumph. That night London was filled with illuminations which outshone those on any other occasion, including Wellington's victory at Waterloo. Cannons and muskets were fired – William Cobbett (who was prone to hyperbole) put the number at 50,000 guns – and the people went "mad with enthusiasm for the Queen," here and there indulging in "looting and all kinds of brutality." Countess Lieven told her servants that they could take off their hats to the Queen as much as they liked, as "when it is a question of being shot, I submit to the law of force." Without a military escort, she said, "the mob is my master." In several streets witnesses against Caroline, in particular Majocchi and Demont, were burned in effigy. (Robins 2006: 289, citing Cobbett's *Political Register* and Lieven correspondence)

In the aftermath, the movement declined except for one last sensational burst. The government fortified its front against the queen. Early in 1821, Parliament refused to restore Caroline's name to the Anglican liturgy's prayers for the royal family. In July, its agents kept her from attending George IV's coronation, despite the crowds that cheered on her attempt to enter Westminster Abbey. In August, a dispirited Caroline died. She had asked that her body be returned to her native Brunswick. The government then faced a dilemma: if they transported the body to the Channel via the Thames, they ran the risk that activists from the City of London would block the river, seize the casket, and display Caroline in state at Guildhall before releasing her for the final voyage.

On the scheduled day, 14 August, the authorities chose instead to conceal their chosen path through north London until the last moment. The stratagem didn't work: supporters of the deceased queen not only gathered en masse at the queen's residence but also diverted the procession through central London before massive crowds. At the Cumberland Gate end of Hyde Park, troops confronted marchers:

Among those watching the affair at Cumberland Gate from his official place in the funeral procession was Maj.-Gen. Sir Robert Wilson, a veteran of the Egyptian and Peninsular Campaigns and of the Irish Rebellion of 1798. The forty-three-year-old Wilson watched as the Life Guards fired into a crowd of unarmed if disorderly Englishmen. The man who earlier had allegedly been involved in the obstruction at Kensington Gardens now intervened to prevent further bloodshed. Wilson rode up to Captain Oakes and publicly rebuked him for firing without the orders of a magistrate. Wilson then reprimanded several soldiers; when one of them, Private Thomas Waite, objected that he was only performing his duty, Wilson bellowed, "You damned rascal. I have a good mind to knock you off your horse." (Palmer 1988: 176)

A magistrate did arrive and ordered Captain Oakes to withdraw his men. But by then the damage was done: two demonstrators died in that confrontation. The funeral procession of those two artisans on 26 August, attended by thousands of London workers in well-disciplined ranks, marked the last great moment of the Queen Caroline affair.

Figure 5-1 reveals the mixture of social movement and older performances that occurred in the London region's 274 CGs of 1820. It separates CGs for which royalty was the principal issue from all the rest. Attacks played only a trivial part in the Queen Caroline events, although they figured more extensively in other CGs. Correspondingly, Control verbs remained relatively rare in either set. In both categories, the verb categories Meet, Move, Bargain, and Support outshadowed other sorts of action. Support, Bargain, and Move characterized gatherings on behalf of royalty even more than other gatherings. Unlike the enormous concentration on petition-generating meetings that appeared in the mobilizations around religious rights and parliamentary reform a decade later (see Chapter 4), British activists were still engaging in a street politics with overtones of the 18th century.

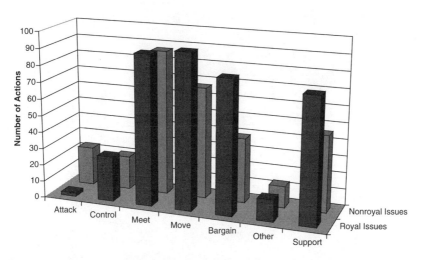

Figure 5-1 Verbs in London-Region CGs, 1820

142

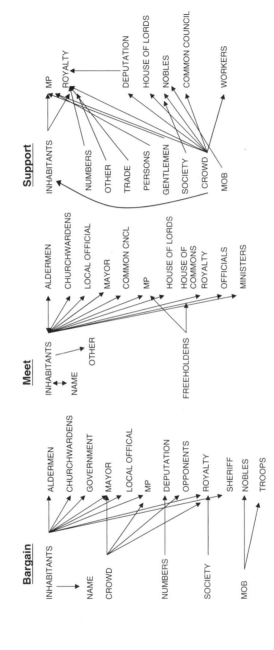

Figure 5-2 Structures of Claims in London-Region CGs, 1820

Figure 5-2 shows more clearly that two separate repertoires were in play. Bargain and (especially) Meet verbs concentrated in assemblies of inhabitants that issued messages to a wide variety of authorities, including the central government. Support verbs, in contrast, aligned an equally wide variety of claimants on parliament and royalty – especially on Queen Caroline herself. To some extent, street crowds substituted for assemblies of inhabitants: they cheered or jeered the day's major public figures.

By 1820, British participants in contentious politics had definitively invented the social movement. But the new repertoire had not entirely swept the field. Radicals, reformers, and organized workers had taken the initiative in making meetings, marches, petitions, and public statements their preferred ways of pressing claims on public authorities. Ordinary people in the street still broke windows, forced illuminations, and took advantage of authorized public ceremonies to voice their preferences. Especially outside of London, revolutionaries and radical workers still plotted insurrections and popular seizures of power. Nevertheless, as in North America and elsewhere in Western Europe, the social movement had moved from being a theoretical possibility to becoming a visibly available alternative to collective violence.

Social movements went on to flourish across most of the democratizing world. As the 19th century wore on, social movements became standard vehicles for claim making in the more democratic Western countries. During the 20th century, the scope of the social movement extended to parts of Asia and Africa as well. During the 21st century, social movements of a global scale began to form (Tilly 2004b: chapter 5). The forms of claim making whose tentative beginnings we have observed in Boston, Charleston, and London during the 1760s became a worldwide force. Some minimum of rights to associate, assemble, and speak underlay that spread of social movements. But once they began to form in one regime or another, they promoted the expansion of democratic practices across the world (Tilly 2004b: chapter 6).

Social movements beautifully exemplify the nature of strong repertoires. Let us review the criteria for a strong repertoire:

- In particular times and places, performances cluster into a limited number of recurrent, well-defined types. Social movements obviously standardize their performances and channel their participants into those performances.

- Within the range defined by all contentious actions that a given set of actors carry on, substantial blanks appear; combinations of actions clearly lying within the technical reach of participants never occur. As a result, performance types have visible boundaries rather than distributing continuously over the space of technically possible performances. From early on, social movements eliminated such actions as attacks on malefactors' dwellings and shaming renegades publicly in favor of disciplined displays of WUNC.
- For a given set of actors and issues, those performances change relatively little from one round of action to the next; what happens in one round of action, furthermore, detectibly constrains what happens in the next round. The available evidence from Great Britain amply confirms both continuity and constraint.
- Participants in contention give evidence that they are aware of those performances by giving names to them, referring to previous actions of the same kind, giving each other instructions, adopting divisions of labor that require prior consultation or experience, anticipating each other's actions, and/or terminating actions more or less simultaneously. The interactions of organizers, participants, authorities, and observers in social movements make that awareness of relevant performances crystal clear.
- Within a set of connected actors, each significant pair of actors has its own repertoire. In the pair, claim-making actors make choices within the existing repertoire. Great Britain's citizen-Parliament interactions, in particular, soon adopted a highly standardized repertoire of meetings and petitions.
- The more connected the histories of actors outside of contention, the more similar their repertoires. Hence a process of increasing connection tends to homogenize performances – that is, make them more modular. With the important exception of the Swing Rebellion, we have witnessed an impressive homogenization of contentious performances in Great Britain after 1820.
- New performances arise chiefly through innovation within existing performances, but tend to crystallize, stabilize, and acquire visible boundaries once they exist. The evidence from Great Britain fully documents innovation within existing performances as well as routinization of such innovations as the petition march, the street demonstration, and the public meeting.

If repertoires in general tend to be strong, the social movement repertoire is super-strong. For two centuries it has dominated public claim making in democratizing and democratic regimes. Although such innovations as Internet organizing and communication by mobile telephone continue to modify the social movement's fine grain, in general the social movement repertoire exhibits impressive continuity from its first partial appearances in the time of John Wilkes and Samuel Adams.

6

Repertoires and Regimes

From 7 July to 8 August 1835 – three years after his return from America and the same year as publication of his *Democracy in America* – Alexis de Tocqueville traveled through Ireland with his friend Gustave de Beaumont. The two vigorous visitors followed a circuit that took in Dublin, Waterford, Killarney, Galway, Castelbar, and back to Dublin. With his nose for idle aristocracies and protracted conflicts, Tocqueville interrogated Protestants and Catholics alike on the prospects for Protestant-Catholic harmony in Ireland. On 11 July Tocqueville interviewed Thomas Kelly, inspector for Ireland's newly established (Anglican) national schools. He asked Kelly whether the restoration of an Irish Parliament (which Irish nationalists, including Daniel O'Connell, were then starting to demand and which would now surely include a Catholic majority) would shift the balance of power. Kelly replied that "it would be a complete revolution, a reverse tyranny just as great as before" (Tocqueville 1991: 523). He meant that Catholics would take vengeance for years of Protestant misrule.

Like Kelly, Tocqueville's Irish informants generally agreed that the Protestant aristocracy had governed Ireland badly for several centuries. But they saw little possibility of a peaceful settlement in which Protestants and Catholics would run the country together. Since Catholic Emancipation (1829), indeed, Protestant landlords had been expelling their small Catholic tenants, who had lost the vote in the deal that gave richer Catholics the right to hold many public offices. Divisions between rich and poor were growing sharper, and even more clearly marked along religious lines.

Toward the end of his tour, Tocqueville reviewed the history of a conquering Anglican aristocracy that displaced Catholics from landownership starting in the time of Henry VIII. He jotted down these reflections:

Give these unlike and unequal people a different religion, so that the noble doesn't merely feel contempt for the people, but hates them, while the people both hates and damns the noble. Far from giving such an aristocracy a reason to unite with the people, give it strong reasons to separate itself in order to remain similar to the nation from which it springs, from which it borrows all its strength, and which it prides itself on resembling. Instead of giving it motivation to compromise with the people, give it motives to oppress the people, confident in foreign support that gives it nothing to fear from tyranny. Give that aristocracy the exclusive power to govern and enrich itself, forbid the people from joining the elite or set unacceptable conditions for that ascent, so that kept to itself, disconnected from the upper classes, object of their enmity, without hope of improving its lot, the people gives up and becomes satisfied when after great effort it survives by working the fields, while the noble, on his side, deprived of everything that stirs a man to grand, generous actions, sleeps in unenlightened egoism. (Tocqueville 1991: 556)

In Tocqueville's bitter reflections on Ireland, we hear echoes of his famous analysis concerning how France's Old Regime nobility – his ancestors – sank into idle exploitation and eventually facilitated revolution (Tocqueville 1952). It took another ninety years, but Ireland did finally break away from Great Britain after World War I.

When Tocqueville and Beaumont visited Ireland, it belonged formally to the same regime as Great Britain. Aided by Britain's enemy France, Ireland had rumbled with revolution during the 1790s. Britain responded by creating the (feebly) United Kingdom in 1801: England, Wales, Scotland, and Ireland now fell under the same crown. In the process, Ireland lost its separate Parliament as one hundred Irish Protestant MPs joined the British Parliament. But that nominal equality masked a colonial relationship: a lord lieutenant governed in the king's name and maintained the Protestant establishment.

As a consequence, the quality of contentious politics differed sharply on the two sides of the Irish Sea. Samuel Clark and James S. Donnelly Jr. put it this way:

Ireland became almost synonymous with rebellion during the later eighteenth and early nineteenth centuries. Every decade between 1760 and 1840 was punctuated by at least one major outbreak of rural discontent. Though these upheavals generally lacked regional organization, they were regional in the sense that the participants pursued broadly similar aims over wide areas of the country. Effective repression was difficult for the government to achieve, largely because the rebels usually adopted clandestine forms of collective action. Some regional movements – the Oakboys of 1763, the Houghers of 1778–9, the Ribbonmen of 1819–20 – were of short duration and had a life measured only in months. But others – the Rightboys of 1785–8, the Rockites of 1821–4 – endured for several years. And in the 1790s a staggering series of popular protests erupted in the Irish countryside, which were not purely agrarian or economic in aim, and which culminated in a vast revolutionary effort dedicated to the establishment of a separatist republic. (Clark and Donnelly 1983: 25)

In Britain, as we have seen, the politics of social movements was coming to prevail when Tocqueville and Beaumont made their tour. In Ireland of the 1830s, however, food seizures continued in times of dearth, landless laborers rebelled against the (Anglican) tithe, agrarian secret societies resisted landlords' extensions of their power, armed bands of Protestants and Catholics confronted each other in public places, local factions battled each other to the death, and O'Connell and his allies agitated for repeal of the Union, while both Irish Catholic nationalists and Orangemen (that is, Protestant supporters of Union and opponents of Emancipation) attacked British-backed forces of order. In these circumstances, Parliament once again resorted to a coercion act – officially known, almost inevitably, as the Peace Preservation Act – that allowed the lord lieutenant to suspend civil liberties and install a kind of martial law in areas he declared in a "state of disturbance" (Broeker 1970: 214).

This chapter uses a comparison of contentious performances in Ireland and Great Britain to raise a much more general question: to what extent, how, and why do the forms of political contention vary from one type of national regime to another? Profound differences in contention occur across regimes, and deep alterations in contention regularly occur as regimes change character.

Regime Space

A regime is the set of relationships among a government and the major political actors within the government's jurisdiction that interact routinely with each other and the government. In Great Britain, for example, the regime of 1750–1840 certainly included Parliament and the crown, but it also included organized workers, the nobility, landlords, constituted local communities, and political parties. During the period it also came to include militant Protestants, militant Catholics, and advocates of parliamentary reform. We have encountered regimes already when considering political opportunity structure (POS). POS is regime structure as considered from the perspective of a potential maker of claims.

Repertoires tend to become uniform within regimes, and therefore to distinguish regimes from each other. On one side, a regime's distinctive political institutions promote emergence of a repertoire adapted to those institutions and widely available throughout the same regime. On the other, those same distinctive political institutions differentiate regimes and therefore their repertoires from each other. Even such similar regimes as those of Canada and the United States nurture their own distinctive performances, such as the demonstration besieging Parliament in Ottawa and the march to the Mall in Washington, DC, or the native drumming that frequently opens Canadian rallies and demonstrations. Uniformity within regimes and differences among regimes result from two interacting influences: 1) actions of central governments that impose limits on collective claim making within the regime and 2) communication and collaboration among claimants (actual or potential) that pool information, beliefs, and practices concerning what forms of claim making work or don't work.

Schematically, every government distinguishes among claim-making performances that it prescribes (e.g., pledges of allegiance), those it tolerates (e.g., petitioning), and those it forbids (e.g., assassination of officials). The exact contours of the three categories vary from regime to regime as a result of accumulated bargains between rulers and their subject populations. We have repeatedly seen British regimes bargaining with their subjects over such questions as the right to assemble publicly or to seize grain destined for the London market. But once the map of required, tolerated, and forbidden performances exists, government agents such as police, troops, officials, and schoolteachers act to reinforce its boundaries.

Makers of claims negotiate with government agents over those same boundaries. Demonstrators and police, for example, contest the boundary between peaceful assembly and disorderly behavior, as villagers who seize food in times of dearth bargain with mayors and constables over the price to set for the public sale of that food. Outside the scope of 18th- and 19th-century Britain, however, claimants bargain with government agents over acceptable forms of resistance to taxation, the right to bear arms collectively, the propriety of killing pariahs, and much more. Regimes vary enormously in their delineations of prescribed, tolerated, and forbidden claim making.

Our basic map of regimes remains very simple. In one dimension we place variations in governmental capacity – roughly speaking, the extent to which rulers' deliberate actions affect distributions of people, activities, and resources within the government's territory. Along the other dimension, we array regimes by their degree of democracy or non-democracy, the extent to which persons subject to the government's authority have broad, equal rights to influence governmental affairs and to receive protection from arbitrary governmental action. That capacity-democracy space allows us, for example, to compare the very different forms of politics that occur in high-capacity democratic regimes and low-capacity undemocratic regimes. It also allows us to trace paths of change in regimes, for instance, the partial democratization and extensive increase in governmental capacity of the British national regime between 1750 and 1840.

Figure 6-1 reduces the space to four crude types of regime: low-capacity undemocratic, high-capacity undemocratic, high-capacity democratic, and low-capacity democratic. A "0" on either dimension represents the lowest known value in some array of regimes, a "1," the highest known value; for present purposes, let us think of each range as including all regimes that exist during the early 21st century. Examples of each type in the diagram then include:

High-capacity undemocratic: North Korea, Morocco
Low-capacity undemocratic: Albania, Democratic Republic of the
    Congo
High-capacity democratic: India, Argentina
Low-capacity democratic: Monaco, Barbados

Over human history regimes have distributed very unevenly across the types. The great bulk of historical regimes have fallen into the low-capacity undemocratic sector. Many of the biggest and most powerful, however, have dwelt in the high-capacity undemocratic sector. High-capacity democratic regimes have been rare and mostly recent. Low-capacity democratic regimes have remained even fewer and farther between.

Regime space makes it possible to think systematically about the relationship between a regime's overall operation and the character of its contentious performances. Struggles among autonomous armed groups such as private armies, for example, concentrate in the low-capacity, low-democracy quadrant. The upper-left quadrant (high capacity, low democracy) contains regimes in which any public, collective making of

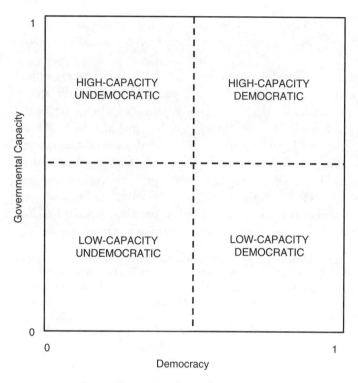

Figure 6-1　Crude Regime Types

claims occurs either within stringent limits imposed by the government or in niches that have somehow escaped governmental surveillance and control. Mark Beissinger's study of contention in the disintegrating Soviet Union from 1987 to 1992 caught the regime as it was moving rapidly from a position firmly in the high-capacity, low-democracy quadrant by democratizing modestly and losing substantial governmental capacity (Beissinger 2002). Mikhail Gorbachev had fostered both shifts.

During the 1990s Russia (the USSR's major successor state) lost even more capacity under the presidency of Boris Yeltsin, but ceased to democratize. Vladimir Putin's arrival as president in 1999 started a dramatic reversal, in which Putin used brutal methods and energy revenues to rebuild capacity while drastically curtailing the democratic gains of the previous decade (Tilly 2007: 133–137). By that time, the burst of popular contention that had followed Mikhail Gorbachev's reforms was subsiding. Meanwhile, regimes that managed to stay in the upper-left quadrant, such as China and Iran, maintained extensive controls over claim making and had few niches that escaped governmental surveillance and intervention.

The lower-right quadrant (low capacity, high democracy) contains turbulent, often violent, forms of public politics that often threaten to overturn governmental control. Consider Jamaica, where the central government clings to the democratic forms bequeathed it by the British colonial regime, but barely governs in the face of criminal gangs, armed supporters of major politicians, and a police force famous for its autonomous brutality. The 2006 report of the New York democracy-monitoring agency Freedom House noted that Jamaica's formal politics keeps to democratic routines but warned about police brutality, judicial backlogs, rampant homophobia, and crime so widespread as to cripple public life:

Jamaica is a main transit point for cocaine shipped from Colombia through the Caribbean to U.S. markets, and the drug trade is now largely controlled by Colombian organized crime syndicates. Violence is the major cause of death in Jamaica, and the murder rate is one of the highest in the world. Much of the violence is the result of warfare between drug gangs known as "posses." Jamaican-born criminal deportees from the United States and a growing illegal weapons trade are major causes of the violence. Mobs have been responsible for numerous vigilante killings of suspected criminals. (Freedom House 2006b)

The contrast with Russia could hardly be greater.

The neighboring lower-left quadrant (low democracy, low capacity) contains regimes that exercise relatively little constraint on collective claim making and give plenty of scope to autonomous centers of power: private armies, dealers in contraband, well-connected religious and kinship networks, large patron-client chains. The bulk of the world's civil wars cluster in the lower left (Tilly 2005b: chapter 6). Violent rivalries concentrate there because control over thin but often brutal governments gives one or another of these autonomous groups tremendous advantages over its impoverished rivals. Desperate Somalia marks an extreme case of fragmenting struggles for power within the quadrant, but at times in recent decades the Democratic Republic of the Congo, Sierra Leone, Ivory Coast, and Liberia have all edged into the same zone and the same sorts of contentious politics. The European decolonization of sub-Saharan Africa obviously left a number of low-capacity states behind.

In the upper-right quadrant (high democracy, high capacity) we find the relatively contained contentious politics of social movements and similar forms of contention. India, the world's most populous democracy, has maintained its distinctive combination of central capacity and democracy since independence (1947) despite numerous armed conflicts in areas that escape the central government's control (Tilly 2007: chapter 3). Freedom House gave India high ratings in 2007, but qualified them: "A wide range of political parties operate freely, and there are no restrictions on peaceful political activism. However, despite the vibrancy of the Indian political system, effective and accountable rule continues to be undermined by political infighting, pervasive criminality in politics, decrepit state institutions, and widespread corruption" (Freedom House 2007c). Thus a location in the upper-right quadrant remains purely relative: no regimes of absolute capacity or complete democracy have ever existed anywhere.

Further political differences appear within regime space. In the space's upper (high-capacity) half, governmental agents figure importantly in collective claim making, often with violent repression on the low-democracy side and with careful containment on the high-democracy side. Below the mid-section, in the territory of low capacity, autonomous wielders of force play larger parts, and much more of contentious politics occurs without effective governmental intervention (Tilly 2005b).

From the viewpoint of violence, regime space also has some powerful implications. Leaving aside government-initiated interstate warfare, overall levels of violence run higher in low-capacity regimes, whether undemocratic or democratic. Democracy depresses violence within domestic politics, if not necessarily in relations among governments. The overall implications for levels of collective violence within regimes look like this:

High violence: low-capacity undemocratic regimes
Medium violence: high-capacity undemocratic and low-capacity democratic regimes
Low violence: high-capacity democratic regimes

If substantial shifts from regime type to regime type occur in the world, we should expect them to affect overall levels of collective violence. If high-capacity undemocratic regimes lose capacity – as happened widely in the disintegrating Soviet Union after 1985 – we should expect levels of violence to increase (Beissinger 1998, 2002). If many regimes democratize without losing capacity, we can expect short-run increases in collective violence as struggles for control intensify, followed by long-term declines in violent encounters.

POS makes pivotal connections between repertoires and regimes. Any government applies facilitation and repression to different available forms of claim making, thus dividing performances into required, tolerated, and forbidden. High-capacity regimes exert more extensive control over the actual use of those performances, and democratic regimes ordinarily use less brutal varieties of control. On the whole, the zone of tolerated performances expands with democratization as the range of required performances shrinks and the forbidden territory narrows to performances that directly threaten the regime's survival. Precisely because low-capacity states back their specifications of required, tolerated, and forbidden performances with less effective facilitation and repression than high-capacity states, low-capacity regimes live with greater variability of claim making from time to time and place to place.

The pace of change in POS also affects levels and forms of contention significantly. Rapidly shifting threats and opportunities generally move power holders toward rigid repertoires and challengers toward more flexible repertoires. Power holders cling to proven performances, including repression of challengers; meanwhile, challengers seek new means to outwit authorities and competitors. (Complication: as the POS argument implies, rivalry among power holders often leads some of them to form alliances with challengers, which limits the power holders' movement toward rigidity as well as the challengers' move toward flexibility.) Since some repertoires link challengers to power holders, rapidly shifting threats and opportunities thus introduce more uncertainties into the relations between claimants and objects of their claims. Programs, identities, and political standing all shift more rapidly.

In times of rapidly changing political opportunity, therefore, we find both recurrent innovation and frequent misapprehension among parties to contention, especially in the case of popular challenges to power holders. A spiral of contention ensues, as each new round of claim making begins to threaten the interests of (or provide new opportunities for) political actors who had previously remained inactive. We have seen just such spirals arise in the Soviet Union (1977–1992) and Mexico (1968–1988). The extreme arrives in a revolutionary situation: a deep split in control of coercive means. During a revolutionary situation, every actor's interest is at risk, and many actors therefore mobilize for action.

Such cycles usually end with rapid demobilization of most actors, especially those who have challenged and lost. At that point, repertoires crystallize as the pace of innovation in performances slows. Some innovations that appeared during the cycle remain in the repertoire, while some old performances or features of performances disappear. Association with the gain or loss of political advantage by one actor or another strongly affects innovations' survival and disappearance, although changes in the conditions of everyday existence and in actors' internal organization as a consequence of the struggle also affect the viability of different performances.

Incremental changes in repertoires are less dramatic, but more decisive in the long run. Incremental changes occur for three main reasons:

1. Because the same sort of innovative response to rapidly changing POS occurs on a smaller scale in lesser crises and confrontations, whence innovations accumulate in a similar manner
2. Because incremental changes in the dispersion of power, the openness of political institutions, the instability of political arrangements, the availability of allies or supporters, and regime repressiveness – that is, in POS – likewise occur
3. Because potential actors' organization, shared understandings, and interests change incrementally as well

In combination, these three effects identify intertwined strands of change in contentious repertoires, attributable to 1) the internal history of struggle, 2) transformations of regimes, 3) alterations of social structure and culture outside the government, and 4) their interaction.

Britain and Ireland in Regime Space

We can see these effects operating in the British and Irish regimes between 1750 and 1840. To do so, we must deny the actual unity of the United Kingdom from 1801 to 1840. England, Wales, and Scotland did operate in relative synchrony. But Ireland still followed different rules. In fact, Ireland continued to occupy a separate semi-colonial position after the 1800 Act of Union. Catholic Emancipation (1829) reduced the political penalties of Catholics, but by no means removed them in Great Britain or in Ireland. Throughout the years from 1750 to 1840, furthermore, Ireland's regime remained both less democratic and lower in governmental capacity than Great Britain's. Figure 6-2 sketches the difference.

According to the sketch, both regimes rose sharply in capacity after 1750, de-democratized somewhat during the repressive years of war with France, then lost some capacity and underwent modest democratization after the wars ended in 1815. But Great Britain preceded and exceeded

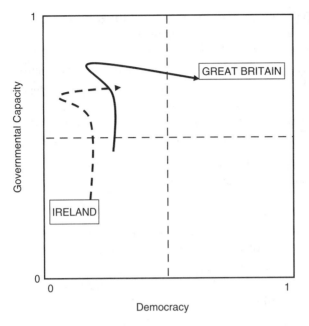

Figure 6-2 Regime Trajectories of Great Britain and Ireland, 1750–1840

Ireland in all these regards. As seen from the bottom up, Britain's commercialization and expansion of communications simultaneously facilitated state capacity and promoted democratization. As seen from the top down, parliamentarization did the same: Parliament's increasing control over state expenditure in the face of expanding wars and rising debt added to the central state's muscle as it took power away from the crown. Because of the connections it formed between local populations and the central state, parliamentarization also provided openings for democratization.

Think back to implications of my earlier generalizations about relationships between contentious repertoires and locations in regime space. We might expect significant increases in state capacity such as occurred in both Great Britain and Ireland to augment involvement of state agents in contentious politics, to expand the scopes of both required and forbidden claim-making performances, and to increase the state's actual enforcement of those limits. During the phases of partial democratization, however, we might expect a further shift, as required and forbidden performances diminished in scope and the range of tolerated performances grew, all within increased monitoring and containment of claim-making performances by the state.

In addition, we might expect the sequence of capacity increase followed by partial democratization first to diminish levels of collective violence and increase the involvement of state agents in all collective violence, then to temper violence overall. Although the much higher levels of collective violence in Ireland than in Great Britain tell us that more was happening than these simple generalizations allow, on the whole the contentious histories of Great Britain and Ireland between 1750 and 1840 fulfill these expectations.

Political opportunity structure necessarily altered significantly. Remember the elements of POS as outlined in Chapter 4: openness of the regime, coherence of the regime's elite, stability of political alignments, availability of allies for potential challengers, repression and facilitation, and the pace of change in any or all of them. Roughly speaking, the period from 1750 to the 1790s modestly increased POS for most challengers in Great Britain through such innovations as the Wilkite mobilization and the rise of militant antislavery. Although the later war years reduced opportunity and increased threat as the state grew more repressive and potential allies for challengers grew more cautious, the postwar years brought renewed opening of POS despite frequent attempts of state authorities to dampen the popular making of claims. Levels of claim making rose dramatically during the postwar years, and contentious claims increasingly took social movement forms.

In the case of Great Britain, momentous changes were occurring in the central state's operation. They help explain Britain's trajectory within the capacity-democracy space. Figure 6-3 underlines the magnitude of the British state's fiscal expansion between 1750 and 1840 (Brewer 1989, Daunton 2001, Mann 1988, Stone 1994; I have interpolated the values for 1800 to adjust for a change in the fiscal year). With a highly commercial economy and heavy reliance on efficient customs and excise services for revenue, the state collected an exceptional share of national income in taxes, compared to other western states of its time. The peak for our period arrived in the war year of 1810, when government expenditure equaled an estimated 23 percent of Britain's gross national product (Daunton 2001: 23). As war-driven taxation expanded,

the crown surrendered its ability to live on its own resources, and depended on grants from parliament which was jealous of its power and independence. The election of taxes rested on a complex process of bargaining, and linked parliament with the concerns of the localities. Unlike in many other European countries, the significant increase in British taxation came in the eighteenth century and some of

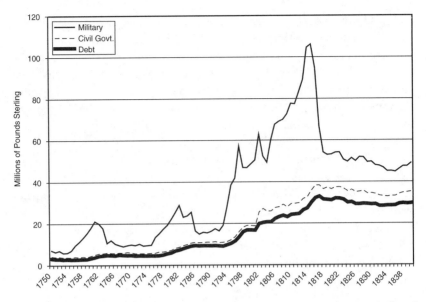

Figure 6-3 British Government Expenditures, 1750–1840 (from Mitchell and Deane 1971: 389–397)

the problems encountered by continental European states in financing land-wars of the seventeenth century were avoided: the sale of offices, extensive use of tax farmers and the granting of fiscal privileges. The collection of taxes embedded the fiscal system in local sources of power and authority, and created a sense of trust between taxpayers and in the central state. The revenue then supported the use of loans which had a high level of security and marketability. (Daunton 2001: 41)

Figure 6-3 doubly displays the impact of war. First, the curve of total expenditure (top line) clearly registers the impact of the Seven Years' War (1756–1763), the American War (1775–1783), and, incomparably, the series of wars with revolutionary and Napoleonic France (1793–1815). It also shows how war built up debt. As the great French wars ended, debt became by far the largest of the three broad categories of governmental expenditure. Despite the rise of debt, nevertheless, overall levels of expenditure – and therefore of taxes – dropped precipitously after 1815. By that time, however, war-driven parliamentarization had done its political work. Parliament had become the center of the British regime.

As the graph shows clearly, direct military expenditure fluctuated far more than did the other two major components: debt and civil government. It did so because in times of war Britain spent mightily on its army and navy, only to cut back drastically when peace arrived. From a peacetime level of about 35 thousand men, the Seven Years' War pushed the army up to 203 thousand troops in 1760, only to shrink to about 33 thousand at war's end. (Irish taxpayers paid for the troops that occupied Ireland, which ran at about 12 thousand men during the 1770s and rose to 60 thousand, not including large militias, in 1800; Foster 1988: 244.)

During the American wars, the army's strength rose again to some 108 thousand men while the navy increased to 82 thousand. Still, the French wars topped all previous efforts; the army reached a maximum of 237 thousand troops toward the end (Barnett 1974). Expenditure on armed force rose and fell accordingly. Table 6-1 shows the rise and fall. It also shows that except for 1770 Britain spent more on the army than the navy, but the navy generally cost more per man.

The British state's military expansion obviously connected servicemen and their families more directly with national politics. The regime's trajectory also had more general effects on popular political participation (Tilly 1995). A bigger and higher-capacity state intervened more aggressively in local life, taxed more heavily, exerted more control over the food supply, and regulated workers' organizations more closely. Parliamentarization shifted power away from the crown, the nobility, and their patron-client networks. It also increased the impact of the legislators'

Table 6-1: *British Governmental Expenditure on Army and Navy, 1750–1840*

Year	Army	Navy
1750	1,566	1,385
1760	8,931	4,539
1770	1,781	2,082
1780	8,540	6,329
1790	2,742	2,482
1800	16,615	13,161
1810	28,900	19,400
1820	10,300	4,400
1830	9,300	4,000
1840	5,300	3,800

Note: Amounts are in thousands of pounds sterling. The values for 1800 are interpolated, and army amounts include ordnance.
Source: Mitchell and Deane 1971: 389–396.

actions on local affairs. These changes gradually undermined the effectiveness of claim-making performances in the 18th-century mode: particular, parochial, and bifurcated. In their place, cosmopolitan, modular, and autonomous performances gained leverage. Social movements came into their own.

Earlier chapters have documented Great Britain's repertoire changes in great detail. Figure 6-4 sums up familiar changes from 1758 to 1834. It presents three series: on meetings as a share of all CGs, on the proportion of all actions having Parliament – that is, the House of Commons, House of Lords, MPs, or Parliament as a whole – as objects, and the percentage of all actions occurring in public meetings and involving claims by local assemblies (electors, freeholders, inhabitants, or parishioners) on Parliament. Meetings in general rose from well below 20 percent of all CGs during the 1750s to substantially above 50 percent of the total after 1801; indeed, only the Swing Rebellion of 1830 brought the share of meetings below three-fifths of all CGs. With the exception of the crisis year 1801, the curve for Parliament as an object of claims rises

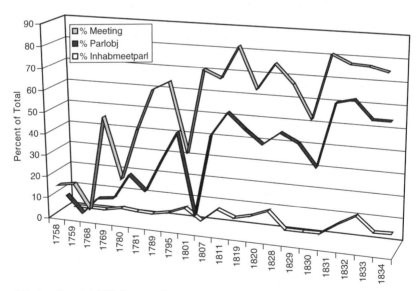

% Meeting = Percent of all CGs in year meetings
% ParlObj = Percent of all actions in year with Parliament (Commons, Lords, Parliament, or MPs) as objects
% Inhabmeetparl = Percent of all actions in year occuring in public meetings and consisting of electors, freeholders, inhabitants, or parishioners making claims on Parliament (Commons, Lords, Parliament, or MPs)

Figure 6-4 Meetings and Parliament in London-Region CGs, 1758–1834

almost uninterruptedly from trivial proportions before 1780 to more than half during the 1830s. Actions in public meetings of local assemblies with Parliament as their object rose modestly, touching 10 percent of all actions during the heated struggle over parliamentary reform in 1832.

The Swing Rebellion qualifies the neat correspondence between repertoires and regimes that this chapter has posited so far. Although repertoires do tend in general to spread through whole regimes, every regime retains some sectors that lead, lag, or otherwise deviate from the prevailing ways of making claims. Swing shows how such deviant sectors work.

In 1830, landless laborers of London's hinterland mounted one last great uprising before declining in despair. Starting at the end of August 1830, laborers who worked for wages on large farms engaged in an impressive range of intimidating actions. They often invoked Captain Swing, a mythical avenger of agricultural workers' rights. They wrote threatening letters, burned farm buildings and hayricks, wrecked threshing machines, drove away overseers of the poor, collectively demanded wage increases, and visited rectories, magistrates' homes, and workhouses to demand higher poor relief or lower tithes.

On a smaller scale, local groups of landless laborers had often done all these things to defend their wages and employment before. The claim-making performances all had their places in the 18th-century repertoire of interchanges among laborers, farmers, and local authorities. In some ways Swing wrought the revenge of the 18th-century moral economy on the 19th-century political economy. No 18th-century laborers' mobilization, however, matched the episode of August to December 1830. Master historians of Swing Eric Hobsbawm and George Rudé sum up the background in these terms:

The condition of the southern labourer was such that he required only some special stimulus – admittedly it would probably have to be exceptionally powerful to overcome his demoralized passivity – to produce a very widespread movement. The economic conditions of 1828–30 produced a situation which made his already bad situation worse, and almost certainly increased both rural unemployment, the attempts to diminish in some way or another the financial burden of poor relief on the rate-payers, and the discontent of farmers and all those who depended on agriculture. The combined effect of continental revolution and British political crisis produced an atmosphere of expectation, of tension, of hope and potential action. (Hobsbawm and Rudé 1968: 91)

The rising began in Kent, but soon spread to Berkshire, Sussex, Buckinghamshire, Dorset, Wiltshire, and especially Hampshire. Hobsbawm and Rudé have shown that the struggle's geography contradicts any picture of remote, backward areas as its settings (Hobsbawm and Rudé 1968; see also Armstrong 1988, Charlesworth 1978, Cirket 1978, Richards 1974, Singleton 1964). On the contrary, they document:

Location of events in London's market region

Concentration in parishes with significant numbers of non-agricultural workers and previous histories of wage-fixing in conjunction with local poor rates

Distribution along major roads

Justification of wage demands by reference to long-established rights as well as to current national politics

National politics mattered in part because Wellington's faltering government was paying more attention to the challenges of reformers than to rural unrest. When a new Whig government arrived in November, it soon took vigorous steps to curb the landless laborers. Open confrontations surged during Wellington's last days in office (after 8 November) and began to decline rapidly two weeks after the Whigs came to power. Clandestine arson attacks behaved differently, correlating closely with confrontations before November, increasing only modestly during the surge of confrontations, but continuing with greater frequency through December. Figure 6-5 (drawn from the Hobsbawm-Rudé event catalog) displays the two configurations.

The graph makes clear that the bomb had a long fuse: attacks, confrontations, and arson occurred at low levels from the end of August until

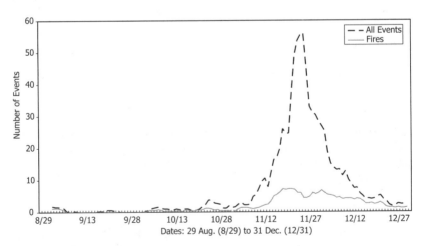

Figure 6-5 Swing Rebellion, 1830: Fires and All Events, 5-Day Moving Average (from Hobsbawm and Rudé 1968)

the end of October, and mainly in Kent. Then arrived a sensational expansion in geographic range and number of events. Eventually Swing attacks, confrontations, and/or arson spread to more than twenty counties, concentrating in southeastern England, London's agricultural supply area. Once Swing ended, clandestine attacks recurred for another decade or so when unemployment and low wages prevailed. But never again did any connected rural rising in the Swing mode repeat itself in Great Britain (Archer 1990). In Ireland, as we will soon see, similar forms of rural pressure and retaliation continued through the 19th century. With contrasting regimes, Ireland and Great Britain produced dramatically different varieties of contentious politics.

The case of landless laborers in the two regimes underlines that not all participants in British contention benefited from the vast repertoire changes of the early 19th century. Landless laborers always lived a precarious existence, but so long as local webs of patronage and control remained predominant, they could exert collective influence by means of the old repertoire's standard performances of pressure, resistance, and retaliation. To the extent that local power holders lost their ability to remedy local conditions, that the central state augmented its repressive means, that Parliament became the principal seat of national decision making, and that potential allies among radicals abandoned agricultural workers as they joined the effort to influence parliamentary decisions, arson, cattle-maiming, and local risings lost effectiveness. Like the industrial machine-breakers whose last collective efforts to save their livelihood sputtered out during the 1830s as well, landless agricultural laborers lost serious leverage with the new repertoire's rising dominance.

The Irish Regime

Ireland did not go through a similar transformation of repertoires until considerably later than most of Great Britain. The timing of Irish regimes helps explain why. Anglo-Norman warriors conquered bits of Ireland during the 11th-century Norman takeover of England, and a century later England's Henry II launched a serious invasion of the island. Over the 13th to 15th centuries, English kings tried repeatedly to subordinate the Irish, but outside of the Dublin region – the famous Pale – they did not succeed for long. Confrontations of Protestants and Catholics continued for centuries. Box 6-1 provides a long-run chronology of Ireland's turbulent Protestant-Catholic relations.

Box 6-1: Landmark Dates of Irish Protestant-Catholic Relations

1520–1602	Tudor invasions; plantations; rebellions; civil wars; establishment of Irish Protestant church
1610–1640	Stuart dispossessions; English and Scottish settlements in Ireland, especially Ulster
1641–1650	Rebellions and civil war in England and Ireland, ending with Cromwell's brutal conquest of Ireland
1689–1691	Glorious Revolution in England; civil war in Ireland; reconquest by William III; sharp abridgement of Catholic political rights; massive seizure of Catholic property continuing to 1703
1782–1783	Partial restoration of Irish political autonomy; Catholic rights to acquire land and to teach (but Irish Parliament still exclusively Protestant)
1791–1795	Propertied Catholics acquire voting rights; United Irishmen (autonomist, increasingly Catholic) and Orange Order (loyalist, Protestant) form
1798	United Irish risings; civil war; massacres; French invasions; bloody suppression
1801	Creation of United Kingdom (England, Wales, Scotland, Ireland); abolition of Irish Parliament; incorporation of one hundred Irish Protestant MPs into U.K. Parliament
1813–1829	Repeated campaigns for Catholic Emancipation in England and Ireland; mass mobilizations for Emancipation in Ireland and against it in England; final passage of parliamentary acts expanding (but not entirely equalizing) Catholic political rights; raising property requirements for the Irish franchise; dissolving Daniel O'Connell's Catholic Association
1830s–1890s	Numerous anti-landlord and anti-tithe actions; failed agitation for Irish home rule
1843–	Major Protestant-Catholic violence in Belfast, especially 1843, 1857, 1864, 1872, 1886, 1893
1845–1850	Potato famine, leading to large-scale emigration
1848	Young Ireland uprising in Munster
1858	Founding of Irish Republic Brotherhood (Fenians) in Dublin and New York
1867	Fenian risings in Ireland; Clan na Gael founded in New York

1869	Church of Ireland (Anglican) disestablished
1884	Franchise Act greatly expands rural (and almost entirely Catholic) electorate
1916	Easter Rising, with German support
1919–1923	Civil wars, first producing separate governments and parliaments for North and South (1921), then creation of Irish Free State, excluding Northern Ireland (1922)
1923–2004	Intermittent Protestant-Catholic struggles in Northern Ireland; frequent involvement of British troops; suspension and restitution of successive Northern Ireland governments
1949	Declaration of independent Irish Republic, still excluding Northern Ireland

Serious English colonization and administration did not begin until the 1550s. Most of the earliest settlers were not English, but Scottish. At the succession of Scottish King James VI to the English crown as James I (1603), royally sponsored settlements of Scots and Englishmen greatly expanded. They concentrated in Ulster, the nine northernmost counties of Ireland. There and elsewhere in Ireland, English rulers regularly dispossessed Catholic landlords; that displacement of Catholics from landownership and political power accelerated during the 17th century.

During the English civil wars of 1640–1690, Irish leaders tried repeatedly to wrest their territories from English rule. From opposite sides, Irish activists still celebrate or execrate the Battle of the Boyne (1690), when Protestant King William defeated his rival, Catholic King James, who fled to France. From that point until the 19th century, English regimes excluded Catholics from almost every form of political power in Ireland, including in Ulster. With minor exceptions, Protestants alone enjoyed the right to bear arms. During the late 1770s, indeed, Anglican landlords emulated American revolutionaries by organizing militias – the Volunteers – 80 thousand strong. Urban equivalents also formed.

In 1778, for example, Belfast formed its own volunteer corps, nominally to protect the coast against a threatened French landing. By 1782, perhaps 90 thousand men had joined these militias (Mac Suibhne 2000: 45). In 1782, "delegates from a number of Ulster Volunteer corps gathered at Dungannon in the parish church and pledged their support to resolutions in favour of [Irish] legislative independence" (McDowell 2001:

191). Although a few landlords recruited Catholics to their companies, the militias became overwhelmingly a Protestant force.

David Miller interprets the increasing Irish military activity of the 1770s as part of a struggle for national power:

The central issue in Irish politics between 1770 and 1829 was the readmission of Catholics to membership in the polity. That process had only just begun when, in the early 1780s, a section of the Protestant gentry allied themselves with their Protestant retainers, who were only marginally within the polity, against the government. Although this Patriot party seemed to have achieved its principal aims with the granting of legislative autonomy and commercial concessions in the early 1780s, their methods had the effect of seriously dividing the polity. (Miller 1983: 187)

For "polity," read "regime." Militant Protestants divided, however, between two contradictory programs: parliamentary reform that would increase the political rights of the Protestant middle classes and alliances with Catholics for even more general democratic programs. In either case, the 1780s and 1790s brought an increasing connection between centuries-old Protestant-Catholic struggles and Irish national politics. From the enfranchisement of the previously disfranchised wealthier Catholics under British pressure in 1793, that connection included electoral politics.

As Tocqueville learned on his Irish journey, the prevailing system of power rested on two huge divisions. In relations with Great Britain, Irish Protestants exercised great priority over Catholics even after Catholic Emancipation. Within Ireland, however, landlords (a small minority of them Catholic) ruled over the great mass of (Catholic) smallholders and landless laborers. To be more precise, large tenants, typically Protestant, ruled the countryside:

Though the land was owned by a relatively small elite numbering perhaps fewer than 10,000 aristocrats and gentry, their estates were generally sublet to such a degree that for the majority of rural dwellers, their landlord was not the proprietor of the soil but rather a large farmer. Such a farmer might sublet part of his holding to small tenants at a stipulated rent; he might give cabins and plots of ground to laborers, who would pay rent for these by working for him at a stated wage; or he might let some of his land in conacre to laborers for the growing of a crop of potatoes. (Clark and Donnelly 1983: 31)

When Irish peasants struck at their rural oppressors, then, they most often targeted large farmers and the local officials who supported their rule. Nevertheless, landowners both dominated the national regime and incurred the ire of mass mobilizations against rural oppression.

At the time of Tocqueville's inquiry, indeed, landlords were responding to the political threat of Emancipation by displacing the Catholic tenants who had previously delivered their votes faithfully for the landlords' candidates. In 1830, the chief secretary for Ireland, Henry Hardinge, wrote to Prime Minister Robert Peel:

When we know that a Protestant gentleman, a Sir Robert Hudson, ejected in the depth of winter 400 Catholics from his estate in [County Cavan] who retired into the mountains, having no means of lawful existence from the difficulty of obtaining work, whilst the farms were chiefly relet to Protestants, can we be surprised at the burnings of houses and maiming of cattle in that neighborhood? On Lord William Beresford's estate ... in Wicklow, arrangements are making to eject about 500 Catholics under the Subletting Act ... The Archdeacon has successfully mediated for the present, but admitting the improvement of the estate, and the liberality and kindness with which the measure will be carried into execution in the spring, can it be matter of wonder, that young men, whose Fathers for two or three generations have lived on the Estate, and who have punctually paid their rents, should become Ribbon-men and outlaws? Whilst the popular discontent has such natural causes for indulging in vengeance and outrage, I do not expect any cessation of midnight hostilities. (Clark 1979: 70)

Hardinge saw a clear connection between regime change and renewed use of the forms of collective pressure Irish countrymen had long employed against miscreant landlords and tenants who violated local codes.

Yet Hardinge's very interest in landlord oppression of Catholics marked an increase in the British government's efforts to control domestic conflict in Ireland. In collaboration with the Protestant elite, British rulers had long attempted to tamp down Irish mobilization by military repression and by establishment of routine policing. In 1786, the government centralized control of Dublin's exclusively Protestant police in Dublin Castle. The following year the Irish Parliament, under strong government influence and against a drumroll of intense controversy, created a nationally controlled police (again exclusively Protestant) for troubled counties (Palmer 1988: 104–115). Chief Secretary for Ireland Arthur Wellesley, the future Duke of Wellington, strengthened the Dublin police in 1808.

As Chief Secretary in 1814, Robert Peel then initiated a Peace Preservation Force for threatened districts that later extended into a national Irish constabulary. By this time, of course, approval depended not on an Irish Parliament but on the Parliament of the United Kingdom. Peel not only got his police, but actively recruited Catholics into its ranks (Palmer 1988: 203). As we might expect, local authorities commonly resisted the arrival of Peel's police in their districts as a challenge to their own power and an unwanted extension of British administration into Ireland. But British intervention was nationalizing Irish political struggles and generating common fronts of Irish Catholics and Protestants.

The simple scheme of relations among changes in regimes, POS, and repertoires that was sketched earlier predicts both parallels and differences between repertoire changes in Great Britain and Ireland from 1750 to 1840. As Irish regime capacity increased during the years of international war, we might expect the intervention of governmental agents in popular struggles to have risen, governmental control over the forms of claim making to have become more effective, and connections between local and national struggles to have multiplied. During the (very) relative democratization of Ireland after the Napoleonic Wars, we might expect the range of tolerated political performances to have broadened, with increased monitoring and containment of claim-making performances by the state.

These generalizations do apply roughly. But they underestimate two crucial aspects of the Irish regime: 1) that the ultimate governmental power, Great Britain, represented for a minority of Irish people their chief defense against a hostile mass, but for an increasing majority it represented an occupying power and 2) that despite strenuous efforts the Irish government never established anything like the control over rural contention that the British government displayed with a vengeance in its suppression of Swing.

Irish Contention

As we might expect, the combination of a contested relationship to the British crown with an exploitative system of domestic domination long bifurcated Irish popular politics. On one side, Irish activists who were well connected internationally made claims on or against Great Britain. On the other side, two kinds of conflicts prevailed: between landlords and tenants or laborers whose livelihoods depended on them and between Protestants and Catholics. Box 6-2 provides a rough chronology of Irish contention over the nine decades from 1750 to 1840.

British and Irish contentious repertoires resembled each other much more closely at the period's start than at its close. On the whole, Irish performances of the 1750s and 1760s, like their British counterparts, belonged to the particular, parochial, and bifurcated categories of contention. The big difference is that during subsequent decades Irish

Box 6-2: A Rough Chronology of Contentious Politics in Ireland, 1750–1840

1750–1759	Violent resistance in Dublin to rumored Act of Union with Great Britain
1760–1769	Whiteboy and Hearts of Oak attacks in Armagh, Monaghan, Tyrone, Tipperary, Cos, Limerick, Waterford, Cork, and Kilkenny; food seizures in dearth of 1766
1770–1779	Formation of Volunteers; Whiteboy and Hearts of Steel attacks, including Steelboys attack on Belfast barracks; rival Protestant-Catholic militia marches begin in Ulster
1780–1789	Catholic Volunteers opposing (Protestant) Peep o' Day Boys, agitating for reform and against proposed Act of Union, Catholic-Protestant battles (including militia marches) in north
1790–1799	Volunteers continue agitation for reform until repressed (1793); formation of United Irishmen (suppressed in 1794, revived in 1797) and Defenders; start of agitation for reform; demonstrations in support of the French Revolution; Catholic-Protestant battles (including rival militia marches) in north; resistance to disarmament in Ulster; two French attempts at invasion in conjunction with Irish rebellion; one of them (1798) temporarily successful but then crushed
1800–1809	Orangemen consolidate power in north, Threshers lead attacks on tithes and Catholic dues in Mayo, lethal faction fighting between (plebeian) Caravats and (middle-class) Shanavests in Munster
1810–1819	Ribbonmen (descendants of Defenders and United Irishmen) fighting with Orangemen in north, Caravats attacking in Munster and midlands
1820–1829	O'Connell and Catholic Association (first formed 1823) organize mass movement for Emancipation; Brunswick Clubs oppose Emancipation in Ulster; Rockites lead attacks in Munster; Terry Alts do likewise in Clare, Galway, Westmeath, and Limerick
1830–1840	Tithe War across much of the country, O'Connell organizes Repeal Association (1840)

contentious performances showed only a weak tendency to move toward modular, cosmopolitan, and autonomous forms such as the public meeting and other elements of the social movement repertoire. The largest exception arrived with Daniel O'Connell's transnational drive for Catholic Emancipation in the 1820s. Like the Repeal Association that O'Connell founded in 1840, the Catholic Association of 1823 and thereafter took many of its cues from the conventions and possibilities of British politics, rather than attending primarily to Irish local concerns. The centrality of Parliament to both campaigns drew O'Connell and his fellow Irish nationalists into the prevailing British repertoire.

We need an old distinction, however. The organizational bases of Irish contention shared more properties than did the claim-making performances that Irish people mounted over the span from 1750 to 1840. Catholic parishes notably figured as organizational bases for a wide variety of contention, from retaliation against rapacious landlords to demands for Catholic political rights. Although parish priests publicly deplored the violence with which their countrymen pursued their aims, those same priests provided much of the connective tissue among scattered parishioners and parishes in a land of dispersed settlement. Militias, secret societies, and local chapters of national associations all organized chiefly on a parish-by-parish basis. Retaliation against renegades occurred mainly within the same parishes. The generalization applies almost as much to Protestant as to Catholic mobilizations.

Any observer of popular contention who went from Great Britain to Ireland during the 18th century would have noticed three remarkable distinctions of Irish claim making. First, militarily organized societies and avenging forces supported a large share of the more visible popular struggles; their larger-scale versions took such names as Whiteboys, Hearts of Oak, and Hearts of Steel. Similar locally based military units consolidated into such nationally sanctioned forces as the Volunteers and the Defenders. The phenomenon is even more surprising because British rulers denied Catholics the right to bear arms into the 19th century, and Protestants fiercely protected their sanctioned right to armed force.

The Volunteers first formed in Belfast (1778) as a middle-class Protestant force, but soon expanded throughout Ulster, to Dublin, and into other parts of Ireland (Jarman 1997: 40). They immediately launched public parades and reviews. But they soon divided between units supporting Protestant hegemony and other units promoting all-Ireland resistance to British control. For Armagh in the 1780s, reports Sean

Farrell, the Patriot attempt to enlist Catholics in the nationalist Volunteers raised powerful Protestant objections:

The prospect of Irish Catholics legally carrying arms was particularly galling to many lower-class Protestants. In an era when citizenship was often defined by the right to bear arms, many plebeian Protestants viewed their exclusive right to carry weapons as the primary mark of their social superiority over Catholics. Efforts to alter this portion of the Penal Code came as a shock to many loyalists, particularly because it was "their" elite that had proposed the hated reforms. The combined sense of threat and abandonment produced the Peep o' Day Boys, who attempted to reimpose their conception of true law by carrying out violent arms searches on Catholic homes between 1784 and 1788. (Farrell 2000: 17–18)

Thus who had the right to join which militarily organized units raised serious questions of solidarity, citizenship, and social superiority.

Second, unlike the continued fragmentation of Britain's Swing Rebellion and the abortiveness of Britain's postwar attempts at armed rebellion, Ireland's avenging actions sometimes cascaded into insurrection or civil war. The two French-backed attempts at island-wide revolutions (1796 and 1798) offer the most salient examples of the first and the Tithe War of 1830–1833 offers the most prominent case of the second. According to B. F. Foster, "the 1798 rising was probably the most concentrated episode of violence in Irish history" (Foster 1988: 280). The insurrections failed miserably, brought on massive repression, and lay behind Britain's abolition of the separate Irish Parliament. Collective resistance to tithes, in contrast, eventually achieved its objects. Parliament consolidated that popular victory in the Tithe Rentcharge Act of 1838.

Not that the Tithe War took the form of a peaceful social movement. Its local actions incited desperate but ultimately ineffectual repression from Irish public authorities. In the two peak years, prosecutions for "outrage" in Ireland ran as follows:

Offense	1831	1832
Homicide	210	248
Robbery	1,478	1,172
Burning	466	571
Cattle maiming	293	295
Illegal notices	1,798	2,086
Illegal meetings	1,792	422
Attacks on houses	2,296	1,675

Source: Townshend 1983: 6

As compared to the contemporaneous Swing, the Tithe War mobilization involved higher levels of interpersonal violence as well as larger-
scale organization. Yet it did not conform to the meetings, petitions, and
press statements of Britain's simultaneous social movements, including
Catholic Emancipation.

Third, public parading in military order not only became a standard
Irish way of showing strength from the 1690s onward but also provided
repeated occasions in which rival forces – often Protestant and Catholic –
competed to demonstrate their superiority in one Irish town or another
(Tilly 2003: 120–127). In Great Britain, religious and craft processions
offered legal and customary precedents for the street demonstration, but
the practice of parade and counter-parade never figured so prominently as
in Ireland. The regime itself contributed to that development when it
authorized public celebrations of the Glorious Revolution starting in
1690. On those occasions, supporters of the British victory would not only
parade but also carouse and fire off guns in displays of Protestant privi-
lege. Elections similarly gave partisans the chance to strut their stuff (Jupp
and Magennis 2000: 20–22).

Participants in the celebrations tended to exceed the wishes of their
rulers:

State processions continued through Dublin into the early nineteenth century,
but it proved ever more difficult to control the exuberance of the popular
celebrations and the meaning of the memory of the victor of the Boyne [i.e.,
King William]. November 4th became the focus for competing claims on
William's memory: on the one side by the representatives of the Crown, and on
the other by the Volunteers, who demanded political reform of Parliament.
(Jarman 1997: 35)

During the mobilization for Catholic Emancipation of the 1820s,
Catholic-Protestant competition for parade routes and dates intensified,
especially in Ulster. At that point, Catholic Ribbonmen repeatedly
confronted parading ranks of the Protestant Orange Order and vice
versa (Jarman 1997: 54). In a nice historical irony, the regime's tolera-
tion of large Orange marches set a precedent for anti-Orange displays as
well as for the mass gatherings of the Catholic Emancipation campaign
(Jupp and Magennis 2000: 23).

By the end of the 1820s, however, the old rules were changing.
Catholic Emancipation made manifest that Protestant exclusion of

Catholics from citizenship and power was failing. Even the Orange Order began to give way:

Unable to slow down the passage of Catholic emancipation, Orangemen were reduced to ritual forms of protest. The largest such demonstration occurred on 13 July 1829, when Orangemen assembled across the north of Ireland to protest the apostasy of the British government and to display their continued ascendancy over their Catholic enemies. With party feelings at their highest pitch since 1798, Orange demonstrations triggered widespread rioting in Ulster; at least forty people died in a series of bloody clashes that day. (Farrell 2000: 101)

Moreover, the mobilization for Catholic Emancipation made available a model of social movement organization and action that not only influenced subsequent O'Connellite campaigns for Repeal but also expanded to such campaigns as opposition to the tithe; if the Tithe War involved plenty of local violence, it also generated peaceful mass meetings that transcended sectarian differences (Cronin 2000). Although Catholic-Protestant competition and hostility continued at a local level, especially in Ulster, government extension of protection to Catholics and the rise of Irish resistance to British control combined ironically to promote Catholic-Protestant alliances in such campaigns as the Tithe War and Repeal. Regime change generated repertoire change.

How much of the British-Irish comparison generalizes to broad principles of correspondence and causal connection between repertoires and regimes? This chapter's answer differs among three levels. First, in the particular cases of Great Britain and Ireland from 1750 to 1840, repertoires and regimes unquestionably shaped each other. The persistence of militarily organized and broadly based political entities in Ireland, for example, responded both to the weaker central control of the government(s) over the Irish countryside and to the anti-British nationalism that swelled after 1780, but it then strongly affected forms of Irish political struggle during the 19th century.

At a second level, other regimes we examined earlier – for instance, those of the Soviet Union, Mexico, France, and the American colonies – give us reason to suppose more generally that regimes differ sharply in contentious repertoires, change repertoires as national structures of power change, respond to repertoire shifts with alterations of national power, and in fact experience continuous interplay between repertoires and regimes.

At the most general level, however, this chapter has simply identified likely sources of regime-repertoire correspondence that deserve much more extensive comparative study (Tilly 2005b). A genuinely systematic analysis of that correspondence will include not only separate evidence on a wide variety of repertoires and regimes but also close inspection of the dynamics of political opportunity structure. Plenty of work remains for future researchers.

7

Contention in Space and Time

The United States holds its Labor Day on the first Monday of September. The radical Knights of Labor started the custom in 1882. In a pattern that should now be familiar to this book's readers, the Knights held a parade in New York City on Tuesday (not Monday) 5 September, then repeated the successful performance in September 1884. Meanwhile, supporters of the Knights' rival, International Workingmen's Association (IWA), opted for the 1st of May – May Day – as the occasion on which to display labor's strength across the world and to strike for an eight-hour day. A Chicago coalition of labor unions declared a general strike for May Day 1886. But a vicious, highly visible confrontation between demonstrators and police at a labor rally in Chicago's Haymarket Square on 6 May (known, depending on the observer's political position, as the Haymarket Riot or the Haymarket Massacre) tainted the date.

U.S. president Grover Cleveland feared that May Day would become a memorial to the Haymarket radicals. Pressed by Cleveland, American state legislatures lined up to designate September's first Monday as Labor Day. Thus they implicitly chose the Knights over the IWA. The holiday (now national) has lost its close connection with shows of working-class strength. Many Americans use the weekend as a last chance for a summer getaway, while college and professional football teams start their fall seasons a few days before or after that first Monday. In 2007, nevertheless, the national unions of mine and steel workers chose Labor Day to announce their support of Democrat John Edwards as candidate for president in the 2008 election. A lingering memory associated Labor Day with organized labor.

Contentious politics took no holiday on Labor Day 2007 in the United States or elsewhere. Box 7-1 lists headlines of the day from the wire

175

Box 7-1: Contentious Politics on the Reuters and BBC Newswires, 3 September 2007

Dhaka	Ex–prime minister of Bangladesh Khaleda arrested on graft charge
Washington, DC	President Bush in Iraq on surprise visit, White House says
Basra	British (military forces) quit Basra city, Iraq
Kabul	Afghan Taliban vows to kidnap, kill more foreigners; one killed in Kabul airport blast; rebels killed in Afghan clashes
Kingston	Jamaicans go to the polls, wary over recent political violence
Kathmandu	Nepal police step up searches after bomb blasts
Khartoum	Sudan detains opposition lawyer for defaming police
Freetown	Sierra Leone presidential rivals agree not to use vigilantes as they urge an end to violent clashes
Kinshasa	"State of war" in eastern Congo; Congo troops sent to quell rebels
Buenos Aires	Hundreds of Argentines protest against a paper mill in Uruguay
Caracas	Venezuela frees twenty-seven Colombians arrested three years ago for plotting against President Hugo Chávez
Copenhagen	Danish police clash with youths
Brussels	Belgian Dutch speakers surround Brussels on mass bike ride
Beirut	Lebanese forces search for remnants of a militant group a day after it was routed from a Palestinian refugee camp
Colombo	Sri Lankan army "takes rebel base"

services of Reuters and the BBC. The headlines established the diversity of contentious performances across the world. They also recall that different sorts of regimes host characteristically different repertoires of contention. In Bangladesh, for example, we see a military regime arresting its opponent, former prime minister Begum Khaleda Zia, under conditions of emergency rule. In the United States, we watch an elected president Bush traveling to occupied Iraq in the company of Secretary of State Condoleezza Rice and Secretary of Defense Robert Gates, thus gesturing simultaneously to the American public, American troops in Iraq, and the beleaguered people of Iraq. Meanwhile British troops withdraw from the Iraqi city of Basra, where they had been exercising military control.

Afghanistan turns out to be even more of a killing ground than Iraq, with a resurgent Taliban and a clutch of semi-independent militias battling for control of their own territories. Nepal, Sudan, Sierra Leone, the Democratic Republic of the Congo, Lebanon, and Sri Lanka all deal with the remnants of civil war as their central governments try to wipe out pockets of armed opposition. In oil-rich and increasingly authoritarian Venezuela, by contrast, President Hugo Chávez makes a grand gesture toward Latin American solidarity by releasing from prison twenty-seven Colombians accused of joining an attempted 2004 coup against him. Two months later, New York's monitoring agency Freedom House includes Venezuela in what it calls a "growing pushback against democracy driven by authoritarian regimes" (Freedom House 2007f).

Placing the regimes of the 3 September 2007 news in the capacity-democracy space identifies further variations. Figure 7-1 presents my judgments of the regimes' locations in 2007. What correspondences can we detect between those locations and prevailing repertoires of contention? In the relatively democratic regimes of Jamaica, Argentina, Denmark, the United States, and Belgium, we witness different versions of the social movement repertoire. Jamaicans carry on electoral campaigns despite the constant risk that armed gangs will disrupt them, Argentines demonstrate more or less peacefully against the pollution they say will flow into their country from a Uruguayan paper mill, Danish police fight with youthful demonstrators who are protesting the closure of an improvised youth center by throwing stones and torching automobiles, and Belgian Dutch speakers devise a novel form of demonstration by surrounding francophone Brussels on a massive bicycle ride.

Although some violence occurs in the more democratic regimes, on the whole makers of claims in those regimes lack arms, and authorities manage to contain their performances without massive use of force. In the top (high-capacity) half of regime space, authorities wield force and either initiate or monitor closely those claim-making performances that occur. Unarmed civilians make up the vast bulk of contentious claims in high-capacity regimes. Below the mid-section, however, autonomous armed

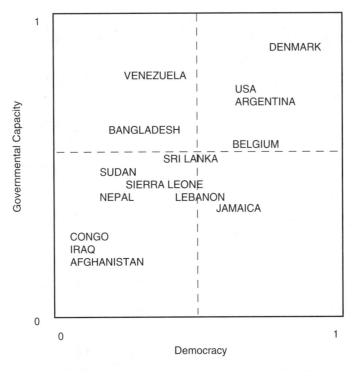

Figure 7-1 Capacity-Democracy Positions of Regimes in the News, 3 September
2007
Source: Compiled from Freedom House 2007b

groups play much larger parts in contention, frequently killing public
authorities or each other as they struggle. Congo, Iraq, and Afghanistan
mark the bottom, but Nepal, Lebanon, and Jamaica all have high rates of
collective violence. Because of weaker central control, they also experience
wider variability in the forms of claim making from time to time and place
to place than occurs in high-capacity regimes.

Chapter 6 worked out the correspondences between contentious performances and regime location for Ireland and Great Britain. This chapter
extends the demonstration by showing more generally that claim-making
performances vary and change systematically (if not perfectly) with regime
locations. The correspondence remains imperfect because a regime's
previous experience with contention and its relations to other regimes also
affect its prevailing repertoires. Yet very large differences in contentious
politics separate the four capacity-democracy quadrants: high-capacity

undemocratic, low-capacity undemocratic, low-capacity democratic, and high-capacity democratic. What is more, any move from quadrant to quadrant reshapes contention fundamentally. How and why are this chapter's questions.

The how and why have top-down and bottom-up versions. From the top, rulers are trying to impose arrays of prescribed, tolerated, and forbidden claim-making performances. On the average, undemocratic regimes prescribe more performances, tolerate fewer performances, and forbid more performances than democratic regimes. But low-capacity regimes lack the ability to enforce those prescriptions; as a result many contentious claims simply escape their control. On the democratic side, in general regimes prescribe few performances, tolerate a great many, but repress energetically those they forbid. Yet again, low-capacity democratic regimes ipso facto tolerate wide ranges of claim-making performances, experience greater variability in performances from time to time as well as from place to place, and are only partially successful in enforcing their interdictions against claims, claimants, and performances their rulers define as unacceptable.

Seen from the bottom, regime characteristics become political opportunity structure. Regime openness, coherence of the elite, stability of political alignments, availability of allies, repression and facilitation, and pace of change in those elements define opportunity and threat for potential claimants. But claimants' ability to take action also depends on available models of claim making (the contentious repertoire) and connections among claimants (the social bases of contention). Repertoires and social bases likewise vary dramatically, as we have seen, according to location within the capacity-democracy space. Even such closely connected regimes as those of 19th-century Ireland and Great Britain differed significantly in repertoires and social bases as well as in political opportunity structure.

Integrating top-down and bottom-up explanations clarifies connections between individual performances and whole regimes. State action sets limits (variable by type of regime) on the feasibility and likely outcomes of different performances that claimants are capable of mounting. Yet incrementally the array of performances that actually occur shapes and reshapes the regime. It does so by inciting facilitation or repression, by creating or breaking alliances between claimants and other actors, and by succeeding or failing in pressing direct demands for regime change. In Great Britain, we saw just such reshaping of the regime in the successive waves of mobilization over Test and Corporation repeal, Catholic Emancipation, and parliamentary reform. If we followed up the Labor Day headlines regime-by-regime in detail, we would find similar reshaping at work in Afghanistan, Lebanon, Argentina, Belgium, and all the other countries on our list.

Democracy, Capacity, and Contention

Annual ratings by New York–based Freedom House provide independent confirmation of my evaluations of the fifteen regimes in Figure 7-1 for democracy, if not for state capacity. Each year since 1972, Freedom House has published ratings for every recognized independent country in the world. It uses detailed questionnaires concerning regime performance and recruits replies to the questionnaires from experienced political analysts. Freedom House sums up its main expert judgments in two categories: political rights and civil liberties. In each category, the countries are rated on a scale from 1 (highly favorable) to 7 (highly unfavorable). Thus a 1,1 (high on both political rights and civil liberties) is the best rating any regime can receive, a 7,7, the worst.

Figure 7-2 graphs the Freedom House ratings for 2006 of the fifteen regimes that appeared in the contentious politics headlines on Labor Day 2007. Clearly regimes tend to fall along the diagonal, receiving similar scores on political rights and civil liberties. That fact surely stems in part from a halo effect (a rater who estimates political rights in a given regime as high or low is more likely to give the same regime a high or low rating for civil liberties, and vice versa) and in part from genuine causes (regime conditions push political rights and civil liberties in the same direction, political rights affect civil liberties, and civil liberties affect political rights). Yet the graph shows some off-diagonal placements: Congo rates even lower (6) on civil liberties than on political rights (5), and Jamaica similarly receives a lower rating for civil liberties (3) than for political rights (2). If we think of the combined ratings – that is, positions along the diagonal – as a rough approximation of democracy, however, the placements in that dimension resemble those proposed in Figure 7-1.

Comparing the two figures brings out the importance of state capacity: it matters for the character of contentious politics that Argentina and Jamaica, similar in extent of democracy, differ dramatically in capacity. The higher-capacity Argentine state, while not quite reaching the political control exercised by Denmark's government, intervenes much more

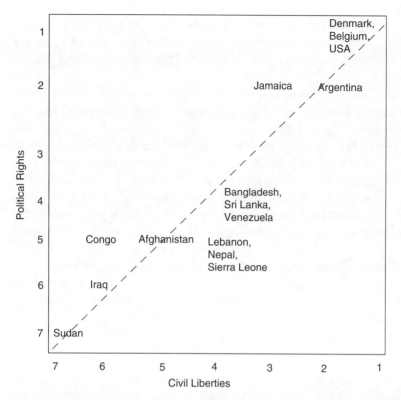

Figure 7-2 Freedom House Ratings of Selected Regimes on Political Rights and Civil Liberties, 2006
Source: Compiled from Freedom House 2007b

effectively in contentious politics than does the Jamaican regime (Tilly 2007: 4–6).

Rather than following all fifteen regimes, let us concentrate on one from each quadrant of the capacity-democracy space: Jamaica, Nepal, Bangladesh, and Denmark. The four occupy very different positions in the Freedom House ratings: 2,3 for Jamaica, 5,4 for Nepal, 4,4 for Bangladesh, but 1,1 for Denmark. According to my rougher estimates of state capacity, however, Denmark exercises much higher capacity than Jamaica, and Bangladesh considerably higher state capacity than Nepal. We can therefore compare reports of contentious politics in the four regimes for 2006 and 2007 to see whether they confirm my general claims about the effects of location within regime space: higher levels of violence, more autonomous actors wielding force, and less effective governmental intervention in the low-capacity-undemocratic quadrant (Nepal); more politics in the social movement form combined with significant autonomy for wielders of violence in the low-capacity-democratic quadrant (Jamaica); and so on.

Jamaica: low-capacity democratic. Jamaica attained independence from the United Kingdom in 1962. It continued as a parliamentary democracy in the British style (it still has a governor general appointed by the British monarch), but its central government never acquired effective power over its population's resources and activities. The Jamaican police often use violence on their own initiative without fear of prosecution or internal discipline; the Colombian cocaine trade thrives on the lucrative trade directed toward the United States; drug-running gangs (commonly called "posses") enjoy political patronage; partisan gang fights often break out during elections; frequent attacks on gays, lesbians, and HIV/AIDS victims go largely unpunished; the judicial system combines inefficiency with arbitrariness; and the country maintains one of the world's highest rates of homicide. In short, Jamaica typifies the popular politics of low-capacity democratic regimes.

In its annual survey of freedom in the world for 2006, Freedom House reported that the government of P. J. Patterson

confronted labor unrest and an increase in violent crime carried out largely by gangs operating a lucrative drug trade that was loosely tied to local party bosses. In 2000, Patterson promised to stanch Jamaica's "rampant criminality" by introducing new gun-control measures, creating a new police strike-force to target organized crime, and reinstating the death penalty. The pledges came after leaders of the vital tourism industry joined Jamaicans from all walks of life in demanding an end to the street crime, which had been spiraling upward over the previous two decades. The crime wave had crippled local businesses and spurred an exodus of middle-class Jamaicans from the island. (Freedom House 2007d: 1)

Despite all this, Jamaica maintains an active two-party system in which the opposition wields considerable influence and occasionally comes to power. In February 2006, Patterson's fellow People's National Party member Portia Simpson Miller won what the *Annual Register* called a "bruising and divisive campaign" and became the country's first female prime minister. She soon got her taste of taint: "In October, the government was accused of impropriety after accepting a US$470,000 donation from a Netherlands-based oil trader. Even though Simpson Miller denied any wrongdoing, the money was returned, and Information Minister Colin Campbell, who was at the centre of the scandal, resigned"

(*Annual Register* 2007: 150). The country's great deficit is not democracy but state capacity.

Nepal: low-capacity undemocratic. For two centuries, Nepal operated as a relatively high-capacity monarchy. Granting elections in 1959, King Mahendra faced a leftist victory and immediately reimposed authoritarian rule. In 1990, however, a communist coalition organized pro-democracy rallies that persuaded King Birendra to open the system up to political parties. (At about the same time, Bhutan and India expelled thousands of ethnic Nepalis into Nepal, where the government settled them in refugee camps that likewise became centers of anti-government mobilization.) In the ensuing party struggles, the state lost capacity massively as a Maoist party raised a widespread rural insurrection (1996).

The king sent his army to combat the insurrection in 2002, which escalated the violence. In 2005, King Gyanendra declared a state of emergency and tried to impose stringent controls over all politically relevant organizations. He used state security forces to suppress political demonstrations (Amnesty International 2007b). But he was unable to quell the Maoists.

Indeed, in 2005 the Maoists joined a coalition with other parties to oppose the government. In 2006, the coalition organized a very effective series of anti-government demonstrations, strikes, and clashes with security forces, a mobilization called the Jana Andolan, or People's Movement. Government forces killed eighteen people and injured something like 4 thousand in those protests. After repeated maneuvers, the king agreed to recall Parliament and reduce royal powers. The *Annual Register*'s report for 2006 described that moment as a minor revolution: "The year was one of great political turmoil and saw the effective side-lining of the monarchy in favour of a party-based government, which in turn reached out to the Maoist rebels and brought them into the fold, ending, at least for the time being, the civil war that had cost over 12,000 lives since 1996" (*Annual Register* 2007: 298).

An uneasy coalition between Maoists and non-Maoists came to power in 2007, but failed to establish control over Nepal's countryside. Although the Maoists officially abandoned their "people's war," they did not disband the shock troops of their Young Communist League (*Economist* 2007: 53). The coalition's draft bill for a Truth and Reconciliation Commission, furthermore, looked more like amnesty for political offenders on both sides than an effort to bring justice to victims (Human Rights Watch 2007d).

Unlike Jamaica, then, Nepal has recently emerged from years of open, fierce civil war. Its central government has not recovered effective power over the country as a whole. As Freedom House reported in 2007:

Both the government and the Maoists have been accused of an array of human rights violations in the context of the insurgency, which affected the entire country and has claimed nearly 13,000 lives since 1996. Prior to April 2006, the army and the poorly equipped police force were regularly implicated in extra-judicial killings, disappearances, arbitrary arrests and detentions, rapes, and the torture of suspected Maoists and their alleged supporters. The [National Human Rights Commission] recorded several thousand extrajudicial executions since 2001 and several hundred disappearances in each of the last few years, giving Nepal the highest number of recorded disappearances worldwide. Nevertheless, a March 2005 Human Rights Watch report detailing the phe-nomenon noted that the incidents may have been underreported. (Freedom House 2007e)

The army, furthermore, continued to resist any effort to make it help account for disappearances. It is as if Nepal cast a much larger shadow on the same dark side of contentious politics as Jamaica, but without any of Jamaica's redeeming democratic features. Conceivably a settlement among Nepal's warring factions will push the regime as a whole toward democracy. But the Katmandu bomb blasts reported in the Labor Day news warn us that Nepal has a long way to go before arriving at low-capacity democracy, much less becoming a high-capacity democratic state. The absence of effective state intervention in the bulk of contentious politics, the power of autonomous wielders of force, and the high levels of collective violence place Nepal squarely in the low-capacity-undemocratic quadrant of the capacity-democracy space.

Bangladesh: (relatively) high-capacity undemocratic. Bangladesh does not provide the perfect example of high-capacity non-democracy because state capacity stands at little more than medium. It also operates one of the world's most corrupt political and economic systems (Human Rights Watch 2007b: 5). Nevertheless, differences from Nepal immediately strike the eye. Far more so than Nepal, the Bangladeshi state simultaneously adopts, manipulates, and subverts the forms of elections and party politics. The government's most zealous opponents are not communists, but Islamists. Yet the two main parties, closely matched in electoral support, willingly make alliances with small Islamist groups.

Instead of exercising control over their own enclaves, opponents actively bid for central power both by participating in electoral politics and by attacking current holders of power. As Freedom House describes the situation:

Political power regularly changes hands, and elections are polarizing events that are competitive and bitterly fought. The winning side often sees little need to build consensus, while the losing side frequently resorts to boycotts, strikes, and demonstrations in order to achieve its aims. In recent years, political violence during demonstrations and general strikes has killed hundreds of people in major cities and injured thousands, and police often use excessive force against opposition protesters. Party leaders are also targeted; in September 2006, five [Awami League] leaders were beaten severely during street protests and sustained serious injuries. Local nongovernmental organizations (NGOs) reported that more than 300 people were killed and almost 9,000 were injured in politically motivated violence in 2005. Student wings of political parties continue to be embroiled in violent campus conflicts. (Freedom House 2007a: 3)

Human Rights Watch adds that elite police units committed hundreds of extrajudicial killings in 2006 (Human Rights Watch 2007b: 2).

Freedom House plausibly places Bangladesh well down its rankings of political rights and civil liberties at 4,4, the very midpoint of possible scores – a step ahead of Nepal and substantially more democratic than Afghanistan, Iraq, or Congo. But the striking difference from the low-capacity undemocratic regimes is the heavy involvement of Bangladeshi government forces, as agents or objects, in the country's varied forms of collective violence.

Unlike very high-capacity undemocratic China and Iran, however, the Bangladeshi state struggles furiously to maintain its control over public politics, and often fails. In 2007, for example, a caretaker government first declared a state of emergency, then announced a total ban on political activity before relenting partially under pressure from the major political parties (Human Rights Watch 2007c: 1). During the state of emergency, government authorities detained more than 250 thousand people (Human Rights Watch 2007a: 2).

Denmark: high-capacity democratic. Denmark does not lack contentious politics, as recent disputes over cartoons of Mohammed and more generally over rights of the country's small Muslim minority have shown. As Amnesty International reported the situation in 2007: "Concern mounted over worsening intolerance and xenophobia against refugees, asylum-seekers, minorities in general and Muslims in particular. The scope and breadth of new legislation with the stated aim of countering terrorism gave rise to concern about its impact on fundamental human rights" (Amnesty International 2007a: 1).

On 5 September, indeed, Danish police arrested eight Muslims on suspicion of planning a bomb attack, then released all but two almost immediately (Reuters, 5 September 2007). A month later: "there were fears of a new crisis in October, when video footage was circulated showing members of the right-wing Danish People's Party youth group holding a competition to draw caricatures of Mohammed at their summer camp. The prime minister intervened quickly to condemn the competition and the video" (*Annual Register* 2007: 55).

But terror and Muslims did not exhaust Denmark's contention. During 2006 and 2007, young people battled police in Copenhagen repeatedly over the closing of a youth collective (note our Labor Day headline on the subject). Nevertheless, successive coalition governments have ruled in relative peace since 1909. On the whole, Denmark displays all the familiar marks of social movement politics in high-capacity democratic regimes.

Incessant turbulence in Jamaica, post–civil war fragmentation in Nepal, constant confrontation in Bangladesh, and contained struggle in Denmark reflect the fundamental variation in the forms of contentious politics generated by different sorts of national regimes. Clearly the broad correspondences between repertoire and regime I sketched earlier hold for cross-sectional comparisons. In Ireland and Great Britain, we saw that the correspondence also appears in longitudinal comparisons: as regimes change, so do repertoires. Another look at change over time, nevertheless, will confirm the causal connections between regime change and repertoire change. Let us look at the rich, fascinating history of contention in Venezuela.

Venezuela's Regimes and Contention, 1905–2007

The history of Venezuela since 1900 documents the influence of changes in state capacity and democracy on public politics, including contentious performances. It shows us a regime that had long existed in the low-capacity undemocratic (hence high-violence) quadrant of the capacity-democracy space, but then switched onto what could have been a strong state path to democracy. The state's control over oil revenues made the difference. It also blocked full democratization and eventually drove the regime's trajectory toward high-capacity non-democracy.

Venezuela became a country independent of the Spanish Empire in several stages: as a rebellious province (1810), as part of Simón Bolívar's Gran Colombia (1819), then as a separate republic at Bolívar's death

(1830). Until the early 20th century Venezuela staged a familiar, dreary Latin American drama of military dictators, caudillos, coups, and occasional civilian rule. Large landlords never succeeded in establishing the armed entente that they achieved in major regions of Argentina and Brazil (Centeno 2002: 156). In 1908, however, a coup led by General Juan Vicente Gómez introduced a new era. Gómez ruled Venezuela for twenty-seven years, until his death in 1935. He built up a national army whose officers came largely from his own region of the Andes (Rouquié 1987: 195). He consolidated his rule by distributing large tracts of land to loyal clients (Collier and Collier 1991: 114). He escaped the constant turnover of earlier Venezuelan regimes.

Gómez lasted longer than his predecessors, at least in part, because Venezuela opened its oil fields in 1918. It soon became one of the world's major producers. Oil shifted the Venezuelan economy's pivot from coffee to energy and, eventually, energy-backed manufacturing as well. As we might expect, it also fortified the dictator's evasion of popular consent for his rule. During his entire tenure, Gómez blocked the formation of any mass popular organizations.

The move away from an agrarian economy, however, inevitably expanded the numbers of workers and students. They supplied recruits for a militant if relatively powerless opposition. At Gómez's death in 1935, Venezuelan elites banded together to create an elected presidency restricted to a single five-year term and simultaneously acted to ban left activists as Communists. The first elected president – another general from the Andes, Eleazar López Contreras – used a portion of the country's oil revenues to finance welfare programs that would buy popular support and shut out leftists.

The pattern continued long after 1935. True, from that point on those who took power in Venezuela – whether by election or by force – always declared they did so to forward democracy. Venezuela institutionalized general adult suffrage in 1947 and never quite rescinded it. The moderately social democratic party Acción Democrática, furthermore, did supply a vehicle for popular mobilization and support for organized labor (Collier and Collier 1991: 251–270). But oil revenues provided rulers with the means of avoiding mutually binding consultation of citizens. The military junta that governed Venezuela from 1948 to 1958 notably declared that it had seized power to reverse the threat to democracy posed by the previous populist-military government. It received support from the church, from heavily taxed foreign companies, and from traditional elites (Rouquié 1987: 196).

But the junta's leaders acted like military technocrats. They used expanding oil revenues to carry on ostentatious public works and welfare programs. The concentration of entrepreneurial and reform activity within Venezuela's state facilitated coordination among the leaders and made it easy to enlist the private sector in state-led programs (Hirschman 1979: 95–96). It also removed citizens at large from debates about economic development and welfare. Oil revenues insulated rulers from ruled.

Increasingly the ruling junta (led from 1954 by Colonel Marcos Pérez Jiménez, long a power behind the scenes) expanded those revenues by selling oil concessions to foreign companies, especially U.S. companies. In tune with American Cold War policy, it also justified itself increasingly as a U.S. ally and a bulwark against communism. Lulled by success, Pérez Jiménez radically narrowed the base of his domestic power, alienating even a substantial share of military officers. In 1958 a military coup, this time backed by significant popular support, drove the junta from power. The golpistas and their civilian allies quickly called for democratic elections, which brought civilian Rómulo Betancourt to the presidency. Betancourt's accession led many observers to think that Venezuela had finally entered the track to democracy.

In fact, the military never strayed far from the seats of power. After 1958, nevertheless, Venezuela lived mostly under civilian rule. The military only intervened directly in national politics one more time: in 1992, a failed pair of coups brought a future president, Lieutenant Colonel Hugo Chávez Frías, into public view. Two elite political parties, one moderately social democratic, the other moderately Christian democratic, alternated uneasily in power. Writing in 1993, Michael Coppedge declared, however, that party rule (especially as coupled with a strong presidential system) actually set severe limits on democracy:

In Venezuela, political parties monopolize the electoral process, dominate the legislative process, and penetrate politically relevant organizations to a degree that violates the spirit of democracy. The sad consequence is that many of the informal channels of representation that are taken for granted in other democracies, such as interest groups, the media, the courts, and independent opinion leaders, are blocked by extreme party domination. Without effective channels for the representation of their interests between elections, citizens become disenchanted with the parties and with the democratic regime. (Coppedge 1994: 2)

Thus presidents working with or against the two parties dominated the rhythms of Venezuelan public politics. Popular voice remained secondary. Exclusion or patronage became the rule for dealing with potential opponents. Officeholders could make strong decisions without fear of effective popular opposition. Without much public consultation, for example, Venezuela became an active organizer of the Organization of Petroleum Exporting States, the cartel OPEC. It also used oil revenues to launch an ambitious, if ultimately ill-fated, campaign to make Venezuela a major automobile producer.

After OPEC septupled oil's price in 1973, President Carlos Andres Pérez expanded the public works programs of earlier regimes. He also nationalized the oil industry (1975) while borrowing internationally against future oil revenues; that foreign debt, including pressure from the International Monetary Fund (IMF), would bedevil Venezuelan governments for two decades. Although a few Venezuelans grew very rich, for the population at large the standard of living declined dramatically from the 1970s onward.

During his second presidential term (1988–1993), Pérez paid the price. Pérez had campaigned for the presidency on a program of public works and price containment, but after election he quickly changed direction under pressure from domestic and international financiers. In 1989, Pérez announced an austerity plan that included cutbacks in governmental expenditure and rising prices for public services. Implementation of the plan soon incited widespread popular resistance.

Caracas's violence of February–March 1989, for example, began with confrontations between commuters, on one side, and, on the other, drivers of public transportation who were charging the new prices. It soon spiraled into sacking and looting of downtown stores. In Caracas, three hundred people died and more than 2 thousand were wounded as the army moved in to clear the streets. During the first two weeks of March, sixteen Venezuelan cities exploded in similar events. The confrontations gained fame as "El Caracazo" (the Events of Caracas) or "El Sacudón" (the Shock). They opened a decade of struggle and regime change.

Chávez and the Bolivarians

Contention did not come only from the streets: during the early 1980s, a group of nationalist army officers organized a secret network called the Revolutionary Bolivarian Movement. Paratroop officer Hugo Chávez became their leader. In 1992, the Bolivarians almost seized power in a military coup whose failure sent Chávez to prison. He was still in jail when another more senior group of officers tried to seize power a few months later. They captured a TV station and broadcast a video. To the coup leaders' consternation, a Chávez supporter had substituted his own video, in which Chávez announced the government's fall, for the junta's announcement. For that media appearance, Chávez spent another two years in prison.

In 1993, while Chávez languished behind bars, the Venezuelan congress impeached President Carlos Andrés Pérez for corruption and removed him from office. But Pérez's successor, Rafael Caldera, soon faced a collapse of the country's banks, a surge of violent crime, rumors of new military coups, and his own charges of corruption. As Chávez left prison and entered politics, popular demands for political housecleaning swelled. Ex-convict Chávez ran for president.

Chávez billed himself as a populist and won by a large majority. As Chávez came to power in 1999, street confrontations between his supporters and his opponents accelerated. The new president's state visit to Fidel Castro's officially socialist Cuba later the same year dramatized his plan to transform the government and its place in the world at large. He renamed his country the Bolivarian Republic of Venezuela. He also began squeezing the state oil company, Petróleos de Venezuela, for more of its revenues and chipped away at its fabled autonomy. Venezuela moved into a new stage of struggle over the country's future. Chávez defined that future as Bolivarian democracy.

When Chávez addressed a June 2000 meeting of the Andean Community in Lima, Peru, he denied that pre-Chávez Venezuela had been democratic. He announced his own version of democracy:

We in Venezuela have had the idea – maybe a daring one – of referring to a Bolivarian democracy; we have taken up Bolivarian thinking to try to direct our people and to try to sow that awareness and to build that new model. Bolívar, for example, on February 15, 1819 at the Congress of Angostura (there the idea of Colombia was born) stated in his speech that the most perfect system of government is that which gives the people the greatest amount of social security, the greatest amount of political stability, and the greatest amount of happiness possible. (Chávez 2000: 3)

Chávez added that Bolivarian democracy promoted political equality and established a "happy balance" between extreme freedom, at one extreme, and autocracy, at the other. In short, he described a familiar Latin American program of top-down populism. In contrast to the Western models of democracy that he vigorously rejected, the program offered plenty of elections, but otherwise made little provision for popular consultation and consent with respect to the means of rule. It followed Bolívar, furthermore, in featuring rebellion against foreign domination, now especially that of the United States.

Over the next eight years, Chávez used his control over oil revenues to consolidate his power, to cramp his opposition, to sponsor populism elsewhere in Latin America, and even to hold off an increasingly hostile United States. He survived a coup in 2002, concerted resistance from the national oil company in 2002–2003, a general strike during the same period, and a U.S.-supported recall referendum in 2004. Step-by-step he responded with tightened repression. A Chávez-dominated legislature packed the Supreme Court, broadened prohibitions on insulting or showing disrespect for the president, and stepped up surveillance of mass media. Meanwhile, the courts prosecuted increasing numbers of regime opponents.

Chávez enjoyed substantial support among Venezuela's numerous poor. But, like heads of rentier states elsewhere, he was relying on his country's oil-generated wealth to bypass resistance to his means of rule. In 2006, the government took control over seven oil fields previously operated by foreign companies and increased royalties paid by the remaining foreign firms from one sixth to one third of their sales. Echoing his 2000 speech to the Andean Community, in 2006 Chávez told a sympathetic interviewer that "we are building a true democracy, with human rights for everyone, social rights, education, health care, pensions, social security, and jobs" (Palast 2006: 2). He did not mention rights to opposition and consent.

That was not happening, of course, for the first time. Figure 7-3 traces Venezuela's zigzag trajectory since 1900. The country entered the 20th century after seven decades as a low-capacity undemocratic regime, with its weak state repeatedly taken over by military officers. Under the Gómez dictatorship, the 1918 opening of Venezuelan oil fields started a spectacular augmentation of state capacity. Those new means of top-down control permitted Gómez to de-democratize an already undemocratic regime. After Gómez' death in 1935, the Venezuelan oligarchy managed modest democratization while continuing to draw on oil wealth to build up state capacity.

The 1948 coup quickly de-democratized the regime, bringing it almost back to its undemocratic condition at Gómez's disappearance. Then a succession of interventionist governments continued to build state capacity while promoting another modest phase of democratization. Despite

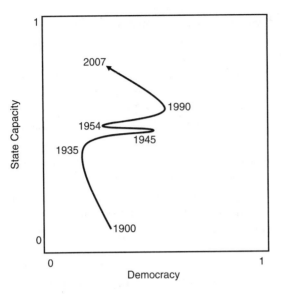

Figure 7-3 Venezuelan Regimes, 1900–2007

arriving as a fierce self-described populist, Chávez continued one trend and reversed the other: at the expense of democracy, he formed the highest-capacity state Venezuela had ever produced. Throughout the entire period from 1900 to 2007, Venezuela barely ever edged into democratic territory. But, fed by oil, it grew into an impressively high-capacity state.

Along with all other independent regimes, Freedom House has rated Venezuela's democracy or non-democracy annually since 1972. Figure 7-4 traces Venezuela's ratings from 1972 to 2007. It shows more than one loop, but an overall decline in political rights and civil liberties. Venezuela never reached either 1,1 or 7,7, but it did move mightily within the two-dimensional rating system. It reached its most favorable rating (1 on political rights, 2 on civil liberties) under President Carlos Andres Pérez in 1976 and maintained that high level to 1986. That rating put Venezuela in the company of such democratic stalwarts as France and Ireland, with civil liberties slightly compromised by their treatment of minorities. The scores plunged to lows of 4,4 in 1999 (the year of Chavez's accession to the presidency) and again in 2006–2007 (as Chávez tightened his grip on executive power).

In short, from what began to look like a democratizing country during the 1970s' burst of oil wealth, Venezuela has regressed irregularly toward fewer political rights and civil liberties – in our terms, it has

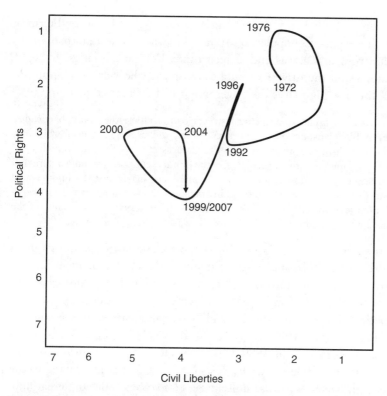

Figure 7-4 Venezuela's Freedom House Ratings, 1972–2007
Source: Compiled from Freedom House 2002, 2007b

de-democratized. At the same time, Venezuelan state capacity has continued to climb. A high-capacity undemocratic regime has emerged. As we might expect, prevailing contentious performances have changed accordingly.

Unfortunately for our purposes, no one has cataloged Venezuelan contention over the entire period from 1972 to 2007. But Margarita López-Maya and her collaborators have done classified event counts of what they define as "protests" in the country as a whole from 1985 through 1999, as well as doing close studies of contention in Caracas during 1999 (López-Maya 1999, 2002, López-Maya, Smilde, and Stephany 2002). Those years take us from the final years of President Jaime Lusinchi through the second presidential term of Carlos Andrés Pérez (1989 to his impeachment in 1993), across the term of the beleaguered Rafael Caldera, to the electoral campaign of Hugo Chávez (1998), and into his arrival as president (1999).

As Pérez adopted austerity measures at the start of his second term in 1989, the extensive popular resistance known as the Caracazo or El Sacudón rose in Caracas and sixteen other Venezuelan cities. It began with attacks on the drivers of public transport, who were attempting to collect the new high fares the government had decreed. But soon

great crowds occupied some central streets of the cities; they built barricades, burning public transport buses, private vehicles, and tires. [They also broke into and looted high-priced shops.] At first the Caracas metropolitan police, who had not been paid for a month, participated in the popular euphoria, helping assure that sacking occurred in good order. People shouted slogans against the high cost of living in general, against the increase in transport fares, and against the government's bundle of austerity measures. Sometimes the attacks followed singing of the national anthem, and in various places people waved flags. (López-Maya 1999: 220)

In their event catalog, López-Maya and collaborators identify six main categories of performances: street marches, blockades of main streets, occupations and invasions of public spaces or buildings, "disturbances" (violent street confrontations between demonstrators, especially students, and police), burning of vehicles and (most often) tires, and sacking of stores (López-Maya 1999: 224–231, 2002: 208–213). López-Maya points out that Venezuelans of 1989 also experimented with shutting out all lights to protest rising electricity costs (*apagones de luz*), and taking to the streets with pots and pans as noisemakers (*cacerolazos*). But the great bulk of public contestation from 1985 through 1999 took the form of marches, blockades, occupations, disturbances, fires, and sacking. Venezuelans had clearly established their own distinctive repertoire of contention.

Figure 7-5 traces fluctuations in the six main performances from 1985 through 1999. It shows clearly that all forms of public claim making rose in the Caracazo year of 1989 and that overall frequencies increased again after 1991, declined during the Caldera years of the later 1990s, but revived rapidly in 1999, as partisans and enemies of Hugo Chávez battled over the presidential succession and Chávez's rapid implementation of his populist programs. We can regret that López-Maya and collaborators have not yet extended their event catalog beyond 1999. Yet we can be sure that contention did not cease as Chávez consolidated his power. On the contrary, the coup of 2002, the general strike of 2002–2003, and the recall referendum of 2004 all signaled the energy of a threatened opposition.

Nevertheless, defeated opposition forces then largely withdrew from Venezuela's electoral politics, claiming that the *chavista* electoral

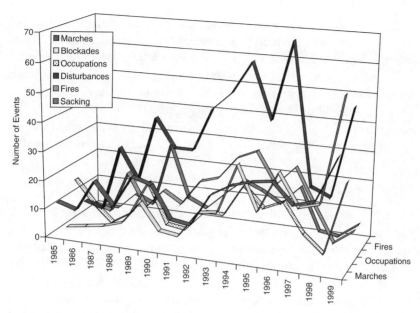

Figure 7-5 Protest Events in Venezuela, 1985–1999
Source: Prepared from table 2 in López-Maya, Smilde, and Stephany 2002: 18, and originally drawn from reports in the newspaper *El Nacional*

authorities would discriminate against them. Less than 30 percent of the adult population has voted in recent elections. After Chávez's 2006 re-election with 62 percent of the vote, he recast the *chavista* political vehicle as the United Socialist Party of Venezuela. Venezuela's middle classes remained largely in opposition, but their massive withdrawal from electoral politics reduced their impact on government performance even further.

The government has outlawed many of the claim-making performances documented by López-Maya for the previous decade, for example, by attaching eight-year prison terms to conviction for road blockades (Freedom House 2006a: 5–6). It has also monitored and intervened in all forms of contention more actively and effectively than previous regimes, even the military regimes of the 1950s. It co-opted and repressed contentious politics. The scattered evidence available indicates that co-optation and repression have worked. By 2007 Chávez had cowed his main opposition within Venezuela. Increasingly public politics followed the forms prescribed and subsidized by the regime.

By then, collective claim making, including its violent forms, had largely moved to Venezuela's periphery. According to Human Rights Watch, rural landlords were hiring contract killers, paramilitaries, and police to attack peasants who were occupying terrain allotted to them under Chávez's land reforms, and kidnappings were occurring frequently near the Colombian border (Human Rights Watch 2007e). With the exception of the periphery, Venezuelan contentious politics had moved into the characteristic patterns of high-capacity undemocratic regimes.

Other Sorts of Regimes

Even in increasingly authoritarian Venezuela, then, some parts of the national territory are escaping central control. For the most part, the analyses in this book have assumed relatively unitary regimes and argued that they produce relatively unitary repertoires. Now I must underline the "relatively." In Mexico, the Zapatistas demonstrated that the southern state of Chiapas escaped in part from central control and produced its own distinct forms of contentious politics. In passing, we have witnessed similar segmentation between northern and southern Ireland, among the republics of the disintegrating Soviet Union, and within most of the fifteen regimes with which this chapter began. Looked at closely, all regimes turn out to be composite, although in variable degrees (Tilly and Tarrow 2006: chapter 8). Contentious performances therefore vary by region and social segment within regimes.

Although national states remain the dominant political organizations in the contemporary world, furthermore, international regimes also form. They influence contentious repertoires. International structures of power that shape contention are nothing new, as a little reflection on the history of empires will reveal. Within Europe alone, the Holy Roman Empire, the Ottoman Empire, the Habsburg Empire, the Austro-Hungarian Empire, and the Papacy at their apogees all exercised great power over individual states. The European Union does not yet wield influence over its member states comparable to that of the Ottoman Empire in its central region at its height, but it certainly creates a political opportunity structure at least as potent as the POS attached to many individual states. In addition, other international institutions such as the United Nations, NATO, the World Bank, and the International Monetary Fund connect with existing states and national actors to create quasi-regimes within which people struggle over issues crossing national borders (Tarrow 2005: chapter 11).

To some extent, such connections mean that domestic claimants facing relatively closed POS at home can appeal to external allies either for direct intervention in their domestic situations or for pressure on their national governments to intervene on behalf of the domestic claimants. Partially successful international campaigns for debt forgiveness in poor countries have followed that pattern (Sikkink 2005: 160). The startling international support system that grew up around Mexico's Zapatistas demonstrates that similar external interventions also occur at a regional level (Olesen 2005). At both the sub-national and the supra-national levels, then, regimes that influence contention wax and wane.

We must tread this treacherous ground cautiously. We need caution for two reasons. First, even where similar claims appear in separate regimes, political and technical barriers to diffusion and brokerage often block collaboration (Hertel 2006). Second, despite Internet coordination of transnational campaigns, the politics of national regimes continues to dominate contentious politics throughout much of the world. When Doug Imig and Sidney Tarrow constructed a catalog of contentious events in the European Union from 1984 through 1997, less than 5 percent of the total took up EU issues and targeted actors outside their own country (Imig and Tarrow 2001). Moreover, Imig, Tarrow, and their collaborators found that "Europrotesters" used essentially the same claim-making performances as their neighbors who were pursuing strictly local or national issues.

Yet the Imig-Tarrow data also show an uptick in European issues and actors during the later 1990s:

Europeans are beginning to recognize more and more that the sources of many of their claims – especially occupational ones – are increasingly found in Europe's integrated market and institutions. And in some cases, they are beginning to organize themselves transnationally. But while business associations have found it relatively easy to influence European decision-making in Brussels, weaker social actors continue to face imposing transaction costs when they attempt to organize across borders. Thus they continue to rely on mainly domestic resources and opportunities to target national decision-makers when they seek redress for their claims against European policies. (Tarrow 2001: 237)

At that point (1997), the transnational mobilizations that Anglophones often call anti-globalization and that Francophones often call *altermondialisme* – another world-ism, with the implication that another, better world is possible if only activists get together – had not attracted the attention that demonstrations at the 1999 Seattle meeting of the

World Trade Organization and later counter-summits would bring them. Since then, world-spanning networks of activists have regularly replied to international financial meetings by organizing large, showy displays of other-worldism (Agrikoliansky, Fillieule, and Mayer 2005, Agrikoliansky and Sommier 2005, della Porta, Andretta, Mosca, and Reiter 2006, Wood 2004). Counter-summits have the largest claim to constitute a new performance distinct from the demonstrations, public meetings, petition drives, press releases, and associational initiatives that became prevalent with the national-level social movement a century and a half ago.

It is at least possible, then, that two momentous changes are occurring: first, creation of new sorts of regimes – sub-national, transnational, and supra-national – that will shape their own patterns of contentious politics; second, emergence of new arrays of contentious performances – new repertoires – that will compete with the repertoires this book has surveyed. Both changes call for comprehensive research programs that students of transnational politics have only begun. We should, however, continue to bet on the argument that has underlain this chapter. We should bet that variation and change in state capacity and degree of democracy at the national scale will continue to exert profound effects on the character of collective contention, regime-by-regime.

Such an interpretation assumes, to be sure, that this book's arguments and findings apply to contentious politics whenever and wherever people contend. Contention takes place in learned performances, runs the argument. It responds and corresponds closely to the regime's character, varies and changes with political opportunity structure, depends on the availability of models for claim making, and builds on existing relations among potential claimants, the argument continues. Chapter after chapter, this book has built that argument and displayed ample evidence to support it.

Skeptics may nevertheless offer two other readings of what the book has offered. First, it could be that the book's framework applies reasonably well to a world in which states remain the dominant organizations within their territories, but not to a weak-state, stateless, or mixed-hegemony world. In that case, the argument's scope would at best encompass the last few centuries of human experience, especially in the Far East and the West. Certainly I have drawn my evidence disproportionately from that experience. It could therefore be that students of contentious politics both outside that experience and in the future can infer no more than interesting hypotheses from the book's analyses.

Second, the book could underestimate the influence of changing organizational technologies on the character of contention and thus underestimate the extent to which contentious politics is now moving away from the apparatus of special-purpose organizations toward flexibly connected transnational networks of activists. After all, Lance Bennett has claimed that

it goes without saying that various technologies greatly magnify the capacity of organizers to reach people and to continue to reach them for future actions. But more than amplifying the mobilizing capacities of organizations, applications of social technologies are beginning to transform organizational forms. For example, the transnational protest network that produced and coordinated dozens of demonstrations around the world at the time of the Seattle WTO event was not an organization at all, in any conventional sense of the term. It was more a meta-organization, or, better, a hyper-organization that existed mainly in the form of the website, e-mail traffic, and linked sites noted above. Such hyper-organizations have now become familiar in transnational and other protest networks. (Bennett 2005: 218)

Bennett directs these remarks toward current changes in the dynamics of transnational mobilizations. But they raise a larger possibility. I am acutely aware that seemingly solid political actors actually consist of fluctuating networks and result from continuous negotiation among political participants; I've even published two whole books on the relevant social processes (Tilly 2002b, 2005a). Yet this book's analyses have proceeded as if organizations, craft groups, and local populations existed and possessed collective interests prior to the contentious performances they carried on.

To the extent that actor constitution, employment of coordinating technologies, and making of claims occur simultaneously and influence each other as they occur, however, this book's arguments may grossly understate the impact of actor and communication processes on performances. Let me shrug my shoulders and mouth a comforting platitude: a book that raises no new unresolved questions is hardly worth writing ... or reading!

8

Conclusions

In the noisy, smelly, turbulent, visually vibrant London of the 1760s, John Wilkes's supporters had no idea that they were helping to create the social movement. As they marched, rallied, and petitioned, however, they knew that they and their hero were pushing the limits of available contentious performances. They centered their claims on public officials, London electors, and Parliament. To that extent they broke with Britain's prevailing parochial, particular, and bifurcated 18th-century repertoire of contention. In comfortable retrospect, we 21st-century observers can think of them as pointing toward the combination of campaigns, performances, and WUNC displays (public enactments of worthiness, unity, numbers, and commitment) we call the social movement. We can therefore conclude that they were helping craft cosmopolitan, autonomous, and modular repertoires. From their own perspective, however, they were opposing tyranny and asserting their collective rights. Our analysis is retrospective; theirs was prospective.

The tension between retrospective and prospective analysis drives this book. On one side, we seek retrospectively to explain how changes in performances and repertoires occur. Chapter 4, for instance, used a comparison of London's Wilkes and Gordon mobilizations (1768 and 1780) to show how the outcome of one campaign affects the shape of the next campaign. On the other side, we seek prospectively to show how previously existing performances and repertoires shape the ways that people make collective contentious claims. The start of Chapter 2, for example, invoked Mark Beissinger's analysis of the Soviet Union's collapse to show that under Mikhail Gorbachev's government of the late 1980s the street demonstration became available as a standard way of making claims for the autonomy or independence of the USSR's titular nationalities.

How can we resolve the tension? We can do so dialectically, by confronting and synthesizing the two perspectives. Here is how the synthesis works:

Decompose contentious episodes into particular interactions.
Detect the sets of interactions that comprise different sorts of episodes.
Identify the learned performances that group certain episodes together.
See how performances cluster within repertoires and campaigns.
Watch how one campaign affects the next.
Then analyze how incremental change from campaign to campaign
    compounds into larger-scale repertoire change.

Following these routines, the book returned again and again to the contentious politics of Great Britain from the 1750s to the 1830s. Yet its subject is not Great Britain, but contentious politics. My research group carefully assembled a large body of evidence on contentious gatherings in 18th- and 19th-century Britain. The evidence includes close observations not just of contentious episodes as wholes but also of individual actions and interactions within episodes. We can therefore use the evidence as a sort of laboratory for the scrutiny of much more general arguments concerning the ebb and flow of contention. Box 8-1 summarizes the general arguments that organize the book.

The arguments run from ontological to methodological to substantive, with a whiff of epistemology as well. Ontologically, they declare that performances and repertoires really exist, rather than consisting simply of useful metaphors; participants in contentious politics learn, follow, and innovate within rough scripts for claim making. Methodologically, they insist that descriptions of interactions within episodes and well-ordered catalogs of episodes greatly facilitate the discovery of contention's systematic properties. Substantively, they propose that top-down actions of regimes and bottom-up interactions of campaigns produce transformations of performances and repertoires. The whiff of epistemology arrives with the claim that event catalogs, for all their obvious simplifications, provide reliable ways of observing the dynamics of contention. Let us go through Box 8-1's principles one by one.

Contentious performances consist of individual actions and interactions; they compound into repertoires, each characterizing some set of political relations.
    The book describes performances in four ways: 1) in narratives of individual episodes, interpreted as performances (e.g., Venezuela's Caracazo

Box 8-1: This Book's Organizing Arguments

- Contentious performances consist of individual actions and interactions; they compound into repertoires, each characterizing some set of political relations.
- In contentious politics, strategizing, learning, and change occur especially at the level of performances rather than at the levels of actions, interactions, or whole repertoires.
- Within contentious politics, performances generally fall into strong repertoires that significantly constrain the choices of potential claim makers.
- Performances and repertoires are causally coherent (similar causes operate over a wide range of instances) and symbolically coherent (once existing, they acquire meanings that facilitate emulation and innovation).
- Systematic study of performances requires close description of interaction among participants rather than simple identification and counting of whole episodes.
- Detailed event catalogs promote systematic study of contention because they allow comparisons among episodes and help identify connections among them.
- Evolution of performances and repertoires occurs especially through campaigns consisting of multiple performances in which interacting alterations of political opportunity structure, models of action, and connections among claimants link one campaign to the next.
- Large repertoire changes, including the emergence of the social movement, therefore occur incrementally rather than in sudden bursts.
- National regimes strongly shape available performances and repertoires through top-down controls over claim making mediated by political opportunity structure.
- But from the bottom up, claim making itself then alters regimes.

uprising of 1989), 2) in summary descriptions of repertoires, either with abstract characteristics or lists of performances (e.g., for Venezuela from 1989 to 1999), 3) by breaking down narratives into subject-object-verb sequences (e.g., in the London gatherings of 1768 and 1834 episodes that opened Chapter 1), and 4) by abstracting actions and interactions from formal accounts, for example, by looking closely at the relations among actors identified by bargaining, as opposed to meeting or supporting, as in Chapter 5's dissection of London gatherings during 1820.

Seen as performances, such routines as food seizures and public meetings have recognizable beginnings, internal sequences, ends, and settings. They involve distinctive sets of players and audiences: participants in local markets who assemble at those markets in food seizures, local residents or adherents to a cause who assemble in a public field or a private hall in public meetings, and so on.

Some performances remain simple and predictable, especially when the object of claims – Parliament, the president, a political hero – is absent. Much of the time, however, the action pits actors against each other, as when strikers battle strikebreakers and customs officers battle smugglers. In these cases, however, the multiple participants typically know and follow available scripts as they struggle. The donkeyed worker knows the routine of donkeying all too well.

By drawing especially on systematic event catalogs, I must admit, the book has obscured one difficult problem in the analysis of performances. An episode in which people assemble, somehow make claims, and then disperse does not necessarily correspond exactly to a performance. That for two reasons: first because people sometimes combine two performances in one outing, as when they meet before marching, second because another party such as troops or opponents sometimes interrupts a performance and converts it into a battle or a rout. The common practice of labeling the episodes in event catalogs by their most visible interactions is understandable, but it exaggerates the correspondence between episode and performance. Nevertheless, the British data establish that close descriptions of contentious events make it feasible, with significant effort, to relate performances coherently to episodes. And in fact the great bulk of contentious episodes do center on a single performance.

In contentious politics, strategizing, learning, and change occur especially at the level of performances rather than at the levels of actions, interactions, or whole repertoires.

The evidence assembled in this book rarely gives us direct information on participants' strategizing and learning. More generally, by concentrating on episodes of collective claim making, the approach I have advocated throughout the book draws attention away from what happens between contentious episodes: alterations in connections among potential claimants, telling experiences among those potential claimants outside of public contention, organizing efforts by political entrepreneurs, and deliberate but secret planning of participation in contention. Narratives of contentious episodes do, however, reveal the outcomes of those intervening processes. Comparisons among successive episodes can therefore make two great contributions: they signal what the intervening processes should explain, and they permit coherent connections with continuous histories of localities, groups, and activist networks.

Within contentious politics, performances generally fall into strong repertoires that significantly constrain the choices of potential claim makers.

Repertoires array two or more performances that characterize some set of political relations, from the small scale of relations between agricultural laborers and the farmers who hire them to the large scale of relations between authorized groups of citizens and national rulers. By concentrating on more frequent performances and grouping similar performances together, this book has tilted its observations toward the larger scale. Yet it has provided enough narratives of individual episodes to convey the flavor of contention at the small scale. Has it established beyond doubt that strong repertoires prevail in contentious politics? No, it has not.

Here are the criteria for strong repertoires:

- In particular times and places, performances cluster into a limited number of recurrent, well-defined types. From beginning to end, the book has demonstrated that clustering.
- Within the range defined by all contentious actions that a given set of actors carry on, substantial blanks appear; combinations of actions clearly lying within the technical reach of participants never occur. As a result, performance types have visible boundaries rather than distributing continuously over the space of technically possible performances. If we look at whole repertoires, we repeatedly discover not only that technically possible acts are missing, but also that the same people engage in very different forms of claim making depending on the political relation at hand. The same people cheer the king and sack the houses of miscreants.

- For a given set of actors and issues, those performances change relatively little from one round of action to the next; what happens in one round of action, furthermore, detectibly constrains what happens in the next round. Chapter 4, "From Campaign to Campaign," makes this book's most serious effort to establish this combination of continuity and constraint.
- Participants in contention give evidence that they are aware of those performances by giving names to them, referring to previous actions of the same kind, giving each other instructions, adopting divisions of labor that require prior consultation or experience, anticipating each other's actions, and/or terminating actions more or less simultaneously. The interactions of organizers, participants, authorities, and observers in social movements make that awareness of relevant performances crystal clear.
- Within a set of connected actors, each significant pair of actors has its own repertoire. In the pair, claim-making actors make choices within the existing repertoire. The book has illustrated, but not conclusively demonstrated, the matching of repertoires with pairs of political actors, for example, craft workers and masters or citizens and legislators.
- The more connected the histories of actors outside of contention, the more similar their repertoires. Hence a process of increasing connection tends to homogenize performances – that is, make them more modular. Again, the book has illustrated the point, but, for lack of continuous histories outside of contention, it falls far short of proving it.
- New performances arise chiefly through innovation within existing performances, but tend to crystallize, stabilize, and acquire visible boundaries once they exist. We have witnessed this sort of innovation and crystallization repeatedly, especially in the emergence of the social movement repertoire from previous arrays of performances. Not all performances mutate, however: food seizures, for example, simply faded away. To some extent, meetings about prices and dearth replaced them. But the models for meetings came from elsewhere.

Let me conclude prudently that the book has failed to make the definitive case for strong repertoires, but has at least strengthened the hypothesis and clarified what sort of additional testing it calls for.

Performances and repertoires are causally coherent (similar causes operate over a wide range of instances) and symbolically coherent (once existing, they acquire meanings that facilitate emulation and innovation).

The book as a whole has built up and applied an explanatory scheme for a wide range of performances, repertoires, and settings from the disintegration of the Soviet Union to the election of Hugo Chávez as president of Venezuela. Readers must judge for themselves how successfully the evidence presented has made the case for that explanatory scheme. But if the scheme works reasonably well, it also supports the claim of causal coherence. As for symbolic coherence, the book's narratives certainly convey the sense that, in setting after setting, participants in contentious politics readily distinguished one performance from another, gave them names, called up precedents, and prepared their actions in the light of previous similar actions. In the Queen Caroline affair of 1820, for example, we witness a spectacular evocation of known models for the expression of collective support.

Systematic study of performances requires close description of interaction among participants rather than simple identification and counting of whole episodes.

Students of contention have often made stark choices between epidemiology and narrative. At the epidemiological extreme, they have analyzed counts of contentious events such as strikes or violent attacks by examining change and variation in their social locations. At the narrative extreme, they have reconstructed single events as one action or interaction after another. This book has identified a middle ground between epidemiology and narrative. The middle ground contains close descriptions of successive interactions within contentious episodes. From the middle ground we can move in three directions: back toward epidemiology by using the interactions to reclassify the events, back toward narrative by reconstructing episodes as sequences of interactions, and toward analytic sequences transcending any particular episode, but identifying recurrent actions and relations. At one point or another, the book has done all three.

In the third vein, I have repeatedly aggregated verb categories – "attack," "control," "end," "meet," "move," "bargain," "support," and "other" – when comparing sets of episodes and have then shown which sets of relations among claimants and objects of claims prevailed within different verb categories. However, I have also tried to locate those analyses in specific historical contexts by offering accounts of campaigns such as the Queen Caroline affair, Catholic Emancipation, and Venezuela's Sacudón of 1989.

Detailed event catalogs promote systematic study of contention because they allow comparisons among episodes and help identify connections among them.

As we have now abundantly seen, detailed event catalogs range from relatively simple event counts in the style of Gerhard Botz on Austria 1918–1938 to the sophisticated subject-verb-object accounts of Roberto Franzosi on Italy 1919–1922. By drawing extensively on evidence from my own studies of Great Britain, I have tipped the book's balance toward event catalogs that specify sequences of interactions within episodes. But the simpler event counts of Mark Beissinger on the Soviet Union and Susan Olzak on ethnic conflicts across the world show how much intelligent analysts can tell us about contentious politics when they handle their crisp classifications well.

To tell the truth, compilers of event catalogs have created three excellent models of analysis, quite different in technique and texture. In the style of Marc Steinberg, some have created catalogs to define what they must explain, but have then plunged deep into the events and their contexts to produce historically rich analytical narratives. When it comes to reconstructing deliberation and meaning, this first approach has great advantages. Others, in the style of Mark Beissinger, have created relatively simple uniform descriptions of their events, but then have undertaken sophisticated treatments of variation in time and space based on extensive data concerning contexts. When it comes to arguments about regularities in change and variation of contention, this second approach has its own distinct advantages. The third approach, illustrated by Roberto Franzosi, Sidney Tarrow, Takeshi Wada, and GBS, decomposes cataloged events into their elements in order to look systematically at their dynamics. At length, this book has displayed the advantages of that approach.

Evolution of performances and repertoires occurs especially through campaigns in which interacting alterations of political opportunity structure (POS), models of action, and connections among claimants link one campaign to the next.

Chapter 4 ("From Campaign to Campaign") made this case most systematically, but then Chapter 5 ("Invention of the Social Movement"), Chapter 6 ("Repertoires and Regimes"), and Chapter 7 ("Contention in Space and Time") all built on the framework of Chapter 4. The simple proposal that campaigns influence subsequent campaigns through alterations of political opportunity structure, of available models for action, of connections among potential claimants, and of interactions among the three nicely disciplines the analysis of repertoire change. Such cases as the 1830 Swing rebellion establish, furthermore, that each of the three components – POS, models, and connections – has a negative version: a massive failure broadcasts a signal that a certain performance, or even a whole repertoire, has lost its effectiveness.

Large repertoire changes, including the emergence of the social movement, therefore occur incrementally rather than in sudden bursts.

Even in turbulent Ireland, as we have seen, militia marches, attacks on landlords, and mobilization for independence only modified incrementally. Elsewhere, the junction of the public meeting and the demonstration within social movements only took place over decades, with many intermediate steps. In Great Britain, the transition from parochial, particular, and bifurcated to cosmopolitan, modular, and autonomous performances did not happen in one revolutionary shift, but through a thousand small alterations in existing performances. Earlier chapters have frequently followed those modifications through incremental shifts of verb categories. Over the long run, for example, we have seen Attack, Control, and Other verbs decline massively as Meet verbs came to prevail in Great Britain.

National regimes strongly shape available performances and repertoires through top-down controls over claim making mediated by political opportunity structure.

I have illustrated and defended this claim mainly through two sorts of national analyses: static comparisons of whole regimes at the same point in time and schematic histories of the same regime over substantial periods of time. Chapter 7, to take a case in point, began with brief comparisons of contemporary Jamaica, Nepal, Bangladesh, and Denmark before turning to changes within Venezuela from 1900 to the recent past. Previous chapters have necessarily spent more time on Great Britain between the 1750s and the 1830s, but the analyses of Ireland, Venezuela, France, and contemporary regimes across the world at least make a suggestive argument for regime effects mediated by POS.

But, from the bottom up, claim making itself then alters regimes.

Brief analyses of Mexico, the Soviet Union, and Venezuela have made the point clear. My comparison of Ireland and Great Britain elaborated it.

Perhaps the most dramatic illustration of the argument, however, comes from British struggles over parliamentary reform during the 1820s and 1830s. The Reform Act of 1832 fell far short of working-class demands, but it deeply altered the character of the British regime, brought the industrial bourgeoisie into positions of power, reinforced the position of Parliament vis-à-vis the king and nobility, set a precedent for subsequent reforms, and made organized workers a force to be reckoned with at a national scale. Claim-making from the bottom up transformed the British political regime.

The end of Chapter 7 raised a new question that previous chapters had hardly touched: to what extent do sub-national and transnational regimes interact with collective claim making in the same ways that we have observed at the national scale? Answering that question will require both new evidence and new theories. Both compel analysts to go beyond the convenience of national states and national boundaries on which the analyses of this book have relied.

Top Down Plus Bottom Up

Regardless of the regime's scale and connection with national states, the book's analyses have repeatedly disciplined explanations by combining top-down and bottom-up perspectives. Top down, we survey contention as seen by powerful actors, including rulers. Bottom up, we examine the situations of potential actors as they face a certain sort of regime. Figure 8-1 schematizes the book's main explanatory elements as they converge from above and below on the strategy of a single actor at the point of deciding whether and how to make claims. It offers a simple explanatory scheme.

The three columns in the scheme could represent different types of regime (e.g., high-capacity undemocratic, low-capacity undemocratic, and high-capacity democratic), three specific regimes (e.g., Ireland, Great Britain, and France in the early 19th century), or the same regime at three points in time (e.g., Venezuela in 1907, 1957, and 2007). In each case, from the top down regime characteristics shape political opportunity structure, which in turn significantly affects strategies considered and adopted by potential claimants. From the bottom up, the experience of contention itself produces arrays of known performances – repertoires – which greatly limit the strategies available to potential claimants. The book's strongest claims and its fullest evidence appear in the diagram's bottom half: that the

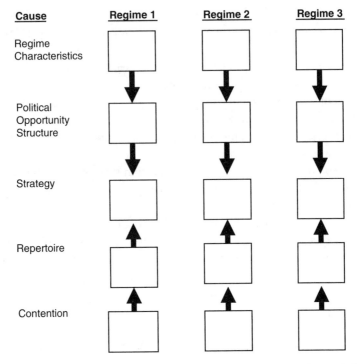

| Cause | Regime 1 | Regime 2 | Regime 3 |

Figure 8-1 Explaining a Single Actor's Strategy under Three Different Regimes

experience of contention itself generates claim-making repertoires, and that existing repertoires decisively constrain the collective making of claims.

Of course we could add more causal arrows, for example, from contention to POS or from regime characteristics to strategy. Over and over again, we have seen regimes responding to certain forms of claim making with effective repression, thus reshaping available repertoires. (Remember how British authorities responded to Irish revolutionary attempts during the 1790s by tightening repression, abolishing the separate Irish Parliament, and integrating one hundred Irish Protestant MPs into a Parliament now governing the so-called United Kingdom.) But the arrows actually included in the scheme identify the most common causal stories this book has told. The diagram therefore contains instructions for applying the book's arguments to cases it has not considered.

For any particular regime, an explanation arrived at this way will remain incomplete but useful. It will remain incomplete because I have deliberately downplayed two major clusters of causes: change and variation in regime political economies on one side, interactions among regimes on the other. As for regime political economies, the huge place of oil production and revenues in the evolution of Venezuelan contention underlines their importance. As for interactions among regimes, the history of Irish-British struggle makes clear how much initiatives coming from one regime can shape contention in a second regime.

I have neglected regime political economies and interaction among regimes in order to concentrate on clarifying causal connections between regime characteristics and the nature of contentious politics. The book as a whole has pursued a thin object of explanation: not the whole of contentious politics and its social bases but the public performances in which people make consequential, collective, public claims on others. Chapters 1 through 7 moved slowly and deliberately from the analysis of individual performances through the interaction and evolution of repertoires to an endpoint: the connection between repertoires and regimes. If those chapters did their work well, you now have the means of explaining change and variation in contentious performances across the world, past and present. But you also have an agenda for new research on the complexities of popular contention.

What agenda? Most of all, the book argues that students of contentious politics should move away from classified event counts and single-episode narratives toward procedures that trace interactions among participants in multiple episodes. They should also look systematically at how alterations in political opportunities, available models for claim making, and connections among potential claimants produce changes in performances and repertoires. This book has described and advocated the construction of fastidiously detailed event catalogs for those purposes. If the weaknesses of that approach inspire my readers to invent different and superior methods for investigating contentious performances, I will cheer them on.

References

Agrikoliansky, Éric, Olivier Fillieule, and Nonna Mayer (2005): *L'Alter-mondialisme en France: La longue histoire d'une nouvelle cause*. Paris: Flammarion.

Agrikoliansky, Éric and Isabelle Sommier (2005): eds., *Radiographie du mouvement altermondialiste*. Paris: La Dispute.

Alexander, John K. (2002): *Samuel Adams: America's Revolutionary Politician*. Lanham, MD: Rowman & Littlefield.

Amenta, Edwin (2006): *When Movements Matter: The Townsend Plan & the Rise of Social Security*. Princeton, NJ: Princeton University Press.

Aminzade, Ronald (1993): *Ballots and Barricades: Class Formation and Republican Politics in France, 1830–1871*. Princeton, NJ: Princeton University Press.

Amnesty International (2007a): "Denmark" www.thereport.amnesty.org/eng/Regions/Europe-and-Central-Asia/Denmark, viewed 13 September 2007.

   (2007b): "Nepal" www.thereport.amnesty.org/eng/Regions/Asia-Pacific/Nepal, viewed 13 September 2007.

Andrews, Kenneth T. (2004): *Freedom Is a Constant Struggle: The Mississippi Civil Rights Movement and Its Legacy*. Chicago: University of Chicago Press.

Archer, John E. (1990): *By a Flash and a Scare: Incendiarism, Animal Maiming, and Poaching in East Anglia, 1815–1870*. Oxford: Clarendon Press.

Armstrong, Alan (1988): *Farmworkers: A Social and Economic History, 1770–1980*. London: Batsford.

Banaszak, Lee Ann (1999): *Why Movements Succeed or Fail: Opportunity, Culture, and the Struggle for Woman Suffrage*. Princeton, NJ: Princeton University Press.

Barber, Lucy G. (2002): *Marching on Washington: The Forging of an American Political Tradition*. Berkeley: University of California Press.

Barnett, Corelli (1974): *Britain and Her Army, 1509–1970: A Military, Political and Social Survey*. Harmondsworth: Penguin.

Beckwith, Karen (2000): "Hinges in Collective Action: Strategic Innovation in the Pittston Coal Strike," *Mobilization* 5: 179–200.

   (2001): "Women's Movements at Century's End: Excavation and Advances in Political Science," *Annual Review of Political Science* 4: 371–390.

Beissinger, Mark (1998): "Nationalist Violence and the State: Political Authority and Contentious Repertoires in the Former USSR," *Comparative Politics* 30: 401–433.

(2002): *Nationalist Mobilization and the Collapse of the Soviet State*. Cambridge: Cambridge University Press.

Belchem, John (1985): *"Orator" Hunt: Henry Hunt and English Working-Class Radicalism*. Oxford: Clarendon Press.

Bennett, W. Lance (2005): "Social Movements beyond Borders: Understanding Two Eras of Transnational Activism" in Donatella della Porta and Sidney Tarrow, eds., *Transnational Protest and Global Activism*. Lanham, MD: Rowman & Littlefield.

Bob, Clifford (2005): *The Marketing of Rebellion: Insurgents, Media, and International Activism*. Cambridge: Cambridge University Press.

Bohstedt, John (1983): *Riots and Community Politics in England and Wales 1790–1810*. Cambridge, MA: Harvard University Press.

Bond, Doug (2006): "IDEA: Integrated Data for Events Analysis" www.vranet.com/idea, viewed 17 January 2007.

Booth, Alan (1977): "Food Riots in the North-West of England 1790–1801," *Past and Present* 77: 84–107.

Borland, Elizabeth (2004): "Cultural Opportunity and Tactical Choice in the Argentine and Chilean Reproductive Rights Movements," *Mobilization* 9: 327–340.

Botz, Gerhard (1983): *Gewalt in der Politik: Attentate, Zusammenstösse, Putschversuche, Unruhen in Österreich 1918–1938*. Munich: Wilhelm Fink.

(1987): *Krisenzonen einer Demokratie: Gewalt, Streik und Konfliktunterdrückung in Österreich seit 1918*. Frankfurt: Campus Verlag.

Bourguinat, Nicolas (2002): *Les Grains du désordre: L'État face aux violences frumentaires dans la première moitié du XIXe siècle*. Paris: Éditions del'École des Hautes Études en Sciences Sociales.

te Brake, Wayne (1989): *Regents and Rebels: The Revolutionary World of the 18th Century Dutch City*. Oxford: Blackwell.

(1990): "How Much in How Little? Dutch Revolution in Comparative Perspective," *Tijdschrift voor Sociale Geschiedenis* 16: 349–363.

Brewer, John (1976): *Party Ideology and Popular Politics at the Accession of George III*. Cambridge: Cambridge University Press.

(1989): *The Sinews of Power: War, Money and the English State, 1688–1783*. New York: Knopf.

Brewer, John and John Styles (1980): eds., *An Ungovernable People: The English and Their Law in the Seventeenth and Eighteenth Centuries*. New Brunswick, NJ: Rutgers University Press.

Brock, Michael (1973): *The Great Reform Act*. London: Hutchinson University Library.

Brockett, Charles D. (2005): *Political Movements and Violence in Central America*. Cambridge: Cambridge University Press.

Broeker, Galen (1970): *Rural Disorder and Police Reform in Ireland, 1812–36*. London: Routledge & Kegan Paul.

Brown, Christopher Leslie (2006): *Moral Capital: Foundations of British Abolitionism*. Chapel Hill: University of North Carolina Press.

Burke, Edmund (1986): *Reflections on the Revolution in France*. London: Penguin.

Burke, Peter (2005): "Performing History: The Importance of Occasions," *Rethinking History* 9: 35–52.

Button, James W. (1978): *Black Violence: Political Impact of the 1960s Riots*. Princeton, NJ: Princeton University Press.

Casquete, Jesús (2006): *El poder de la calle: Ensayos sobre acción colectiva*. Madrid: Centro de Estudios Políticos y Constitucionales.

Centeno, Miguel Angel (2002): *Blood and Debt: War and the Nation-State in Latin America*. University Park: Pennsylvania State University Press.

Chabot, Sean (2000): "Transnational Diffusion and the African American Reinvention of the Gandhian Repertoire," *Mobilization* 5: 201–216.

Chabot, Sean and Jan Willem Duyvendak (2002): "Globalization and Transnational Diffusion between Social Movements: Reconceptualizing the Dissemination of the Gandhian Repertoire and the 'Coming Out' Routine," *Theory and Society* 31: 697–740.

Charlesworth, Andrew (1978): *Social Protest in a Rural Society: The Spatial Diffusion of the Captain Swing Disturbances of 1830–1831*. Liverpool: Department of Geography, University of Liverpool. Historical Geography Research Series, no. 1.

(1983): ed., *An Atlas of Rural Protest in Britain, 1548–1900*. London: Croom Helm.

Charlesworth, Andrew, David Gilbert, Adrian Randall, Humphrey Southall, and Chris Wrigley (1996): *An Atlas of Industrial Protest in Britain 1750–1990*. London: Macmillan.

Chávez, Hugo (2000): "Address by the President of the Bolivarian Republic of Venezuela, Hugo Chávez" www.comunidadandina.org/INGLES/speeches/chavez1, viewed 11 May 2007.

Cioffi-Revilla, Claudio (1990): *The Scientific Measurement of International Conflict: Handbook of Datasets on Crises and Wars, 1495–1988 A.D.* Boulder, CO: Lynne Rienner.

Cirket, A. F. (1978): "The 1830 Riots in Bedfordshire: Background and Events," *Publications of the Bedfordshire Historical Record Society* 57: 75–112.

Clark, Samuel (1979): *Social Origins of the Irish Land War*. Princeton, NJ: Princeton University Press.

Clark, Samuel and James S. Donnelly, Jr. (1983): "Introduction" to Clark and Donnelly, eds., *Irish Peasants. Violence and Political Unrest 1780–1914*. Madison: University of Wisconsin Press.

Collier, Ruth Berins and David Collier (1991): *Shaping the Political Arena: Critical Junctures, the Labor Movement, and Regime Dynamics in Latin America*. Princeton, NJ: Princeton University Press.

Conser, Walter H. Jr. (1986): "The Stamp Act Resistance" in Walter H. Conser, Jr., Ronald M. McCarthy, David J. Toscano, and Gene Sharp, eds., *Resistance, Politics, and the American Struggle for Independence, 1765–1775*. Boulder, CO: Lynne Rienner.

Coppedge, Michael (1994): *Presidential Partyarchy and Factionalism in Venezuela.* Stanford, CA: Stanford University Press.

Cronin, Maura (2000): "'Of One Mind'? O'Connellite Crowds in the 1830s and 1840s" in Peter Jupp and Eoin Magennis, eds., *Crowds in Ireland, c. 1720–1920.* London: Macmillan.

Daunton, Martin (2001): *Trusting Leviathan. The Politics of Taxation in Britain, 1799–1914.* Cambridge: Cambridge University Press.

Davenport, Christian (2007): *State Repression and the Domestic Democratic Peace.* Cambridge: Cambridge University Press.

Davenport, Christian, Hank Johnston, and Carol Mueller (2005): eds., *Repression and Mobilization.* Minneapolis: University of Minnesota Press.

Davis, David Brion (1987): "Capitalism, Abolitionism, and Hegemony" in Barbara Solow and Stanley Engerman, eds., *British Capitalism and Caribbean Slavery: The Legacy of Eric Williams.* Cambridge: Cambridge University Press.

Dekker, Rudolf (1982): *Holland in beroering: Oproeren in de 17de en 18de eeuw.* Baarn: Amboeken.

   (1987): "Women in Revolt: Popular Protest and Its Social Bases in Holland in the 17th and 18th Centuries. *Theory and Society* 16: 3 (May): 337–362.

della Porta, Donatella, Massimiliano Andretta, Lorenzo Mosca, and Herbert Reiter (2006): *Globalization from Below: Transnational Activists and Protest Networks.* Minneapolis: University of Minnesota Press.

DeNardo, James (1985): *Power in Numbers.* Princeton, NJ: Princeton University Press.

Drescher, Seymour (1982): "Public Opinion and the Destruction of British Colonial Slavery" in James Walvin, ed., *Slavery and British Society, 1776–1946.* Baton Rouge: Louisiana State University Press.

   (1986): *Capitalism and Antislavery: British Mobilization in Comparative Perspective.* London: Macmillan.

   (1994): "Whose Abolition? Popular Pressure and the Ending of the British Slave Trade," *Past and Present* 143: 136–166.

Duyvendak, Jan Willem (1994): *Le poids du politique. Nouveaux mouvements sociaux en France.* Paris: L'Harmattan.

Duyvendak, Jan Willem, Hein-Anton van der Heijden, Ruud Koopmans, and Luuk Wijmans (1992): eds., *Tussen Verbeelding en Macht: 25 jaar nieuwe social bewegingen in Nederland.* Amsterdam: Sua.

Economist (2007): "Flying the Revolutionary Flag Again," *The Economist,* 22 September: 53.

Ekiert, Grzegorz and Jan Kubik (1999): *Rebellious Civil Society: Popular Protest and Democratic Consolidation in Poland, 1989–1993.* Ann Arbor: University of Michigan Press.

Ellingson, Stephen (1995): "Understanding the Dialectic of Discourse and Collective Action: Public Debate and Rioting in Antebellum Cincinnati," *American Journal of Sociology* 101: 100–144.

Ennis, James G. (1987): "Fields of Action: Structure in Movements' Tactical Repertoires," *Sociological Forum* 2: 520–533.

Esherick, Joseph W. and Jeffrey N. Wasserstrom (1990): "Acting Out Democracy: Political Theater in Modern China," *Journal of Asian Studies* 49: 835–865.

Eyerman, Ron (2006): "Performing Opposition or, How Social Movements Move" in Jeffrey C. Alexander, Bernhard Giesen, and Jason L. Mast, eds., *Social Performance: Symbolic Action, Cultural Pragmatics, and Ritual*. Cambridge: Cambridge University Press.

Farrell, Sean (2000): *Rituals and Riots: Sectarian Violence and Political Culture in Ulster, 1784–1886*. Lexington: University Press of Kentucky.

Favre, Pierre (1990): "Introduction" to Pierre Favre, ed., *La Manifestation*. Paris: Presses de la Fondation Nationale des Sciences Politiques.

Fillieule, Olivier (1997): *Stratégies de la rue: Les manifestations en France*. Paris: Presses de la Fondation Nationale des Sciences Politiques.

Foster, R. F. (1988): *Modern Ireland 1600–1972*. London: Penguin.

Franzosi, Roberto (1989): "One Hundred Years of Strike Statistics: Methodological and Theoretical Issues in Quantitative Strike Research," *Industrial and Labor Relations Review* 42: 348–362.

(1995): *The Puzzle of Strikes: Class and State Strategies in Postwar Italy*. Cambridge: Cambridge University Press.

(1998): "Narrative as Data: Linguistic and Statistical Tools for the Quantitative Study of Historical Events," *International Review of Social History* 43: 81–104.

(2004a): *From Words to Numbers: Narrative, Data, and Social Science*. Cambridge: Cambridge University Press.

(2004b): "PC-ACE (Program for Computer-Assisted Coding of Events)" www.pc-ace.com, viewed 9 April 2008.

Freedom House (2002): "Freedom in the World 2002: The Democracy Gap" www.freedomhouse.org/research/survey2002.htm, viewed 29 March 2002.

(2006a): "Countries at the Crossroads 2006, Country Report – Venezuela" www.freedomhouse.org/modules/publications/ccr, viewed 13 September 2007.

(2006b): "Freedom in the World – Jamaica (2006)" www.freedomhouse.org/ inc/content/pubs/fiw, viewed 26 August 2007.

(2007a): "Freedom in the World – Bangladesh (2007)" www.freedomhouse.org/ inc/content/pubs/fiw, viewed 14 September 2007.

(2007b): "Freedom in the World, Country Ratings" www.freedomhouse.org/ template.cfm?, viewed 13 September 2007.

(2007c): "Freedom in the World – India (2007)" www.freedomhouse.org/inc/ content/pubs/fiw, viewed 26 August 2007.

(2007d): "Freedom in the World – Nepal (2007)" www.freedomhouse.org/inc/ content/pubs/fiw, viewed 14 August 2007.

(2007e): "Freedom in the World – Nepal (2007)" www.freedomhouse.org/inc/ content/pubs/fiw, viewed 14 September 2007.

(2007f): "Freedom in the World 2007: Year Marked by Global 'Freedom Stagnation'" www.freedomhouse.org, press release viewed 3 September 2007.

Frey, Bruno S. and Alois Stutzer (2002): "What Can Economists Learn from Happiness Research?" *Journal of Economic Literature* 40: 400–435.

Gaillard, Jeanne (1971): *Communes de province, Commune de Paris 1870–1871*. Paris: Flammarion.

Gamson, William A. (1990): *The Strategy of Social Protest*. Belmont, CA: Wadsworth. 2nd ed.

Garrett, R. Kelly (2006): "Protest in an Information Society: A Review of Literature on Social Movements and New ICTs," *Information, Communication and Society* 9: 202–224.

Giugni, Marco (1995): *Entre stratégie et opportunité: Les nouveaux mouvements sociaux en Suisse*. Zürich: Seismo.

   (1998): "Was It Worth the Effort? The Outcomes and Consequences of Social Movements," *Annual Review of Sociology* 24: 371–393.

Giugni, Marco G., Doug McAdam, and Charles Tilly (1999): eds., *How Social Movements Matter*. Minneapolis: University of Minnesota Press.

Goldstone, Jack and Charles Tilly (2001): "Threat (and Opportunity): Popular Action and State Response in the Dynamics of Contentious Action" in Ronald Aminzade et al., *Silence and Voice in Contentious Politics*. Cambridge: Cambridge University Press.

Goodwin, Albert (1979): *The Friends of Liberty: The English Democratic Movement in the Age of the French Revolution*. Cambridge, MA: Harvard University Press.

Goodwin, Jeff and James M. Jasper (1999): "Caught in a Winding, Snarling Vine: The Structural Bias of Political Process Theory," *Sociological Forum* 14: 27–54.

   (2004): *Rethinking Social Movements: Structure, Meaning and Emotion*. Lanham, MD: Rowman & Littlefield.

Gran, Brian K. and Jeremy Hein (2005): "The Preconditions and Consequences of Social Movement Actions: Opinions of Immigrant Assimilation among Local Polity Members in France," *Sociological Focus* 38: 25–39.

Granjon, Fabien (2002): "Les répertoires d'action télémathiques du néo-militantisme," *Le Mouvement Social* 200: 11–32.

Greenberg, Louis (1971): *Sisters of Liberty: Paris, Marseille, Lyon and the Reaction to the Centralized State*. Cambridge, MA: Harvard University Press.

Greiff, Mats (1997): "'Marching Through the Streets Singing and Shouting' Industrial Struggles and Trade Unions Among Female Linen Workers in Belfast and Lurgan, 1872–1910," *Saothar 22. Journal of the Irish Labour History Society:* 29–44.

Haimson, Leopold and Charles Tilly (1989): eds., *Strikes, Wars, and Revolutions in an International Perspective: Strike Waves in the Late Nineteenth and Early Twentieth Centuries*. Cambridge: Cambridge University Press.

Hall, Simon (2007): "Marching on Washington: The Civil Rights and Anti-War Movements of the 1960s" in Matthias Reiss, ed., *The Street as Stage: Protest Marches and Public Rallies since the Nineteenth Century*. Oxford: Oxford University Press.

Hanagan, Michael (1999): "Industrial versus Preindustrial Forms of Violence" in Lester Kurtz, ed., *Encyclopedia of Violence, Peace, and Conflict*. San Diego, CA: Academic Press. Vol. II, 197–210.

Harrison, Mark (1988): *Crowds and History: Mass Phenomena in English Towns, 1790–1835*. Cambridge: Cambridge University Press.

Hayter, Anthony (1978): *The Army and the Crowd in Mid-Georgian England*. Totowa, NJ: Rowman & Littlefield.

Heerma van Voss, Lex (2001): ed., "Petitions in Social History," *International Review of Social History*, Supplement 9, entire issue.

Hertel, Shareen (2006): *Unexpected Power: Conflict and Change among Transnational Activists*. Ithaca, NY: ILR Press.

Hinde, Wendy (1992): *Catholic Emancipation: A Shake to Men's Minds*. Oxford: Blackwell.

Hirschman, Albert O. (1979): "The Turn to Authoritarianism in Latin America and the Search for Its Economic Determinants" in David Collier, ed., *The New Authoritarianism in Latin America*. Princeton, NJ: Princeton University Press.

Hobsbawm, Eric and George Rudé (1968): *Captain Swing: A Social History of the Great English Agricultural Uprisings of 1830*. New York: Pantheon.

Hochschild, Adam (2005): *Bury the Chains: Prophets and Rebels in the Fight to Free an Empire's Slaves*. Boston: Houghton Mifflin.

Hoerder, Dirk (1977): *Crowd Action in Revolutionary Massachusetts, 1765–1780*. New York: Academic Press.

Hollis, Patricia (1973): ed., *Class and Conflict in Nineteenth-Century England 1815–1850*. London: Routledge & Kegan Paul.

van Honacker, Karin (1994): *Lokaal Verzet en Oproer in de 17de en 18de Eeuw: Collectieve Acties tegen het centraal gezag in Brussel, Antwerpen en Leuven*. Heule: UGA.

   (2000): "Résistance locale et émeutes dans les chef-villes brabançonnes aux XVIIe et XVIIIe siècles," *Revue d'Histoire Moderne et Contemporaine* 47: 37–68.

Human Rights Watch (2007a): "Bangladesh: Abuses Grow in Crackdown on Protests" www.hrw.org/english/docs/2007/8/25/bangla, viewed 14 September 2007.

   (2007c): "Bangladesh: Partial Lifting of Ban on Politics Falls Far Short" www.hrw.org/english/docts/2007/09/11/bangla, viewed 14 September 2007.

   (2007b): "Bangladesh, Events of 2006" [in World Report 2007] www.hrw.org/englishwr2k7, viewed 14 September 2007.

   (2007d): "Nepal: Truth Commission Bill Disregards Victims' Rights" www.hrw.org/english/docs/2007/08/22/nepal, viewed 14 September 2007.

   (2007e): "Venezuela, Events of 2006" [in World Report 2007] www.hrw.org/englishwr2k7, viewed 13 September 2007.

Hunt, Lynn (1978): *Revolution and Urban Politics in Provincial France: Troyes and Reims, 1786–1790*. Stanford, CA: Stanford University Press.

   (1984): *Politics, Culture, and Class in the French Revolution*. Berkeley: University of California Press.

Ibarra, Pedro (2003): ed., *Social Movements and Democracy*. New York: Palgrave Macmillan.

Imig, Doug and Sidney Tarrow (2001): "Mapping the Europeanization of Contention: Evidence from a Quantitative Data Analysis" in Doug Imig and Sidney Tarrow, eds., *Contentious Europeans: Protest and Politics in an Emerging Polity*. Lanham, MD: Rowman & Littlefield.

Jarman, Neil (1997): *Material Conflicts: Parades and Visual Displays in Northern Ireland*. Oxford: Berg.

Jenkins, J. Craig (1985): *The Politics of Insurgency: The Farm Worker Movement in the 1960s*. New York: Columbia University Press. First published in 1975.

Jones, Peter (2003): *Liberty and Locality in Revolutionary France: Six Villages Compared,* *1760–1820.* Cambridge: Cambridge University Press.

Jupp, Peter (1998): *British Politics on the Eve of Reform: The Duke of Wellington's* *Administration, 1828–30.* New York: St. Martin's.

Jupp, Peter and Eoin Magennis (2000): "Introduction: Crowds in Ireland, c. 1720–1920" in Jupp and Magennis, *Crowds in Ireland, c. 1720–1920.* London: Macmillan.

Katzenstein, Mary F. (1998): *Faithful and Fearless: Moving Feminist Protest Inside the* *Church and Military.* Princeton, NJ: Princeton University Press.

Koller, Christian (2007): "Demonstrating in Zurich between 1830 and 1940: From Bourgeois Protest to Proletarian Street Politics" in Matthias Reiss, ed., *The Street as Stage: Protest Marches and Public Rallies since the Nineteenth* *Century.* Oxford: Oxford University Press for the German Historical Institute London.

Koopmans, Ruud (1995): *Democracy from Below: New Social Movements and the* *Political System in West Germany.* Boulder, CO: Westview.

Korpi, Walter and Michael Shalev (1979): "Strikes, Industrial Relations and Class Conflict in Capitalist Societies," *British Journal of Sociology* 30: 164–187.

   (1980): "Strikes, Power and Politics in the Western Nations, 1900–1976" in Maurice Zeitlin, ed., *Political Power and Social Theory.* Greenwich, CT: JAI Press.

Kriesi, Hanspeter (1993): *Political Mobilization and Social Change: The Dutch Case in* *Comparative Perspective.* Aldershot: Avebury.

Kriesi, Hanspeter, Ruud Koopmans, Jan Willem Duyvendak, and Marco G. Giugni (1995): *New Social Movements in Western Europe: A Comparative* *Analysis.* Minneapolis: University of Minnesota Press.

Kriesi, Hanspeter, René Levy, Gilbert Ganguillet, and Heinz Zwicky (1981): *Politische Aktivierung in der Schweiz, 1945–1978.* Diessenhofen: Verlag Ruegger.

Lafargue, Jérôme (1996): *Contestations démocratiques en Afrique: Sociologie de la* *protestation au Kenya et en Zambie.* Paris: Karthala.

Lee, Ching Kwan (2007): *Against the Law: Labor Protests in China's Rustbelt and* *Sunbelt.* Berkeley: University of California Press.

Lindenberger, Thomas (1995): *Strassenpolitik: Zur Sozialgeschichte der öffentlichen* *Ordnung in Berlin 1900 bis 1914.* Bonn: Dietz.

Linders, Annulla (2004): "Victory and Beyond: A Historical Comparative Analysis of the Outcomes of the Abortion Movements in Sweden and the United States," *Sociological Forum* 19: 371–404.

Lofland, John and Michael Fink (1982): *Symbolic Sit-Ins: Protest Occupations at the* *California Capitol.* New York: University Press of America.

López-Maya, Margarita (1999): "La protesta popular venezolana entre 1989 y 1993 (en el umbro del neoliberalismo)" in Margarita López-Maya, ed., *Lucha* *Popular, democracia, neoliberalismo: Protesta popular en América Latina en los años* *de ajuste.* Caracas: Nueva Sociedad.

   (2002): "Venezuela after the Caracazo: Forms of Protest in a Deinstitutionalized Context," *Bulletin of Latin American Research* 21: 199–218.

López-Maya, Margarita, David Smilde, and Keta Stephany (2002): *Protesta y Cultura en Venezuela: Los Marcos de Acción Colectiva en 1999.* Caracas: FACES-UCV, CENDES, and FONACIT.

Luders, Joseph (2006): "The Economics of Movement Success: Business Responses to Civil Rights Mobilization," *American Journal of Sociology* 111: 963–998.

Mac Suibhne, Breandán (2000): "Whiskey, Potatoes and Paddies: Volunteering and the Construction of the Irish Nation in Northwest Ulster, 1778–1782" in Peter Jupp and Eoin Magennis, eds., *Crowds in Ireland, c. 1720–1920.* London: Macmillan.

Maier, Pauline (1972): *From Resistance to Revolution: Colonial Radicals and the Development of American Opposition to Britain, 1765–1776.* New York: Vintage.

Mann, Michael (1988): "State and Society, 1130–1815: An Analysis of English State Finances" in Michael Mann, ed., *States, War and Capitalism: Studies in Political Sociology.* Oxford: Blackwell.

Mansbridge, Jane J. (1986): *Why We Lost the ERA.* Chicago: University of Chicago Press.

Markoff, John (1996a): *The Abolition of Feudalism: Peasants, Lords, and Legislators in the French Revolution.* University Park: Pennsylvania State University Press.

(1996b): *Waves of Democracy: Social Movements and Political Change.* Thousand Oaks, CA: Pine Grove Press.

(1997): "Peasants Help Destroy an Old Regime and Defy a New One: Some Lessons from (and for) the Study of Social Movements," *American Journal of Sociology* 102: 1113–1142.

McAdam, Doug (1999): *Political Process and the Development of Black Insurgency, 1930–1970.* Chicago: University of Chicago Press. Revised ed.

McAdam, Doug and Yang Su (2002): "The War at Home: The Impact of Anti-War Protests, 1965–1973," *American Sociological Review* 67: 696–721.

McCammon, Holly J., Karen E. Campbell, Ellen M. Granberg, and Christine Mowery (2001): "How Movements Win: Gendered Opportunity Structures and U.S. Women's Suffrage Movements, 1866 to 1919," *American Sociological Review* 66: 49–70.

McDowell, R. B. (2001): "The Protestant Nation 1775–1800" in T. W. Moody and F. X. Martin, eds., *The Course of Irish History.* Lanham, MD: Roberts Rinehart. 4th ed. First published in 1967.

McPhail, Clark (1991): *The Myth of the Madding Crowd.* New York: Aldine De Gruyter.

(2006): "The Crowd and Collective Behavior: Bringing Symbolic Interaction Back In," *Symbolic Interaction* 29: 433–464.

McPhail, Clark and David Miller (1973): "The Assembling Process: A Theoretical and Empirical Examination," *American Sociological Review* 38: 721–735.

McPhail, Clark, David D. Schweingruber, and Alin Mihai Ceobanu (2006): "Bridging the Collective Behavior/Social Movement Gap." Paper presented to the annual meeting of the American Sociological Association, Montreal.

McPhail, Clark and Ronald T. Wohlstein (1983): "Individual and Collective Behaviors within Gatherings, Demonstrations, and Riots," *Annual Review of Sociology* 9: 579–600.

McPhee, Peter (1988): "Les formes d'intervention populaire en Roussillon: L'exemple de Collioure, 1789–1815" in Centre d'Histoire Contemporaine du Languedoc Méditerranéen et du Roussillon, *Les pratiques politiques en province à l' époque de la Révolution française*. Montpellier: Publications de la Recherche, Université de Montpellier.

McVeigh, Rory, Michael R. Welch, and Thoroddur Bjarnason (2003): "Hate Crime Reporting as a Successful Social Movement Outcome," *American Sociological Review* 68: 843–867.

Miller, David W. (1983): "The Armagh Troubles, 1784–95" in Samuel Clark and James S. Donnelly, Jr., eds., *Irish Peasants: Violence and Political Unrest 1780–1914*. Madison: University of Wisconsin Press.

Mitchell, B.R. and Phyllis Deane (1971): *Abstract of British Historical Statistics*. Cambridge: Cambridge University Press.

Mobilization (2003): "Book Symposium: Focus on Dynamics of Contention." *Mobilization* 8: 107–141.

Mueller, Carol (1999): "Escape from the GDR, 1961–1989: Hybrid Exit Repertoires in a Disintegrating Leninist Regime," *American Journal of Sociology* 105: 697–735.

Munro, Lyle (2005): "Strategies, Action Repertoires and DIY Activism in the Animal Rights Movement," *Social Movement Studies* 4: 75–94.

Oberschall, Anthony (1994): "Protest Demonstrations and the End of Communist Regimes in 1989," *Research in Social Movements, Conflicts and Change* 17: 1–24.

O'Farrell, Fergus (1981): *Catholic Emancipation: Daniel O'Connell and the Birth of Irish Democracy 1820–30*. Dublin: Gill and Macmillan.

Olesen, Thomas (2005): *International Zapatismo: The Construction of Solidarity in the Age of Globalization*. London: Zed.

Olzak, Susan (1989): "Analysis of Events in the Study of Collective Action," *Annual Review of Sociology* 15: 119–141.

   (1992): *The Dynamics of Ethnic Competition and Conflict*. Stanford, CA: Stanford University Press.

Palast, Greg (2006): "Hugo Chávez" www.progressive.org/mag__intv0706, viewed 11 May 2007.

Palmer, Stanley H. (1988): *Police and Protest in England and Ireland 1780–1850*. Cambridge: Cambridge University Press.

Parssinen, T.M. (1973): "Association, Convention and Anti-Parliament in British Radical Politics, 1771–1848," *English Historical Review* 88: 504–533.

Péchu, Cécile (2006): *Droit au Logement, genèse et sociologie d'une mobilisation*. Paris: Dalloz.

Pigenet, Michel and Danielle Tartakowsky (2003): eds., "Les marches," *Le mouvement social* 202 (January–March), entire issue.

Plotz, John M. (2000): *The Crowd: British Literature and Public Politics*. Berkeley: University of California Press.

Plows, Alexandra, Derek Wall, and Brian Doherty (2004): "Covert Repertoires: Ecotage in the U.K.," *Social Movement Studies* 3: 199–220.

Poell, Thomas (2007): "The Democratic Paradox: Dutch Revolutionary Struggles over Democratisation and Centralisation (1780–1813)." Doctoral dissertation, University of Utrecht.

Polletta, Francesca (2006): *It Was Like a Fever: Storytelling in Protest and Politics.* Chicago: University of Chicago Press.

Prothero, Iorwerth J. (1979): *Artisans and Politics in Early Nineteenth-Century London: John Gast and His Times.* Folkestone: Dawson.

Randall, Adrian and Andrew Charlesworth (1996): eds., *Markets, Market Culture and Popular Protest in Eighteenth-Century Britain and Ireland.* Liverpool: Liverpool University Press.

(2000): "The Moral Economy: Riots, Markets and Social Conflict" in Randall and Charlesworth, eds., *Moral Economy and Popular Protest: Crowds, Conflict and Authority.* London: Macmillan.

Reiss, Matthias (2007a): "Marching on the Capital: National Protest Marches of the British Unemployed in the 1920s and 1930s" in Matthias Reiss, ed., *The Street as Stage: Protest Marches and Public Rallies since the Nineteenth Century.* Oxford: Oxford University Press.

(2007b): ed., *The Street as Stage: Protest Marches and Public Rallies since the Nineteenth Century.* Oxford: Oxford University Press.

Richards, Eric (1974): "Captain Swing in the West Midlands," *International Review of Social History* 19: 86–99.

Robert, Vincent (1996): *Les chemins de la manifestation, 1848–1914.* Lyon: Presses Universitaires de Lyon.

Robins, Jane (2006): *The Trial of Queen Caroline: The Scandalous Affair That Nearly Ended a Monarchy.* New York: Free Press.

Rogers, Nicholas (1998): *Crowds, Culture, and Politics in Georgian Britain.* Oxford: Clarendon Press.

Rolfe, Brett (2005): "Building an Electronic Repertoire of Contention," *Social Movement Studies* 4: 65–74.

Rouquié, Alain (1987): *The Military and the State in Latin America.* Berkeley: University of California Press.

Rowe, D.J. (1970): ed., *London Radicalism 1830–1843: A Selection from the Papers of Francis Place.* London: London Record Society.

(1977): "London Radicalism in the Era of the Great Reform Bill" in John Stevenson, ed., *London in the Age of Reform.* Oxford: Blackwell.

Rucht, Dieter (1991): "The Study of Social Movements in Western Germany: Between Activism and Social Science" in Dieter Rucht, ed., *Research on Social Movements: The State of the Art in Western Europe and the USA.* Boulder, CO: Westview.

(2007): "On the Sociology of Protest Marches" in Matthias Reiss, ed., *The Street as Stage: Protest Marches and Public Rallies since the Nineteenth Century.* Oxford: Oxford University Press.

Rucht, Dieter and Ruud Koopmans (1999): eds., "Protest Event Analysis," *Mobilization* 4, no. 2, entire issue.

Rucht, Dieter, Ruud Koopmans, and Friedhelm Neidhardt (1999): eds., *Acts of Dissent: New Developments in the Study of Protest.* Lanham, MD: Rowman & Littlefield.

Rucht, Dieter and Friedhelm Neidhardt (1998): "Methodological Issues in Collecting Protest Event Data: Units of Analysis, Sources and Sampling, Coding Problems" in Dieter Rucht, Ruud Koopmans, and Friedhelm Neidhardt, eds., *Acts of Dissent: New Developments in the Study of Protest*. Lanham, MD: Rowman & Littlefield.

Rucht, Dieter and Thomas Ohlemacher (1992): "Protest Event Data: Collection, Uses and Perspectives" in Mario Diani and Ron Eyerman, eds., *Studying Collective Action*. London: Sage Publications.

Rude, Fernand (1969): *L'Insurrection lyonnaise de novembre 1831: Le mouvement ouvrier à Lyon de 1827–1832*. Paris: Anthropos.

Rudé, George (1971): *Hanoverian London 1714–1808*. London: Secker & Warburg.

Rule, James and Charles Tilly (1965): *Measuring Political Upheaval*. Princeton, NJ: Center of International Studies, Princeton University.

Salvatore, Ricardo (2001): "Repertoires of Coercion and Market Culture in Nineteenth-Century Buenos Aires Province," *International Review of Social History* 45: 409–448.

Sarkees, Meredith Reid, Frank Whelon Wayman, and J. David Singer (2003): "Inter-State, Intra-State, and Extra-State Wars: A Comprehensive Look at Their Distribution over Time, 1816–1997," *International Studies Quarterly* 47: 49–70.

Sawyer, R. Keith (2001): *Creating Conversations: Improvisation in Everyday Discourse*. Cresskill, NJ: Hampton Press.

Scalmer, Sean (2002a): *Dissent Events: Protest, the Media and the Political Gimmick in Australia*. Sydney: University of New South Wales Press.

(2002b): "The Labor of Diffusion: The Peace Pledge Union and the Adaptation of the Gandhian Repertoire," *Mobilization* 7: 269–285.

Schama, Simon (1977): *Patriots and Liberators: Revolution in the Netherlands 1780–1813*. London: Collins.

Schrodt, Philip A. (2006): "Twenty Years of the Kansas Event Data System Project" www.ku.edu/~keds, viewed 17 January 2007.

Schumaker, Paul D. (1978): "The Scope of Political Conflict and the Effectiveness of Constraints in Contemporary Urban Protest," *Sociological Quarterly* 19: 168–184.

Schwedler, Jillian (2005): "Cop Rock: Protest, Identity, and Dancing Riot Police in Jordan," *Social Movement Studies* 4: 155–175.

Schweingruber, David and Clark McPhail (1999): "A Method for Systematically Observing and Recording Collective Action," *Sociological Methods & Research* 27: 451–498.

Schweitzer, R. A. and Steven C. Simmons (1981): "Interactive, Direct-Entry Approaches to Contentious Gathering Event Files," *Social Science History* 5: 317–342.

Shorter, Edward and Charles Tilly (1974): *Strikes in France, 1830 to 1968*. Cambridge: Cambridge University Press.

Sikkink, Kathryn (2005): "Patterns of Dynamic Multilevel Governance and the Insider-Outsider Coalition" in Donatalla della Porta and Sidney Tarrow, eds., *Transnational Protest & Global Activism*. Lanham, MD: Rowman & Littlefield.

Singleton, F. (1964): "Captain Swing in East Anglia," *Bulletin of the Society for the Study of Labour History* 9: 13–15.

Skocpol, Theda (1992): *Protecting Soldiers and Mothers: The Political Origins of Social Policy in the United States.* Cambridge, MA: Harvard University Press.

Snyder, David (1976): "Theoretical and Methodological Problems in the Analysis of Governmental Coercion and Collective Violence," *Journal of Political and Military Sociology* 4: 277–293.

(1978): "Collective Violence: A Research Agenda and Some Strategic Considerations," *Journal of Conflict Resolution* 22: 499–534.

Sorokin, Pitirim A. (1962 [1937]): *Social and Cultural Dynamics. III. Fluctuation of Social Relationships, War, and Revolution.* New York: Bedminster.

Soule, Sarah A. (1997): "The Student Divestment Movement in the United States and Tactical Diffusion: The Shantytown Protest," *Social Forces* 75: 855–883.

(1999): "The Diffusion of an Unsuccessful Innovation," *Annals of the American Academy of Political and Social Science* 566: 121–131.

Soule, Sarah A. and Susan Olzak (2004): "When Do Movements Matter? The Politics of Contingency and the Equal Rights Amendment," *American Sociological Review* 69: 473–497.

Sowell, David (1998): "Repertoires of Contention in Urban Colombia, 1760s–1940s: An Inquiry into Latin American Social Violence," *Journal of Urban History* 24: 302–336.

Stearns, Linda Brewster and Paul D. Almeida (2004): "The Formation of State Actor-Social Movement Coalitions and Favorable Policy Outcomes," *Social Problems* 51: 478–504.

Steinberg, Marc W. (1994): "The Dialogue of Struggle: The Contest over Ideological Boundaries in the Case of London Silk Weavers in the Early Nineteenth Century," *Social Science History* 18: 505–542.

(1996): "'The Labour of the Country Is the Wealth of the Country': Class Identity, Consciousness, and the Role of Discourse in the Making of the English Working Class," *International Labor and Working-Class History* 49: 1–25.

(1998): "Tilting the Frame: Considerations on Collective Action Framing from a Discursive Turn," *Theory and Society* 27: 845–872.

(1999a): *Fighting Words: Working-Class Formation, Collective Action, and Discourse in Early Nineteenth-Century England.* Ithaca, NY: Cornell University Press.

(1999b): "The Talk and Back Talk of Collective Action: A Dialogic Analysis of Repertoires of Discourse among Nineteenth-Century English Cotton Spinners," *American Journal of Sociology* 105: 736–780.

Stevenson, John (1979): *Popular Disturbances in England, 1700–1870.* London: Longman.

Stinchcombe, Arthur L. (1999): "Ending Revolutions and Building New Governments," *Annual Review of Political Science* 2: 49–73.

Stone, Lawrence (1994): ed., *An Imperial State at War: Britain from 1689 to 1815.* London: Routledge.

Sugimoto, Yoshio (1981): *Popular Disturbance in Postwar Japan.* Hong Kong: Asian Research Service.

Szabó, Máté (1996): "Repertoires of Contention in Post-Communist Protest Cultures: An East Central European Comparative Survey," *Social Research* 63: 1155–1182.

Tamayo, Sergio (1999): *Los veinte octubres mexicanos: La transición a la modernización y la democracia, 1968–1988*. Mexico City: Universidad Autónoma Metropolitana-Azcapotzalco.

Tarrow, Sidney (1989): *Democracy and Disorder: Social Conflict, Political Protest and Democracy in Italy, 1965–1975*. New York: Oxford University Press.

(1998): *Power in Movement*. New York: Cambridge University Press. 2nd ed.

(2001): "Contentious Politics in a Composite Polity" in Doug Imig and Sidney Tarrow, eds., *Contentious Europeans: Protest and Politics in an Emerging Polity*. Lanham, MD: Rowman & Littlefield.

(2005): *The New Transnational Activism*. Cambridge: Cambridge University Press.

Tartakowsky, Danielle (1997): *Les Manifestations de rue en France, 1918–1968*. Paris: Publications de la Sorbonne.

(2004): *La Manif en éclats*. Paris: La Dispute.

(2007): "Is the French Manif Still Specific? Changes in French Street Demonstrations" in Matthias Reiss, ed., *The Street as Stage: Protest Marches and Public Rallies since the Nineteenth Century*. Oxford: Oxford University Press.

Temperley, Howard (1981): "The Ideology of Antislavery" in David Eltis and James Walvin, eds., *The Abolition of the Atlantic Slave Trade: Origins and Effects in Europe, Africa, and the Americas*. Madison: University of Wisconsin Press.

Thompson, E. P. (1963): *The Making of the English Working Class*. London: Gollancz.

(1965): "Foreword" to A. J. Peacock, *Bread or Blood: A Study of the Agrarian Riots in East Anglia in 1816*. London: Gollancz.

(1971): "The Moral Economy of the English Crowd in the Eighteenth Century," *Past and Present* 50: 76–136.

(1991): *Customs in Common*. London: Merlin.

Thornton, Patricia M. (2002): "Insinuation, Insult, and Invective: The Threshold of Power and Protest in Modern China," *Comparative Studies in Society and History* 44: 597–619.

Tillema, Herbert K. (1991): *International Armed Conflict since 1945: A Bibliographic Handbook of Wars and Military Interventions*. Boulder, CO: Westview.

Tilly, Charles (1969): "Methods for the Study of Collective Violence" in Ralph W. Conant and Molly Apple Levin, eds., *Problems in Research on Community Violence*. New York: Praeger.

(1975): "Food Supply and Public Order in Modern Europe" in Charles Tilly, ed., *The Formation of National States in Western Europe*. Princeton, NJ: Princeton University Press.

(1986): *The Contentious French*. Cambridge, MA: Harvard University Press.

(1993): *European Revolutions, 1492–1992*. Oxford: Blackwell.

(1995): *Popular Contention in Great Britain, 1758–1834*. Cambridge, MA: Harvard University Press.

(1997): "Parliamentarization of Popular Contention in Great Britain, 1758–1834," *Theory and Society* 26: 245–273.

(2001): "Mechanisms in Political Processes," *Annual Review of Political Science* 4: 21–41.

(2002a): "Event Catalogs as Theories," *Sociological Theory* 20: 248–254.

(2002b): *Stories, Identities, and Political Change*. Lanham, MD: Rowman & Littlefield.

(2003): *The Politics of Collective Violence*. Cambridge: Cambridge University Press.

(2004a): "Observations of Social Processes and Their Formal Representations," *Sociological Theory* 22: 595–602.

(2004b): *Social Movements, 1768–2004*. Boulder, CO: Paradigm Publishers.

(2005a): *Identities, Boundaries, and Social Ties*. Boulder, CO: Paradigm Publishers.

(2005b): *Regimes and Repertoires*. Chicago: University of Chicago Press.

(2006): "WUNC" in Jeffrey T. Schnapp and Matthew Tiews, eds., *Crowds*. Stanford, CA: Stanford University Press.

(2007): *Democracy*. Cambridge: Cambridge University Press.

Tilly, Charles and Robert E. Goodin (2006): "It Depends" in Robert E. Goodin and Charles Tilly, eds., *The Oxford Handbook of Contextual Political Analysis*. Oxford: Oxford University Press.

Tilly, Charles and Sidney Tarrow (2006): *Contentious Politics*. Boulder, CO: Paradigm Press.

Tilly, Charles, Louise A. Tilly, and Richard Tilly (1975): *The Rebellious Century, 1830–1930*. Cambridge, MA: Harvard University Press.

Tilly, Charles and Lesley Wood (2003): "Contentious Connections in Great Britain, 1828–1834" in Mario Diani and Doug McAdam, eds., *Social Movements and Networks: Relational Approaches to Collective Action*. New York: Oxford University Press.

de Tocqueville, Alexis (1952): *L'Ancien Régime et la Révolution*. Paris: Gallimard.

(1991): André Jardin, ed., *Oeuvres, I*. Paris: Gallimard.

Townshend, Charles (1983): *Political Violence in Ireland: Government and Resistance since 1848*. Oxford: Clarendon Press.

Traugott, Mark (1995): ed., *Repertoires and Cycles of Collective Action*. Durham, NC: Duke University Press.

Trechsel, Alexander (2000): *Feuerwerk Volksrechte: Die Volksabtimmungen in den scheizerischen Kantonen 1970–1996*. Basel: Helbing & Lichtenhahn.

Turbiville, Graham H. (1997): "Mexico's Other Insurgents," *Military Review* 77 (May–June), online version: www-cgsc.army.mil/milrev/milrvweb/html/mayne/tur.html.

Urbina, Ian (2007): "Protest Focuses on Troop Increase for Iraq," *New York Times*, 28 January, N22.

Vasi, Ian Bogdan (2006): "The New Anti-War Protests and Miscible Mobilizations," *Social Movement Studies* 5: 137–154.

Wada, Takeshi (2003): "A Historical and Network Analysis of Popular Contention in the Age of Globalization in Mexico." Unpublished doctoral dissertation in sociology, Columbia University.

(2004): "Event Analysis of Claim Making in Mexico: How Are Social Protests Transformed into Political Protests?" *Mobilization* 9: 241–258.

Wallas, Graham (1898): *The Life of Francis Place, 1771–1854*. London: Longmans.

Walvin, James (1980): "The Rise of British Popular Sentiment for Abolition, 1787–1832" in Christine Bolt and Seymour Drescher, eds., *Anti-Slavery, Religion, and Reform: Essays in Memory of Roger Anstey*. Folkestone: Dawson/Archon.

   (1981): "The Public Campaign in England against Slavery, 1787–1834" in David Eltis and James Walvin, eds., *The Abolition of the Atlantic Slave Trade: Origins and Effects in Europe, Africa, and the Americas*. Madison: University of Wisconsin Press.

   (1988): *Wretched Faces: Famine in Wartime England 1793–1801*. Gloucester: Alan Sutton.

   (1990): "Social Protest, Class, Conflict and Consciousness, in the English Countryside, 1700–1880" in Mick Reed and Roger Wells, eds., *Class, Conflict and Protest in the English Countryside, 1700–1880*. London: Frank Cass.

   (2000): "The Moral Economy of the English Countryside" in Adrian Randall and Andrew Charlesworth, eds., *Moral Economy and Popular Protest*. London: Macmillan.

Whittier, Nancy (1995): *Feminist Generations: The Persistence of the Radical Women's Movement*. Philadelphia: Temple University Press.

Wisler, Dominique and Marco Giugni (1999): "Under the Spotlight: The Impact of Media Attention on Protest Policing," *Mobilization* 4: 203–222.

Woloch, Isser (1970): *Jacobin Legacy: The Democratic Movement Under the Directory*. Princeton, NJ: Princeton University Press.

   (1994): *The New Regime: Transformations of the French Civic Order, 1789–1820s*. New York: Norton.

Wood, Lesley J. (2004): "Breaking the Bank and Taking to the Streets: How Protesters Target Neoliberalism," *Journal of World Systems Research* 10: 69–89.

Index

Act Against Unlawful Oaths (1797), 134
Act for the Defence of the Realm (1798), 134
actors. *See* potential actors, connections among
Adams, John, 130
Adams, Samuel, 127, 144–5
affinity groups. *See* like-minded people
altermondialisme, 197
American Revolution, 119, 126–130. *See also* revolutions
Amnesty International, 185
Andres Pérez, Carlos, 189, 190, 192, 193
antislavery campaigns, 132–4, 157

Bangladesh, 184–5
Beissinger, Mark, 31–5, 120–2, 151, 207
Bennett, Lance, 199
Betancourt, Rómulo, 188
Birendra of Nepal (King), 183
Bolívar, Simon, 186–7
Bolivarian Movement, 189–90
Botz, Gerhard, 20, 21–3, 207
brokerage, 12, 16, 33, 111
Burdett, Francis, 107, 110, 111, 135
Bush, George W., 176–7
Bute (Lord), 2, 46, 74

Caldera, Rafael, 190, 193
campaigns, claim-making. *See* claim-making campaigns
Campbell, Colin, 182–3
El Caracazo (Events of Caracas), 189, 194
Caroline of Brunswick (Queen). *See* claim-making campaigns, Queen Caroline affair
catalogs of events. *See also* Great Britain Study
  European Union, 197

food riot actions, 67, 69–70
French demonstrations, 84
future research recommendations, 211
models of analysis, 207
performance relationship, 201–3
quantitative work, 13
Soviet/post-Soviet contention, 31–5
Venezuelan contention, 193, 194
Catholic Emancipation (1829). *See also* Test and Corporations Acts (1828)
advocates for, 110
anti-Catholic activists, 103–4
Daniel O'Connell, 102–3
insurrection threats, 105–7
Parliament, 104
popular opinion/politics, 101–2
religious lines/restrictions, 102, 146
resistance to, 103
Catholic rights/Relief Act of 1778, 97–9
change and variation
contention-connected interaction, 8
contentious gatherings, 13
epidemiologic/narrative choices, 206
European contention, 53
event catalogs, 207
as explanation, 9
historical retrospect, 29
national/regime political economies, 79–80, 210–11
repertoires, 46
social movements, 7
Chávez Frías, Hugo, 177, 188, 189–95
Civil Rights Movement (American), 8, 12. *See also* social movements
claim-making campaigns. *See also* Gordon, George (Lord); Wilkes, John
causal channels, crossflow of, 113–15
political opportunity structure, 94–5, 101

229